LEXICOGRAPHICA Series Maior

LEXICOGRAPHICA

Series Maior

Supplementary Volumes to the International Annual for Lexicography
Suppléments à la Revue Internationale de Lexicographie
Supplementbände zum Internationalen Jahrbuch für Lexikographie

Edited by
Pierre Corbin, Ulrich Heid, Thomas Herbst, Sven-Göran Malmgren,
Oskar Reichmann, Wolfgang Schweickard, Herbert Ernst Wiegand

141

Dennis Spohr

Towards a Multifunctional Lexical Resource

Design and Implementation of a Graph-based Lexicon Model

De Gruyter

D 93

ISBN 978-3-11-027115-7
e-ISBN 978-3-11-027123-3
ISSN 0175-9264

Library of Congress Cataloging-in-Publication Data
A CIP catalog record for this book has been applied for at the Library of Congress

Bibliografische Information der Deutschen Nationalbibliothek
Die Deutsche Nationalbibliothek verzeichnet diese Publikation in der Deutschen Nationalbibliografie; detaillierte bibliografische Daten sind im Internet über http://dnb.d-nb.de abrufbar.

Druck: Hubert & Co., Göttingen
♾ Gedruckt auf säurefreiem Papier

Printed in Germany

www.degruyter.com

Table of contents

List of tables

List of figures

List of abbreviations

AI	Artificial Intelligence
DB	Database
DTD	Document Type Definition
ED	Electronic Dictionary
GUI	Graphical User Interface
HTML	HyperText Markup Language
HTTP	HyperText Transfer Protocol
ISO	International Organisation for Standardisation
KB	Knowledge Base
KR	Knowledge Representation
LMF	Lexical Markup Framework
MWE	Multi-Word Expression
NLP	Natural Language Processing
OWL	Web Ontology Language
OWL DL	OWL Description Logic
RDBMS	Relational DataBase Management System
RDF	Resource Description Framework
RDFS	RDF Schema
SALSA	SAarbrücken Lexical Semantics Acquistion
SeRQL	Sesame RDF Query Language
SGML	Standard Generalised Markup Language
SPARQL	SPARQL Protocol and RDF Query Language
SW	Semantic Web
SWRL	Semantic Web Rule Language
TFS	Typed Feature Structure
UML	Unified Modelling Language
VDE	Valency Dictionary of English
W3C	World Wide Web Consortium
WWW	World Wide Web
XML	eXtensible Markup Language
XSL	eXtensible Stylesheet Language
XSLT	XSL Transformations

1 Preface

In 2005, while I was working as a student assistant at the Institute for Natural Language Processing at the University of Stuttgart, my then supervisor Ulrich Heid returned from a meeting with Günther Görz at University Erlangen-Nürnberg, impressed by the research done there on using knowledge representation formalisms for modelling computational lexica. Convinced that these formalisms would provide interesting solutions to current issues in computational lexicography, in particular the representation of multi-word expressions in electronic dictionaries, Heid offered a diploma thesis project on representing lexicographic descriptions of collocations in these formalisms. I subsequently took up this subject and wrote my diploma thesis entitled »A Description Logic Approach to Modelling Collocations«, which described the use of the Web Ontology Language OWL in order to represent the properties and relations of collocations. Very early on in this project, it became apparent that OWL opened up new ways of dealing with more general lexicographic questions, such as the relation between electronic dictionaries for human use on the one hand and computational lexica designed to support natural language processing (NLP) applications on the other, as well as (in)consistency and inference in lexicographic descriptions. Inspired by this, and backed by further experience gained during a position as a research assistant at Saarland University in Saarbrücken, I started working on a PhD project elaborating on these ideas.

This book, which represents an updated version of the doctoral dissertation that I had submitted to the Faculty of Humanities of the University of Stuttgart and successfully defended on July 16, 2010, deals with the development of a model for a lexical resource that can be used to serve both human users and NLP applications. While this suggests its immediate classification as a purely lexicographic work, several central aspects of this book go beyond what would traditionally be referred to as »lexicographic research«. As was mentioned above, it describes the application of important recent results of a branch of computer science known as *artificial intelligence* (AI) to the field of dictionary research, such as knowledge representation formalisms and description logic reasoning, and discusses the solutions they offer to specific lexicographic issues. One of these is that they allow for viewing lexica as *labelled graphs*, i. e. net-like resources in which entities (*nodes*) are linked by means of labelled arcs (*edges*). This view of lexical resources has been proven to be very suitable for capturing the highly relational nature of lexical data (see e. g. Polguère (2006); Trippel (2006); Spohr and Heid (2006)), and is in opposition to the traditional text-based view. These advances are complemented by a strong focus on *computational linguistic* methods, including the mining of existing lexical resources for lexicographically relevant information, as well as the utilisation of this information for applications of NLP. This »multifunctionality« – both with respect to the usability of lexicographic information for NLP applications and human users, as well as with respect to the different types within these two categories – is at the heart of this work. Conceptually, this study is thus to be classified as a bridge between the areas of lexicography and computational linguistics on the one hand (often referred to as *computational lexicography*), and AI on the other.

Many people have influenced this work in one way or another. I am indebted to Ulrich Heid for giving me the opportunity to carry out this research and benefit from his expertise, as well as for his constant support and interest in my work over the years. I highly appreciate that he has always taken the time to comment on my work, despite his obligations at different universities and in various committees.

The idea of a »Mutterwörterbuch« formulated by Rufus Gouws from Stellenbosch Institute for Advanced Study has had a profound influence on this work, and I would like to thank him for sharing his ideas with me. Similarly, the works of Henning Bergenholtz and Sven Tarp have had a deep impact on the theoretical aspects of this work, and I am grateful for our very fruitful discussions at the e-Lexicography workshop in Valladolid, which was organised by Pedro A. Fuertes Olivera in 2010.

The audiences at several conferences have provided very useful feedback to different development stages of this work. I would like to thank in particular the audience at eLEX 2009 in Louvain-la-Neuve for their critical comments, which have resulted in a refined argumentation regarding different aspects of this approach.

My former office mates, colleagues and friends in Stuttgart, Saarbrücken and Bielefeld have always created a very cordial and inspiring work environment. For this reason, André Blessing, Regine Brandtner, Aljoscha Burchardt, Philipp Cimiano, Anette Frank, Steffen Heidinger, Simone Heinold, Christian Hying, Katja Lapshinova-Koltunski, Fabienne Martin, Benjamin Massot, Lukas Michelbacher, Florian Niebling, Sebastian Padó, Klaus Rothenhäusler, Achim Stein and Melanie Uth have contributed to this work much more than they are aware of, and I thank them very much.

Further thanks go to Günther Görz, Ulrich Heid, Stefan Schierholz and Achim Stein for reviewing previous drafts of this book. I also appreciate that the coordinators of the International Graduate School 609 »Linguistic representations and their interpretation« have given me the opportunity to share my preliminary results and ideas with experienced researchers as well as fellow young researchers.

On a personal note, I would like to thank my parents, who have encouraged me to study in the first place, and who have always loved and supported me over the years. Finally, none of this would have been possible without my wonderful wife María, whose patience, encouragement, love and understanding have helped me to stay on track when necessary, and to leave this track whenever possible.

I am very grateful to the »Center of Excellence in Cognitive Interaction Technology« (CITEC) at Bielefeld University for providing financial support for the publication of this book.

Nürnberg, September 2011[1] Dennis Spohr

[1] All URLs in this book are valid as of September 4, 2011.

2 Introduction

2.1 Computational Lexicography

According to Tarp (2008: p. 4), lexicography is the »science of dictionaries«, which is meant to be interpreted in direct opposition to the views of researchers who attribute to lexicography the status of a subdiscipline of linguistics. However, while Tarp provides several justifications for his claim (*ibid.*, pp. 4-6), it seems very strong to conceive of lexicography as a science which is *independent* of linguistics. These doubts come from the observation that – irrespective of the particular type of dictionary and the principles that are used to structure it – dictionaries commonly deal with the representation of the items of a language. Moreover, given the amount of linguistic analysis that is typically involved in the initial stages of the compilation of a dictionary, it seems equally plausible to follow the view e. g. of Gibbon (2000), who classifies lexicography as a branch of applied linguistics that deals with the design and construction of dictionaries and the representation of linguistic information.

Irrespective of the debate as to the scientific status of lexicography, which is of no further relevance to the core ideas of this study, there seems to be general agreement on the internal structure of a dictionary. According to Hausmann and Wiegand (1989), for example, it consists of a *microstructure*, a *macrostructure* and a *mediostructure*. While the microstructure refers to the structure of dictionary entries in terms of the descriptions they contain, the macrostructure refers to the sequence of these dictionary entries and the access to them. The mediostructure describes the links between entities, both in terms of references between entries and – in the context of a graph-based lexicon – links between any kind of lexical or descriptive entity.

In addition to these general lexicographic aspects, however, it seems that the definition of lexicography presented above needs to be extended. In particular, it is restricted to dictionaries for human usage only, and does not take into account the structuring of lexical resources for computational use, nor the computational methods which are used to create or process these structures. In addition to the tools which »assist the various lexicographical tasks« (Atkins and Zampolli, 1994: p. 4), these aspects are part of the field of *computational lexicography*, which is classified as a subdiscipline of computational linguistics by Heid (1997). However, in contrast to the debatable position with respect to the independence of lexicography and linguistics, it seems even more difficult to view computational lexicography as separated from computational linguistics. Among others, this is due to the fact that computational lexicography is closely interlinked with other subdisciplines of computational linguistics, such as corpus linguistics for the extraction of lexicographically relevant information from corpora, as well as any branch of computational linguistics that relies to a considerable extent on structured representations of linguistic information, e. g. machine translation. As such, computational lexicography plays a central role in both applied and theoretical respects, in the sense that it applies lexicographic principles and the results of lexicographic research with respect to the structuring of dictionaries in a computational scenario. Therefore, it is not equivalent to the recently emerging *e-lexicography*, is centered around user-oriented electronic dictionaries and thus considered to be subsumed by computational lexicography.

A considerable amount of research in computational lexicography focuses on the conception of structured data models for the definition of machine-readable resources (see e. g. Ide *et al.*, 2003; Polguère, 2006; Trippel, 2006; ISO/FDIS 24613, 2008), as well as the various ways in which the stored information can be processed and *reused* in order to serve several purposes (cf. Heid, 1997). In this respect, recent years have seen a clear tendency towards investigating how descriptions of lexical phenomena can be presented such that they serve different users and their needs in a satisfactory way (see e. g. Gouws, 2007; Gouws and Prinsloo, 2008; Verlinde, 2010; Bothma, 2011). This development is not at all surprising, since these aspects have also been at the centre of attention in theoretical lexicography. In particular, the comparatively recent *function theory* puts very strong emphasis on the needs of different types of users in various kinds of situations (cf. Bergenholtz and Tarp (1995, 2002) and especially Tarp (2008)). Without doubt, function theory is state of the art in theoretical lexicography, and due to its focus on user needs, it defines a number of essential theoretical notions that need to be considered in the context of a model for a multifunctional lexical resource. In the following, we will introduce the main characteristics of function theory, its definition of *lexicographical functions* as well as the concept of a *leximat*, before presenting the main aspects of a *multifunctional* lexical resource.

2.2 Function Theory

As was just mentioned, *function theory* is a rather recent general lexicographic theory that has been developed by Henning Bergenholtz and Sven Tarp (see e. g. Bergenholtz and Tarp, 2002) and published in its latest version by Tarp (2008). In his book, Tarp evaluates the influences that existing lexicographic theories have had on the evolution of function theory by providing a critical account of the predominant directions up to that point. In this contrastive survey, it becomes evident that while function theory has initially built on existing theories such as Wiegand's general lexicographic theory (see e. g. Wiegand, 1988, 1998), it has developed into its own independent theoretical branch.

2.2.1 Definition of a Lexicographical Function

The central aspect of function theory is that it starts from »dictionary users as an object of research« (Tarp, 2008: p. 33) and derives from this analysis requirements on the representation of lexicographic data in dictionaries. In particular, Tarp analyses the needs that users may have in different cognitive and communicative situations, where *cognitive* situations are those in which a user wishes to learn more about a given topic, while *communicative* situations refer to cases »in connection with current or planned communication« (Tarp, 2008: p. 45). Here, the emphasis is on the fact that these situations are essentially *extra-lexicographical situations*, which means that they arise in *potential* users before any dictionary consultation takes place, i. e. before they might turn into *actual* dictionary users. In this vein, a lexicographical function is defined as follows.

> »A lexicographical function is the satisfaction of the specific types of lexicographically relevant need that may arise in a specific type of potential user in a specific type of extra-lexicographical situation.« (Tarp, 2008: p. 81)

Correspondingly, Tarp classifies these lexicographically relevant needs as *function-related* (*primary*) needs which precede any *intra*-lexicographical situation, and distinguishes them from *usage-related* (*secondary*) needs, which do not arise until the potential user has turned into an actual one. Based on this definition, Tarp goes on to define a superior concept of the *genuine purpose* of a dictionary as follows.

> »The genuine purpose of dictionaries is to satisfy the types of lexicographically relevant need that may arise in one or more types of potential user in one or more types of extra-lexicographical situation.« (Tarp, 2008: p. 88)

According to this definition, a *multifunctional* electronic dictionary could be defined as one whose genuine purpose is exactly to satisfy the needs of *several* types of users and situations. As will be seen below, the definition of multifunctionality as applied in the context of computational lexicography even goes beyond this.

In addition to the definitions of these important notions, Tarp's work provides an extensive discussion of different types of situations (e. g. text reception and production in both the mother tongue and a second language), as well as a very detailed presentation of the needs associated with each of these functions (*ibid.*, pp. 69-79 and 146-171). As pointed out by Lew (2008), Tarp's approach to actually arriving at these needs is more pragmatic and in the end not as different from Wiegand's reconstructivist approach as he may have preferred (cf. Tarp, 2008: p. 44; cited in Lew, 2008: p. 115). As criticised e. g. by Piotrowski (2009), however, Tarp does not base his analysis on extensive empirical investigations, and approaches many highly complex cognitive tasks, such as translation and language acquisition, in a somewhat simplistic manner. Despite these issues, which do not affect the core focus of this study, Tarp's analysis offers a comprehensive overview of the various needs that may arise in potential users, and is thus a suitable background for approaching the definition of a multifunctional lexical resource.

2.2.2 The Concept of a Leximat

Besides the theoretical contribution of function theory, Tarp's work introduces the concept of a *leximat*. This term, »which has connotations of both lexicography [...] and mechanics«, is defined as follows.

> »A leximat is a lexicographical tool consisting of a search engine with access to a database and/or the internet, enabling users with a specific type of communicative or cognitive need to gain access via active or passive searching to lexicographical data, from which they can extract the type of information required to cover their specific needs.« (Tarp, 2008: p. 123)

On the one hand, this definition includes lexicographical tools which are labelled as *passive leximats*, as they perform tasks without the user having asked for them (e. g. correction of misspelled user input; cf. the »invisible dictionary« of Bergenholtz, 2005). On the other hand, it includes *active leximats*, which refers to tools that point users to knowledge sources which are capable of satisfying their needs. In the case of cognitive needs, this may involve external resources on the internet.

Tarp deliberately introduces the term leximat in order to differentiate it from an electronic dictionary, mostly due to the traditional connotation of dictionaries as printed reference works. However, due to the strong focus on user-oriented lexicography in his work, the definition of a leximat ignores its use in an NLP scenario. As it is not clear whether this interpretation has been intended – or is simply the result of omission – the term *leximat* will only be used occasionally in order to refer to certain aspects of the work presented in this book. Instead, the more general term *multifunctional lexical resource* will be used, which – as pointed out by Heid (1997) – may include dictionaries, grammars as well as text corpora and even certain NLP tools (*ibid.*, p. 21; see also Trippel, 2010: p. 166), and is thus taken to subsume the key notions of a leximat.

2.3 Multifunctionality

Taking into account the definition of a lexicographical function as proposed by Tarp (2008), one could say that a *multifunctional* lexical resource is one whose genuine purpose is to serve more than one of these functions. As was indicated above, however, multifunctionality goes beyond this. dictionary. In particular, the term is borrowed from literature of the late 1980's and early 1990's on *reusable lexical resources* (see e. g. Heid and McNaught, 1991; Bläser *et al.*, 1992) and has been discussed in great detail in Heid (1997). Here, a multifunctional lexical resource is defined as follows.

> »Der Begriff ›wiederverwendbare lexikalische Ressource‹ bezeichnet eine linguistische Wissensquelle, die schon von ihrer Konzeption an so spezifiziert und realisiert worden ist, daß die Benutzung in verschiedenen Situationen oder Systemen (sowohl verschiedenen Sprachverarbeitungsanwendungen, als auch verschiedenen (interaktiven) Benutzungssituationen mit ›menschlichen Benutzern‹) in die Design-Kriterien miteinfließt. Solche linguistischen Wissensquellen werden auch als ›multifunktionale‹ Ressourcen bezeichnet.« (Heid, 1997: p. 21)

> [»The term ›reusable lexical resource‹ denotes a source of linguistic knowledge whose conception has been specified and realised such that its use in different situations or systems (both different NLP applications and different (interactive) usage situations with ›human users‹) is incorporated in the design criteria. Such sources of linguistic knowledge are also referred to as ›multifunctional‹ resources.«]

According to this definition, and taking into account the analysis presented above, one can say that multifunctionality extends along several dimensions. On the one hand, it refers to the utilisation of the contents of a lexical resource for human users as well as NLP tools. On the other hand, it further needs to cater for the needs of *different types* of users in different situations (e. g. text-productive vs. text-receptive; see above), as well as *different types* of NLP applications (e. g. syntactic parsing or machine translation). Finally, a third dimension can be identified which is concerned with user-specific characteristics like their mother tongue or their language proficiency on the one hand (cf. Tarp, 2008), and application-specific paradigms and terminologies on the other. This means that in order to be truly multifunctional, the model of a lexical resource needs to offer the formal means to define a specific point in this space with respect to the *domain* (e. g. a human user vs. an NLP application), the *function* (e. g. a text-receptive situation vs. syntactic parsing) and an *idiosyncratic* property (e. g. with German mother tongue vs. Lexical-Functional Grammar), and to serve the needs associated with this point. assumed to be overlapping. This is due to the fact that although some of the needs are shared by human users and NLP applications, the criteria to identify them are not. For example, although one could say that proof-reading and syntactic parsing are to some extent related in the sense that both of them need e. g. syntactic valence information (for human users see Tarp (2008): p. 77), one would not say that syntactic parsing is a relevant function of its own in the context of human users. Therefore, we assume that these two functions are located in different ranges, and that the tools used in order to serve the needs associated with them are not necessarily the same.

With reference to function theory, Gouws (2007) states that the »compilation of any dictionary needs to be preceded by a clear identification of the functions that should prevail in the dictionary« (Gouws, 2007: p. 66). However, as the complete range of potential users and applications of a *multifunctional* lexical resource are not necessarily known at the time the lexicon model is compiled, this does not apply completely in this context. In fact, such a lexicon is in direct opposition to application-specific lexical resources on the one hand and human-readable electronic dictionaries on the other. According to de Schryver (2003: p. 145) these two »seem worlds apart«, which is exemplified by the fact that each has typically been designed to serve one particular purpose or a small set of predefined ones and requires considerable effort when trying to adapt it to serving unforeseen purposes (see e. g. Asmussen and Ørsnes, 2005; Spohr, 2004).

Based on the assumption that the internal structure of a lexicon model circumstances does not need to differ along with the purposes that the corresponding lexical resource is to serve, multifunctionality thus refers to the ability to extract different »dictionaries« from a common lexical data collection, i. e. to allow for different views on the lexical data. Each of these views comes with its own lexicographic needs, and thus, the definition of a multifunctional lexical resource presupposes an extensible mechanism that enables its use in various scenarios. Such considerations suggest an architecture according to the notion of »Mutterwörterbuch« (≈ »*mother dictionary*«) as conceived of by Gouws (2006), in which entities are marked on a macro- and microstructural level for their inclusion in a particular usage situation. As a result, the traditional view of lexical entries as static entities needs to be replaced by one which conceives them as *dynamic* entities that are generated according to the needs in this situation.

2.4 Objectives and Contributions of this Book

The central objectives of this study are to design and implement a model for a multifunctional lexical resource that is capable of satisfying the needs of different types of users in different types of communicative and cognitive situations, as well as to provide the mechanisms which are necessary in order to serve different types of NLP applications. In addition to presenting the details of this model, a further major objective is to show how the representations therein can be integrated into the architecture of a multifunctional lexical resource and support the definition of its access functionality, as well as the function-based presentation of its content. However, it should be emphasised that the model as presented in this study does not make any claims as to its completeness with respect to the range of linguistic phenomena that can be represented. Rather, its objective is to be general enough as to enable later extension to further phenomena, and to show the ways in which this can be accomplished.

In the course of achieving these objectives, this study makes contributions in the following respects, which are – in terms of Wiegand (1989) – situated on the methodological side of lexicographic research. First, it provides the implementation of a model that is inspired by the primarily theoretical considerations of Gouws (2006) and Heid and Gouws (2006), and proposes a general and extensible architecture for dealing with user needs in the context of a multifunctional lexical resource. In addition to mere inclusion marks in the sense of Gouws (2006), this mechanism takes into account the user need status as proposed by Tarp (2008) as well as the language background and proficiency of the user. On a conceptual level, this study thus contributes to the view of a lexical entry as a dynamic entity that is generated at the time of the consultation, as opposed to the traditional view of lexical entries as static text-based entities (see Polguère, 2006: p. 51). Moreover, the thoughts presented in the afore-mentioned works are applied not only in the context of human users, but extended to applications in the field of natural language processing.

On a more abstract level, this study introduces concepts from artificial intelligence to the field of computational lexicography, and highlights the support of standard knowledge representation formalisms and reasoning in the definition of a consistent and integer lexical resource. While the general approach of using AI-related formalisms in a lexicographical setting is not a recent one (Evans and Gazdar, 1996; see also Görz, in prep), it seems to be undocumented to use them in a context that (i) includes electronic dictionaries which serve both human users as well as NLP applications, and (ii) views these dictionaries as graphs. By touching upon the results of a recent AI-related project like the semantic web and the range of possibilities opened up by such technologies, this book thus makes an important contribution to research on the internal structure of electronic lexical resources. This is exemplified by means of a prototype implementation of a multifunctional lexical resource which contains unified representations of lexicographically relevant information from the SALSA corpus (Burchardt *et al.*, 2006) and a recently developed database of automatically extracted collocations (Weller and Heid, 2010).

This book is structured as follows. Chapter 3 discusses general requirements on the design of a lexicon model, as well as more specific ones arising in the context of a multifunctional lexical resource. In addition to this, it analyses the implications that these requirements have on different components of the multifunctional lexical resource, as well as on the choice of the formalism that is used for its definition. Finally, the chapter gives an overview of recent other approaches in this field and assesses their performance regarding the identified requirements.

Chapter 4 is devoted to the discussion of the formalism that is used for the definition of the lexicon model. After a short introduction to the *semantic web*, an AI-related project that deals among others with the development of knowledge representation formalisms, the main properties of the *Resource Description Framework* (RDF) and the *Web Ontology Language* (OWL) are presented and positioned with respect to the more widely known and used formalism XML. In particular, the chapter focusses on the formal characteristics of OWL DL, a sublanguage of OWL that is based on a decidable fragment of first-order logics. Moreover, it provides a brief review of the relevant tools that have been developed for querying and processing resources defined in these formalisms, such as inference engines and scalable storage solutions. This section, which provides a rather formal account of the properties of semantic web formalisms, is directed towards more technically interested readers, and may be skipped by readers who focus more on the philological aspects of lexicographic research. Section 4.2 is, however, necessary to support some of the claims made in later chapters, which is why it needs to be part of this book. Section 4.3 closes this chapter with a discussion of the benefits that the tools and formalisms developed in the semantic web offer for specific lexicographic issues. As such, it represents a central section of this book that is recommended to be read by any reader of this book.

Chapter 5 discusses in great detail the lexicon model that has been developed, as well as the motivation behind specific modelling decisions, and provides details on the formalisation of a fragment of the model in description logics. A central section of this chapter deals with the multifunctional aspects of the lexicon model, i. e. the modelling of lexicographical functions and NLP requirements, and presents an extensible mechanism for modelling user profiles in a way that achieves a complete independence of the *object language* (the »described« language), *metalanguage* (the vocabulary used for the description), and *interface language* (the language in which it is presented to the user), and which thus leaves the actual lexical data untouched. Finally, the architecture of the multifunctional lexicon model is shown and discussed in the context of monolingual data, and with a view to bilingual and multilingual perspectives.

Chapter 6 presents the multifunctional lexical resource that can be defined by means of the model introduced in the previous chapter, starting with the extraction and unification of lexicographically relevant information from two existing lexical resources. A large portion of the chapter deals with suggestions for a custom graphical user interface and reports on the ongoing development of such. After providing details on the definition of a mechanism for generating lexical entries for specific lexicographical functions, the NLP-oriented access routes are discussed, which includes details on the implementation of an application programming interface as well as the definition of an exchange format. The chapter closes with a proposal for an architecture of a multifunctional lexical resource.

Chapter 7 summarises the main aspects presented in Chapters 3 to 6 and discusses further improvements as well as possible future developments.

3 Requirements Analysis and State of the Art

In this chapter, we will first discuss the main requirements for the design of the multifunctional lexical resource model (MLR model) as well as requirements which address different components of the MLR as a whole (Section 3.1). Here, we will focus on those requirements which we consider underrepresented both in current models for computational lexicons and electronic dictionaries. This is not to say, however, that each of these requirements in isolation is not treated adequately anywhere, but rather that it is not possible to find a resource that offers a balanced combination of them. Justifications for this claim will be given in Section 3.2, which provides an overview of the state of the art of approaches to defining electronic dictionaries and models for computational lexical resources[1].

3.1 Requirements Analysis

Most of the requirements have been discussed at large in the literature and can, in the context of an MLR, be classified as *requirements on the description, formal and technical requirements*, as well as *requirements with respect to multifunctionality* (see also Spohr, 2008). In the following sections, we will discuss a number of these requirements in more detail, focussing on particular aspects of the description in Section 3.1.1 and the formal and technical aspects in Section 3.1.2. As the main emphasis of this work is on the definition of a model for an MLR, requirements which are centered around the coverage in terms of lexical items are largely ignored. Requirements which originate from the multifunctionality of the MLR will be discussed in Section 3.1.3. Finally, Section 3.1.4 summarises the implications of these requirements on the choice of the formalism for defining the MLR model as well as the other components which make up the MLR.

3.1.1 Requirements on the Description

The first complex of requirements to be discussed refers to various kinds of descriptions, such as linguistic properties of lexical items or multimedia elements for illustrative purposes. In contrast to traditional print dictionaries, the electronic medium does not impose space restrictions on the presentation of dictionary content. Thus, there is no need for text condensation or »traditional space-saving mechanisms« (Gouws, 2007: p. 66), and the descriptions should be stored and indicated in their unabbreviated form (see »decompression« in de Schryver, 2003; Schall, 2007). Moreover, the detail of the descriptions has to be such that the MLR is capable of serving as useful input to both specialised NLP tasks and human expert users, while retaining the possibility to generate or extract less detailed descriptions from the data if required. In addition to this, the MLR model should provide a typology of lexical items, in

[1] Resources which are only commercially available will not be considered.

order to allow for example for *»search by lemma type«* (Schall, 2007: p. 59), such as search restricted to compounds or idioms.

As the mere reproduction of a comprehensive list of phenomena to be covered is not necessary in the context of this work, the following subsections explain three particular phenomena which we consider immediately relevant to both human users and several NLP applications, namely valence, collocations and preferences. The section closes with a few remarks on multilinguality.

3.1.1.1 Valence description

Heid (2006) emphasises the importance of detailed valence descriptions with respect to both human users and NLP applications. From the viewpoint of text production, for example, he notes that it is vital to make explicit reference to the valence differences between (quasi-) synonyms such as *»treffen«* and *»begegnen«* (*»encounter, meet«*), where the direct accusative object of *»treffen«* (»that which is encountered«) is mapped onto the indirect dative object of *»begegnen«*. In addition to this, Heid lists machine translation as an example of NLP technology which relies heavily on (and greatly benefits from) detailed valence description: a machine translation system needs to have the information that e. g. the direct object of *»remember«* is mapped onto the prepositional object of its translation equivalent *»erinnern«*.

A number of researchers have suggested to use the three-layered approach to valence description proposed by FrameNet (Baker *et al.*, 1998; see e. g. Heid and Krüger, 1996; Atkins *et al.*, 2003; Boas, 2005; Heid, 2006) in order to provide adequate treatment of valence phenomena in the lexicon. In this approach, the subcategorised (as well as optional) arguments of a predicate are not only assigned a *phrasal category* (as in many current valence dictionaries; see Herbst *et al.* (2005) for an example) and a *grammatical function* (as in NLP lexica such as traditional LFG subcategorisation lexica; see e. g. Kaplan and Bresnan, 1982), but also a *semantic role* (*»frame element«* in FrameNet). A valence pattern thus consists of one or several such category-function-role triples. This combination of both syntactic and semantic information in the FrameNet approach provides »an analysis of meaning far more granular than is normally possible in commercial lexicography« (Atkins *et al.*, 2003: p. 340).

A crucial point made by Heid (2006) – in the context of valence dictionaries – is that valence descriptions should not only be provided for »prototypical predicates« like verbs, but that this treatment should be extended to cover nouns and multi-word expressions as well (see e. g. Heid and Gouws, 2006). In line with what has been discussed for (lexical-)semantically related items, the differences in valence patterns as well as the mapping of valence arguments (i) between morphologically related items (e. g. verbs and their nominalisations), and (ii) between »collocationally related« items (e. g. nouns and their occurrences in support-verb-constructions) are of central importance. Therefore, the points that have been made in this section so far do also apply to non-verbal lexical items and multi-word expressions.

3.1.1.2 Collocations

Although collocations are highly relevant to both NLP and language-learning tasks (see e. g. Heid, 2006; Tarp, 2008), adequate treatment has been largely neglected in past dictionary design. Apart from specialised collocation dictionaries which have been specifically designed to deal with multi-word expressions (see e. g. Crowther *et al.*, 2003; DiCE[2]), many current electronic dictionaries (e. g. ELDIT: Abel and Weber, 2000) assign to them the status of usage examples in the microstructure of a lexical entry. As a result, it is in such dictionaries difficult – if not impossible – to obtain more detailed information about collocations, such as valence descriptions (see above) or preferences (see below). Such information is, however, indispensable in order for a dictionary to be a useful tool. In other words, the MLR model needs to promote collocations to the status of »treatment units« (Gouws and Prinsloo, 2005: pp. 134f), i. e. they should become part of the macrostructure of the dictionary and receive their own microstructural description (see also Heid and Gouws (2006) and Spohr (2005)). Moreover, due to their relevance as well as the fact that their descriptions are generally more complex than those of single-word entities, the features of collocations will be picked up very frequently throughout the discussions in this work.

3.1.1.3 Preferences and frequency descriptions

Describing preference phenomena is important e. g. for the production of texts, irrespective of whether they are to be automatically generated by an NLP component or produced by a foreign language learner. An approach to detecting morphosyntactic preferences of collocations has e. g. been discussed in Evert *et al.* (2004). The main focus there was on extracting distributional preferences, such as quantifications about how often the base of a collocation is used in the singular or the plural form (e. g. *»sich Hoffnungen machen«* (*»to have hopes«*), where the base is most frequently used in the plural form; Evert *et al.*, 2004: p. 907).

While it is, of course, not only multi-word expressions which show this kind of distributional preferences with respect to morphosyntactic features[3], lexical items in general do further show selectional preferences in terms of valence. The focus here is not on subcategorised arguments, but rather preferences as far as lexical fillers of specific argument slots are concerned. Heid lists *»er hält* X *von jemandem«* (*»he thinks* X *of someone«*) as an example, where *X* may only be replaced by a quite restricted set of lexical fillers, such as *»viel«*, *»nichts«* or *»eine Menge«* (*»much«*, *»nothing«*, *»a lot«*; Heid, 2006: p. 77).

In addition to preference phenomena, it is desirable to be able to assign corpus-based frequency counts to different kinds of indications. For example, in order to be able to present the senses in a lexical entry ordered according to their frequency, it is necessary to be able to represent this kind of information in the MLR model. However, frequency descriptions should also be attributable to more complex descriptions, such as the frequency of a syntactic valence frame with respect to a sense, or the frequency of a particular orthographic form of a lemma. Again, since the kinds of descriptions for which corpus frequency should be stored is not necessarily known at the time of defining the model, a general approach is needed.

3.1.1.4 Multilinguality

Citing Atkins (1996), de Schryver (2003) states that bi- and multilingual dictionaries should offer monolingual functions as well (e. g. definitions or usage notes), and that the second

---

2 http://www.dicesp.com

3 Cf. *»er hat berechnet, dass ... «* (*»he has calculated that ... «*), where in almost every observable corpus instance *»berechnen«* is used in a past tense form (Heid, 2006: p. 76).

language should receive »full treatment« (p. 164f). Moreover, Tarp points out that »traditional learner's dictionaries that are *either* monolingual or bilingual only have a limited useful value« (Tarp, 2008: p. 151). Following the approach of viewing bilingual dictionaries as combinations of two monolingual dictionaries as in Spohr and Heid (2006), this requirement can be met by the general design of the MLR structure. In addition to this bilingual view, the approach presented there can be extended to allow for a general view on multilingual dictionaries as combinations of several monolingual ones (cf. Section 4.3.2 and 5.5.2).

3.1.2 Formal and Technical Requirements

Formal and technical requirements refer to formal properties of the MLR model, as well as the technical aspects of the lexical resource. One of the requirements that is to be discussed in more detail below refers to *access and retrieval*, which should be scalable and performed very efficiently. Moreover, it should allow for complete exploration of all sorts of data contained in the lexicon, their relations as well as complex combinations of both. In addition to this, the model should support an *explicit* organisation of the descriptions mentioned above, in the sense that it should be possible to identify different types of indications unambiguously (cf. Heid, 1997: p. 12f[4]). Such *typed links* can also refer to entities outside the lexicon, such as a query to another lexical resource, a thesaurus or an online search engine (de Schryver, 2003; Tarp, 2008; Verlinde, 2010).

In addition to this, formal requirements include issues of *consistency and integrity*, which become increasingly important when dealing with large amounts of lexicographical data, and even more if these have been acquired and inserted both automatically and manually. Relevant questions in this context are e. g. which properties or relations are used to describe which kinds of items, and how it is possible to ensure that these items actually make use of only the properties they are supposed to. Further technical requirements include the integration of a morphological analyser that processes the input of the user – for word-form-based search or orthographically tolerant search – as well as the logging of a user's search behaviour in order to be able to analyse and improve the interface of the lexical resource (Verlinde (2010); see also Knapp (2004); Bergenholtz and Johnsen (2005); de Schryver *et al.* (2006)).

In the following subsections, we deal in more detail with the formal and technical requirements with respect to access and retrieval as well as consistency and integrity. However, they will be discussed only insofar as they directly affect the internal structure of the MLR model. Further aspects, such as how users should have access to the data, will be discussed in Section 3.1.3.

3.1.2.1 Access and retrieval

Tarp (2008) lists a number of minimal features that should be retrievable from an ED, such as idioms, lemmas, irregular forms, word class or gender. In addition to this, Chiari (2006) states that combinations of such features should also be queryable, e. g. »all nouns and verbs which are rare or frequent and specific of any field except physics« (Chiari, 2006: p. 144). Of course,

[4] See also the criterion »*Konsistenz und Eindeutigkeit der Informationskodierung*« (»*consistency and unambiguity of information encoding*«) in (Schall, 2007: p. 40).

such expressions can be arbitrarily extended (»..., and which subcategorise prepositional phrases except ones with 'auf' ...«), meaning that for all items in the lexical resource that are connected in some way, these connections should be explorable (see e. g. Dodd, 1989; Schall, 2007). In addition, this should be possible by different search modes, such as orthographically tolerant search (fuzzy search), search with Boolean operators and wildcards, or even by voice (cf. de Schryver, 2003; Schall, 2007; see also Section 3.1.3.1).

Chiari's ideas are in line with what is more generally labelled as »Ad-hoc-Abfrage« (*»ad-hoc querying«*) in (Heid, 1997: pp. 145ff) or »non-standard access« in Spohr and Heid (2006), i. e. »access via paths involving other properties and relations than just lemmas« (Spohr and Heid, 2006: p. 71). In a related way, de Schryver mentions »access aspects for which the outer search path (leading to a lemma sign) does not necessarily precede the inner search path (leading to data within articles)« (de Schryver, 2003: p. 173), and Atkins even talked about the »iron grip of the alphabet«, calling for »new methods of access« (Atkins, 1992: p. 521). In this vein, it should in principle be possible to access the data at any arbitrary point in the model. In other words, there should not be a predefined entry point or access point to the data – as is usually the case with standard lemma-based query access[5]. In contrast to the traditional view on dictionaries as lists of entries – which are according to Polguère simply »texts, in the most general sense« (Polguère, 2006: p. 51) – this requires to view dictionaries as graphs in which, among others, »implicit references, in fact, all words [...] should be hyperlinked to the relevant lemma« (Prinsloo, 2005: p. 18; cf. Knapp, 2004: pp. 87-89), and where all nodes and edges in the graph may serve as potential access points (see e. g. Spohr and Heid, 2006; Trippel, 2006). Moreover, the MLR should enable access to external and complementary sources of information, such as online search engines and text corpora, in the sense of Tarp's *leximat* which is capable of serving both communicative and cognitive functions (cf. Tarp, 2008: p. 120ff; see also de Schryver, 2003; Gelpí, 2007).

3.1.2.2 Consistency and integrity

The next requirement on the MLR model that is to be discussed here refers to rather formal aspects, namely the means that are necessary in order to ensure *consistency* and *integrity* of the MLR. In a certain sense, the notion of integrity is subsumed by the notion of consistency. However, we choose to use these two terms in order to describe two separate things. For us, consistency refers to the question as to whether the underlying model of the MLR is *satisfiable* – i. e. whether it is at all *possible* for lexical data to satisfy the conditions defined in the lexicon model without causing any contradictions – as well as whether the data *actually* satisfy the conditions.

Integrity, on the other hand, refers to the question as to whether their descriptions are complete. In order to achieve this, it is necessary to be able to (i) identify and distinguish between different types of data in an MLR, (ii) define different wellformedness constraints and properties for these types, (iii) restrict the set of items that can occur as values of these properties, and (iv) make sure that the data adhere to these restrictions. A very basic kind of consistency check is e. g. to ensure that the values of a part-of-speech property of lexical items are actu-

[5] Whether this is desirable for all kinds of users is not the question here. We believe, however, that it is better to set the stage for »unrestricted access« to the data and constrain it e. g. by means of the graphical user interface than to allow only for restricted access in the first place.

ally made up of part-of-speech tags, and not of grammatical gender, case, or misspelt variants (e. g. *Nn* instead of *NN*), and this should probably be possible in any »mildly« structured formalism. However, more intricate cases are conceivable e. g. for collocations of the type »V + N_{Obj}« (i. e. collocations with a verbal collocator and a nominal base that represents the object of the verb, such as *»eine Rede$_N$ halten$_V$«* (*»to give$_V$ a speech$_N$«*)), where the part of speech of the base of the collocation (*»Rede«*) has to be »N«, and the collocator (*»halten«*) has to be a transitive verb that subcategorises an object. Such restrictions have to be formalisable and verifiable in the MLR model, and traditional approaches that rely on document type definitions (DTD) or XML schemata do not have the formal means to express these kinds of restrictions.

3.1.3 Multifunctional Requirements

Multifunctional requirements denote those requirements that have been derived from the intended multifunctionality of the lexical resource. In particular, they refer to the lexicographical functions that the MLR is to serve, and thus both to specific users' needs and to needs of NLP applications. As the functions are not necessarily known a priori, a general and extensible mechanism for modelling these needs is required. Moreover, multifunctional requirements refer to the ways in which the content of the lexical resource is presented to different types of users, e. g. by means of complete vs. (gradually) reduced article views, as well as the possibility to generate a printable PDF version of the lexical entry (cf. Bartels and Spieß, 2002; de Schryver, 2003; Schall, 2007). As the points of departure are rather different for addressing the needs of human users and the needs of NLP applications, we will discuss below the multifunctional requirements on the MLR first from a user-oriented perspective and then from an NLP-oriented perspective.

3.1.3.1 User-oriented perspective

As was mentioned above, there is an abundance of literature focussing on the needs of users, and many of the requirements discussed there deal with the interaction between users and the lexical resource. At the time of writing, probably the most comprehensive overview is provided by de Schryver (2003), who analysed in detail the relevant literature up to this point and produced a list of no less than 118 desiderata, with emphasis on the advantages that electronic dictionaries offer compared to their printed counterparts. A more recent publication in this field is the dissertation by Schall, who elaborates – among others on the basis of de Schryver's more abstract analysis – a condensed catalogue of 95 criteria according to which electronic dictionaries should be evaluated (cf. Schall, 2007: pp. 81–84). These criteria cover aspects of both content, access and presentation, and after introducing detailed guidelines as to how this evaluation can be carried out, Schall goes on to evaluate several English and German monolingual electronic dictionaries according to her guidelines (Schall, 2007: chap. 3).

Although most of the requirements mentioned in these works have their justification and are relevant to the task at hand, it would not be reasonable to reproduce a discussion of every single one of them. This is mainly due to the fact that many of them merely represent »reminders« of small but more or less important details that should be paid attention to. For example, criterion 16 mentioned by Schall states that for entries containing several graphical illustrations (e. g. *»fruit«*) one should adhere to the proportions of the depicted items (cf. Schall, 2007: p. 44). Therefore, we refer the curious reader to the respective publications and instead focus on a subset of these requirements that rather relate to the conception of the *model* that underlies the MLR with respect to its users.

The most important requirement – and the most obvious one, one might assume – is that the MLR should have a *user-friendly* user interface. De Schryver notes that »if the contents one needs at a particular point in time cannot be accessed in a quick and straightforward way, the dictionary [...] fails to be a good dictionary« (de Schryver, 2003: p. 173). However, Chiari (2006) points out that although user-friendliness in terms of ease of access is a core goal, it should not affect the overall performance and flexibility of the dictionary, such as user customisation and the need to create user-defined dictionaries – a view she shares with a number of other researchers. For example, Atkins (1996) defines the notion of a »virtual dictionary« that is created at the time of dictionary consultation (see de Schryver, 2003: p. 162), and Gouws speaks in terms of a »Mutterwörterbuch« (≈ *»mother dictionary«*), i. e. an abstract dictionary model from which several different (and more specialised) dictionaries can be generated (Gouws, 2006). What these approaches have in common is the demand to be able to define individual dictionaries on the basis of the needs of specific types of users (cf. the criterion *»Individualisierung«* (*»customisation«*) in Schall, 2007: p. 83; see also Gelpí (2007)). On the one hand, this can be partially realised using search forms that allow users to mark the kinds of information they want to retrieve (see e. g. DiCouèbe[6]). On the other hand, not every type of user can be expected to define their output indications in that way. Moreover, when it comes to mapping a query to (both micro- and macrostructural) subsets of the data based on the type of user and the needs associated with this type, a more general and principled approach is needed.

As was mentioned in Section 2.2 above, Tarp (2008) provides useful insights in this respect. In contrast to de Schryver (2003) and Schall (2007), which might to a large extent be considered as comprehensive reviews of the literature at that time, Tarp (2008) presents a more theoretical analysis based on his own general theory of lexicographical functions (*function theory*; see Section 2.2 above; cf. Bergenholtz and Tarp, 2002). Departing from a notion similar to that of Atkins, who stated that »[e]very good dictionary starts from a clear idea of who its users are and what they are going to do with it« (Atkins, 1996: p. 525), Tarp puts particular emphasis on the needs of *potential users*, i. e. needs arising in cognitive or communicative situations which precede the actual consultation of the dictionary (cf. Tarp, 2008: pp. 47ff). According to this view, dictionaries should be conceived of with the needs of users in particular usage situations in mind (e. g. text reception vs. production). Moreover, Storrer (2001) states the following.

> »Lexikalische Daten können so modelliert werden, dass in Abhängigkeit von Nutzerinteressen und Nutzungssituationen die jeweils relevanten lexikographischen Angaben und Verweise herausgegriffen und in ästhetisch ansprechender Weise am Bildschirm dargestellt werden.«(Storrer, 2001: p. 53f)

> [»Lexical data can be modelled such that, depending on users' interests and usage situations, the respectively relevant lexicographic indications and links are extracted and presented on screen in an aesthetically appealing way.«]

6 http://olst.ling.umontreal.ca/dicouebe/main.php

Therefore, what is necessary for an MLR is a formal tool that states (i) which elements of the lexical description are needed in a particular usage situation, and (ii) how these are presented to the user. Here, the analyses in Tarp (2008) can be used primarily for (i), by means of specifying the status of a specific kind of indication e. g. as *primary need* or *secondary need*. For (ii), the tool needs to provide specifications which allow for the presentation of the same content to different users in different ways. This involves e. g. different interface languages depending on the mother tongue of the users, as well as varying amounts of expert terminology, depending on their lexicographic proficiency.

3.1.3.2 NLP-oriented perspective

In addition to serving the needs of different types of users as outlined in the previous section, a truly *multifunctional* lexical resource has to be able to serve NLP applications as well. Although de Schryver notes that the data structures of large-scale NLP lexicons on the one hand and human-readable electronic dictionaries on the other »seem worlds apart«, he notices a clear tendency towards combinations of the two (de Schryver, 2003: p. 145). Similar to the human users of a dictionary, one could say that most NLP applications »speak« their own language. However, while in the case of human users this issue can be resolved e. g. by offering the presentation of the content in several different languages, in the case of NLP it typically involves completely different structures. For example, if a particular NLP application expects input in XML, it does not automatically mean that it can reasonably process any arbitrary XML format that it is provided with.

On the one hand, this can be overcome by providing – ideally standardised – formats for the exchange of data with NLP applications, such as LMF (ISO/FDIS 24613, 2008; see Section 3.2.2.1) or PAULA (Potsdam interchange format for linguistic annotation; Dipper *et al.*, 2006). Here, the dictionary content is converted into the respective exchange format, which can in turn be converted into the format that is needed for the NLP tool. In the case of standardised exchange formats, the NLP application either has the routines necessary for conversion from the standard format into the application-specific format already, or they need to be implemented by the developer of the application. A slightly different view on this issue is to give NLP applications direct access to the lexical resource by means of an *application programming interface* (API), which enables the developer of an NLP application to immediately retrieve and process information from the MLR in a form that suits the respective NLP tool. Here, the most important prerequisite for wide usability is that this API is ideally defined in a platform-independent programming language, such as Java.

The extent to which these requirements can be met by the model of an MLR is rather limited. In fact, it does not go beyond the need to enable the definition of APIs and exchange formats or, at best, support them e. g. by making use of existing APIs. The MLR as a whole should provide access for NLP applications though, and therefore needs to provide mechanisms for exporting the content of the lexical resource in a standardised exchange format as well as an API for direct access to the lexicon.

3.1.4 Implications on the Design of the MLR

The different types of requirements mentioned above have direct implications on various aspects of the MLR. The requirements on the description primarily affect the linguistic model that underlies the lexical resource. As this involves the way in which lexical entities and their descriptions are represented, linguistic requirements determine, on a more abstract level, the choice of the formalism that is used for defining the MLR model. While formal and technical requirements affect the internal structure of the model as well, they further have an effect on the interface between the MLR and human users, as well as between the MLR and NLP applications. Therefore, we can say that in addition to affecting the underlying model, they also influence the general architecture of the MLR and its components. Multifunctional requirements have implications on all of the aspects just mentioned, namely the choice of the formalism, the MLR model, as well as the lexicon architecture. In particular, however, they also have a more theoretical implication with respect to the concept of a *lexical entry*. The various implications will be discussed in the following.

3.1.4.1 Implications on the choice of the formalism

One of the implications which can be directly derived from the above analysis is the fact that the underlying formalism – in addition to being graph-based – cannot be entirely unconstrained, but rather has to be strongly typed. In this respect, very general approaches as those described e. g. by Trippel (2006) and Polguère (2006) do not seem to provide for the appropriate structural means for ensuring consistency and integrity in the sense discussed above – such as relations with defined domain and range – as they rather focus on a very general and unconstrained graph structure (see also Section 3.2.2). In contrast to this, typed formalisms based on the Resource Description Framework (RDF; Manola and Miller, 2004), such as RDF Schema (Brickley and Guha, 2004) or the Web Ontology Language (OWL; Bechhofer *et al.*, 2004), offer among others the formal devices needed to address the issues mentioned above. In addition to this, if one attempts to define a new graph-based framework or metalanguage, it is not unlikely to arrive at a point where one starts »remodelling« subsets of RDF – the description of items in a lexicon can very well be considered as a specific case of describing resources in general –, except for the fact that then large parts of the existing technical infrastructure are no longer available, such as tools which interpret the vocabulary that is needed for this description. This means that all but very basic infrastructure has to be reimplemented in order to be able to interpret the new vocabulary, e. g. the semantics of specific XML element tags[7]. This is not to say that all these issues dissolve once RDF is used. It rather means that using a common metalanguage that has been defined in a declarative and standard framework entails some advantages, such as the fact that – e. g. in the case of OWL – the formal characteristics and complexity have been investigated extensively and are well-known, and that even at the most abstract level more than just very basic infrastructure is available (see Section 4.3). In addition to this, consistency control is one of the strongest claims of Burchardt *et al.* (2008b) in favour of using a typed framework for

[7] Cf. the joint project between the Universities of Tübingen (SFB 441), Hamburg (SFB 538) and Potsdam (SFB 632), which addresses, among others, the issue of *sustainability* of linguistic data (see e. g. Dipper *et al.*, 2006; see also Trippel, 2006: p. 37).

the definition of models for lexical resources. In essence, they have proposed a combination of general knowledge representation methods (e. g. theorem provers for axiom-based consistency checking) with a graph-based query language (see also Section 6.1.2). In doing so, they have been able to express highly complex consistency queries involving several distinct layers, such as the formal definition of FrameNet, the frame semantic annotation scheme, as well as syntactic corpus annotations.

Finally, the point made by Heid (1997) in the context of explicitly vs. implicitly organised dictionaries is a further argument in favour of using a typed formalism. Here, explicitly organised dictionaries are those in which the type of every indication can be identified separately, whereas in implicitly organised dictionaries the type of an indication, as well as e. g. its spacial boundaries in a dictionary entry, needs to be determined on the basis of metalexicographic analysis. As a result, implicit (i. e. untyped) resources may possibly contain ambiguous indications (Heid, 1997: pp. 12f).

3.1.4.2 Implications on the MLR model

In addition to the implications on the choice of the formalism, the different kinds of requirements directly affect the internal structure of the MLR model and its immediate infrastructure. For example, in order to be able to retrieve arbitrary combinations of items from the lexical resource, the relations between these entities have to be expressible in the model in the first place. In other words, the model should be very powerful and offer representations for a wide range of phenomena. On the other hand, however, it is very important to keep an eye on the complexity of the descriptions in the lexicon. Since the data have to be retrievable with an adequate amount of effort, the MLR model should not be more complex than necessary and, ideally, support the development of other components of the lexicon, such as a graphical user interface.

With regard to the modelling of valence information, it needs to be said that although FrameNet (Baker *et al.*, 1998) offers a number of attractive solutions for the description of valence phenomena, a complete adaptation of their paradigm would produce a rather specific and theory-dependent lexicon model. Therefore, while it is reasonable to follow the FrameNet approach in principle and to adhere to three levels of valence description – syntactic category, syntactic function and semantic role – the MLR model should, for the sake of theory-independence, deviate as far as the formalisation of frames and roles is concerned. In other words, it should not rely on frame semantics as a theoretical framework and be extensible such that it can express valence information also on the basis of a different set of semantic roles, such as the one defined by Sowa (2000), if this is desired. Nonetheless, in view of the existence of resources such as the Berkeley FrameNet database for English (Ruppenhofer *et al.*, 2002) and the SALSA lexicon for German (Burchardt *et al.*, 2006; Spohr *et al.*, 2007), it would certainly be inconsiderate to ignore FrameNet and not make use of the lexical knowledge contained in these resources. Therefore, it seems reasonable to use FrameNet as a first basis for the description of valence information.

3.1.4.3 Implications on the architecture of the MLR and its components

As was mentioned in the analysis above, a model is needed which formalises the needs of different types of users in terms of the entities in the MLR. This component should ideally be kept separate from the actual data, in the sense that it provides user-specific *views* on the data, instead of manipulating them directly. The specifications in this model should be represented in a format that enables them to be processed by the components of the user interface that deal with the access by querying as well as the presentation of the content of the lexical resource to the user. In addition to this, the analysis above suggests that the MLR should allow for the embedding of several NLP tools – such as a morphological analyser that processes the input given by the user and a generator for generating inflected forms – as well as a tool that enables orthographically tolerant search, e. g. by means of calculating the Levenshtein distance (Levenshtein, 1966).

Finally, one of the most important implications of the above analysis – in particular of Tarp's account of lexicographic functions (Tarp, 2008) and the concept of multifunctionality as suggested e. g. by Heid and Gouws (2006) – is that lexical entries are not uniform across different types of users, since the same indications may need to be presented to different kinds of users in different ways. Therefore, a lexical entry is not a static entity that is stored as a text in some database. Rather, it is to be conceived of as an entity that is determined on the basis of the needs of a user, and that has to be generated dynamically from the statements which make up the MLR graph. In Chapter 5 and especially Chapter 6 of this work, we present ideas as to how the dynamic notion of lexical entries can be supported by the underlying model, in the sense that a lexical entry is generated at the moment the consultation takes place. An architecture which caters for this would be conceptually very close to Gouws' notion of a »*mother dictionary*« (Gouws, 2006) as well as the concept of a *leximat* as conceived of by Tarp (2008).

3.2 Overview of the State of the Art

This section will assess the performance of related approaches in the field of lexical resources, covering both electronic dictionaries for human users, models for computational lexicons designed for NLP purposes, as well as approaches for combining the two. As the focus of the discussion in this section is on *recent* approaches, however, we will just give a brief introduction and review of the main points of criticism that had been identified with respect to the more »traditional« approaches, before discussing in detail the more recent proposals.[8] The predominant approaches of the 1980's and 1990's have been described and analysed at length in the relevant literature (see e. g. Menon and Modiano (1993); Heid (1997); Hellwig (1997)).

[8] In order to highlight the differences and problems with some of these proposals, a certain amount of formal detail in terms of XML representations is at times required. A very basic introduction to the main characteristics of XML can be found in Section 4.2.2.

3.2.1 Traditional Approaches

The 1980's and 1990's have seen a large number of projects aiming at the definition of standardised formats for reusable lexical resources. Among the most prominent ones are probably the (then EC-funded) projects ACQUILEX[9], GENELEX[10], MULTILEX[11], as well as the more recent PAROLE[12] and its follow-up [13]. What all of these approaches share is that they aimed at the definition of lexical resources and standard representation formats for computational use only. Hence, *reusability* had the sole interpretation of »being usable for more than one NLP application«. The ACQUILEX project, for example, has dealt with the acquisition of lexical knowledge from machine-readable versions of printed dictionaries, as well as their representation in a format that would serve different NLP applications. However, as the emphasis has been on computational use, no investigation as to how these representations could in turn support the production of user-oriented dictionaries has been carried out. In addition to this, due to the focus on the computational processing efficiency, as well as storage bandwidth restrictions which were much more of an issue at that time, the developed formats largely fail to be supportive as far as their naming schemes are concerned. For example, the definition of the SIMPLE format provides rather opaque element names like `combuf` and `inp`, which stand for *»combination of usage feature«* and *»inflection paradigm«* respectively. This impedes the process of getting familiar with the format and the semantics of its elements enormously, in particular for application developers who consider using the respective format for interchange. This is also true of frameworks like COMLEX (Grishman *et al.*, 1994), whose interface language has been inspired by the Lisp programming language family. Besides, many formats have been defined in formalisms which are no longer in use, and not all of them have made the transition to current representation languages like XML. As a result, the tools that support them are no longer actively developed and can therefore not be considered state-of-the-art.

On a more conceptual level, Heid (1997) criticises a number of these approaches for their lack of a »content model« (»Inhaltsmodell«: p. 28), i. e. a set of formal specifications that define the well-formedness of a lexical description (*ibid.*, pp. 37f), which in turn demands a high level of familiarity with the »intended« structures in order to add representations to the resource. This criticism applies as well to the EAGLES project, which aimed at the definition of a »multilingual and multifunctional model for a dictionary viewed as a resource out of which to extract specific application lexicons« (Menon and Modiano, 1993: p. 4) on the basis of the results of ACQUILEX, MULTILEX and GENELEX (cf. Hellwig, 1997). Although such lexical specifications had been developed at a later stage in the project, the formal tools for processing the constraints were still missing. This was different in the DELIS[14] project, which used the constraint-based formalism TFS (*Typed Feature Structure*; Emele, 1994) to define lexical specifications, suffering however from scalability issues (Heid, 1997: pp. 88f).

---

9 *»ACQUIsition of LEXical knowledge for natural language processing systems«*, 1989-1995, Copestake (1992).

10 *»GENEric LEXicon«*, 1989-1994, Antoni-Lay *et al.* (1994).

11 *»MULTIlingual LEXical representation«*, 1991-1993, Paprotté and Schumacher (1993).

12 *»Preparatory Action for linguistic Resources Organisation for Language Engineering«*, 1996-1998, Ruimy *et al.* (1998).

13 *»Semantic Information for Multifunctional Plurilingual Lexica«*, 1999-2000, Lenci *et al.* (2000).

14 *»Descriptive Lexical Specification and tools for corpus-based lexicon building«*, 1993-1995.

Even if the formal tools existed in the form of SGML (and later XML) *document type definitions* (DTDs), the respective projects made use of these formalisms in a way that did not fully exploit their defining power. The CONCEDE[15] project, which is based on the »*Text Encoding Initiative*« (The TEI Consortium, 2009) and is, in fact, a more restrictive encoding of it, has produced an XML DTD.[16] that defines structures like the one in (3.1), which shows part of the English/Slovene entry for »*although*« (taken from Erjavec *et al.*, 2003)

(3.1)
```
<entry id="ensl.44">
  <hw>although</hw>
  <pos>conj</pos>
  <pron>O:l"D@U</pron>
  <struc type="sense" id="ensl.44.3">
   <trans>
    <alt type="orth">
     <orth>&ccaron;eprav</orth>
     <orth>&ccaron;etudi</orth>
    </alt>
   </trans>
  </struc>
   ...
</entry>
```

As can be seen in (3.1), information like the part-of-speech is represented in text form (i. e. *character data* in XML terminology). The DTD, however, is not capable of constraining the content of the `pos` element, which means that it was in principle possible to enter any kind of character data here.[17] Moreover, the value of the `type` attribute in the `alt` element is intended to constrain the elements that can occur as its children. However, there is no formal means that would check for the equality of the text value of the `type` attribute and the names of the children of the `alt` element. While such modelling decisions have certainly been made in order to keep the format as flexible as possible, they undermine the structural means that a formalism like XML offers for representing consistent data. As will be shown in the next section, this is also characteristic of some of the very recent approaches.

3.2.2 Recent Computational Lexical Resources and Models

3.2.2.1 Lexical Markup Framework

The *Lexical Markup Framework* (LMF; ISO/FDIS 24613, 2008) is a very recent ISO initiative which is devoted to the definition of a framework for modelling lexical resources, and which has reached standard status by the end of 2008. Its main goals have been defined as follows.

> »Lexical Markup Framework (LMF) is an abstract metamodel that provides a common, standardized framework for the construction of computational lexicons. LMF ensures the encoding of linguistic information in a way that enables reusability in different applications and for different tasks. LMF

---

[15] »*CONsortium for Central European Dictionary Encoding*«, 1998-2000, Erjavec *et al.* (2003).

[16] See http://www.itri.brighton.ac.uk/projects/concede/DR2.1/XML/xcesDic.dtd.

[17] This could only be achieved at a later stage with a move to XML Schema.

> provides a common, shared representation of lexical objects, including morphological, syntactic and semantic aspects.« (*ibid.*, p. vi)

LMF provides the so-called LMF *core package*, which contains very basic classes like *LexicalEntry*, *Form* and *Sense* (*ibid.*, p. 8). This core package serves as a basis for various extensions, such as packages for morphological, syntactic and semantic descriptions, all of which depend directly or indirectly on the core package (cf. *ibid.*, p. 10). These have been defined by means of diagrams in the *Unified Modelling Language* (UML), although informative XML specifications have been added at a later stage. Since the example fragments that are available on the LMF website[18] are all provided in this XML format, it is assumed that the XML specification is intended to be used as the main interchange format. At the time of writing, it seems that the first large-scale use of encoding lexical data in LMF is being done in the KYOTO project (WordNet-LMF; see Soria *et al.*, 2009).

As the above definition suggests, one of the primary goals of LMF is to achieve interoperability between lexical resources and applications exchanging content with lexical resources. However, although LMF intends to facilitate »true content interoperability across all aspects of electronic lexical resources« (ISO/FDIS 24613, 2008: p. vi), it remains rather vague on its application in the various contexts, and in particular of its application in human usage situations[19]. Despite these restrictions, however, LMF represents a very powerful and promising framework that proposes modelling solutions for a wide range of linguistic phenomena. Moreover, due to the fact that it is the result of several years of work of a group of experts and has been published as an ISO standard, it can be considered as reference for the definition of a multifunctional lexical resource. For this reason, comparisons between the representations chosen in the lexicon model proposed here and the representations provided by LMF will recur very frequently throughout this work, in particular in the context of the modelling of collocations (Section 5.1.2) and valence information (Section 5.2.3). In the following, we will comment on some of the general design patterns in the XML specification that have been identified as problematic with respect to the requirements discussed above.

Similar to what has been mentioned in the context of the traditional approaches, it seems that LMF sacrifices the typing power of XML for flexibility. This is among others reflected in the definition of the `feat` element, which is used for representing attribute-value pairs by means of the two attributes `att` and `val`. The following is a fragment of a representation available from the LMF website.

(3.2)
```
<Lexicon>
 <LexicalEntry>
  <feat att="partOfSpeech" val="verb"/>
  <Lemma>
   <feat att="writtenForm" val="boil"/>
  </Lemma>
  <SubcategorizationFrame id="regularSVO">
   <SyntacticArgument id="synArgX">
    <feat att="syntacticFunction" val="subject"/>
```

[18] See http://www.lexicalmarkupframework.org/.

[19] Francopoulo *et al.* (2006) even state that LMF is a »framework for the construction of NLP lexicons« (*ibid.*, p. 233), whereas the standard document does not seem to be as restrictive.

```
    <feat att="syntacticConstituent" val="NP"/>
  </SyntacticArgument>
...
```

As can be seen in (3.2), the `feat` element is used to encode all sorts of properties, such as the part-of-speech property or the syntactic functions and categories in a subcategorisation frame. According to ISO/FDIS 24613 (2008), the values of `att` and `val` are meant to be taken from the ISO/FDIS 12620 (2009) *Data Category Registry* (DCR; see below). However, there is no inherent mechanism for ensuring that this is actually the case. In particular, the non-normative LMF DTD specifies the following for the attributes of `feat`.

(3.3)
```
<!ATTLIST feat
    att                  CDATA  #REQUIRED
    val                  CDATA  #REQUIRED>
```

In essence, this means that the values of the two attributes are simply made up of character data. While this has advantages in terms of flexibility and extensibility, it does not suffice to make sure that the values of these attributes have actually been taken from the DCR. Moreover, it does not suffice to differentiate between attributes which have a fixed number of admissible values, like `partOfSpeech`, and those which can take any value, such as `writtenForm`. Finally, the number of occurrences of a particular value of `att` is not restricted this way (e. g. `att="partOfSpeech"` could occur more than once), nor is the »type« of the data category with respect to the elements in which it can occur (e. g. `att="writtenForm"` inside of `SyntacticArgument`), and therefore, all of these constraints would need to be checked by an external application. This has been improved in the aforementioned implementation in the KYOTO project, where the data categories have been modelled as XML attributes themselves. Instead of the representation in (3.2), a WordNet-LMF representation would look e. g. as follows[20].

(3.4)
```
<Lemma partOfSpeech="verb" writtenForm="boil"/>
```

In addition to these issues, LMF makes heavy use of *implicit references*. Consider the UML diagram shown in Figure 3.1, which is a reproduction of Figure N.1 in ISO/FDIS 24613 (2008: p. 66).

As can be seen in the figure, the white boxes in the top-lefthand corner represent the components of an MWE, while the boxes at the bottom of the figure represent the lexical realisations of the constituents of the MWE pattern by the components. In the example, the components *»to«*, *»the«* and *»lions«* are meant to represent the PP constituent of the MWE pattern. However, the respective instances are not referenced directly by means of `IDREF`, as one would expect, »but, on the contrary, they are referenced by their respective ordering« (ISO/FDIS 24613, 2008: p. 64). In Figure 3.1, this is shown by means of the attribute `componentRank` of the `MWE Lex` instance. For the component *»lions«*, for example, this indirect reference would be represented in the XML specification as follows.

---

[20] This is based on the WordNet-LMF DTD available from http://www2.let.vu.nl/twiki/pub/Kyoto/LexicalResourceRepresentation/kyoto_wn.dtd. Note, however, that in this DTD the value of the `partOfSpeech` attribute is still defined as `CDATA`, which makes it hard to restrict possible values.

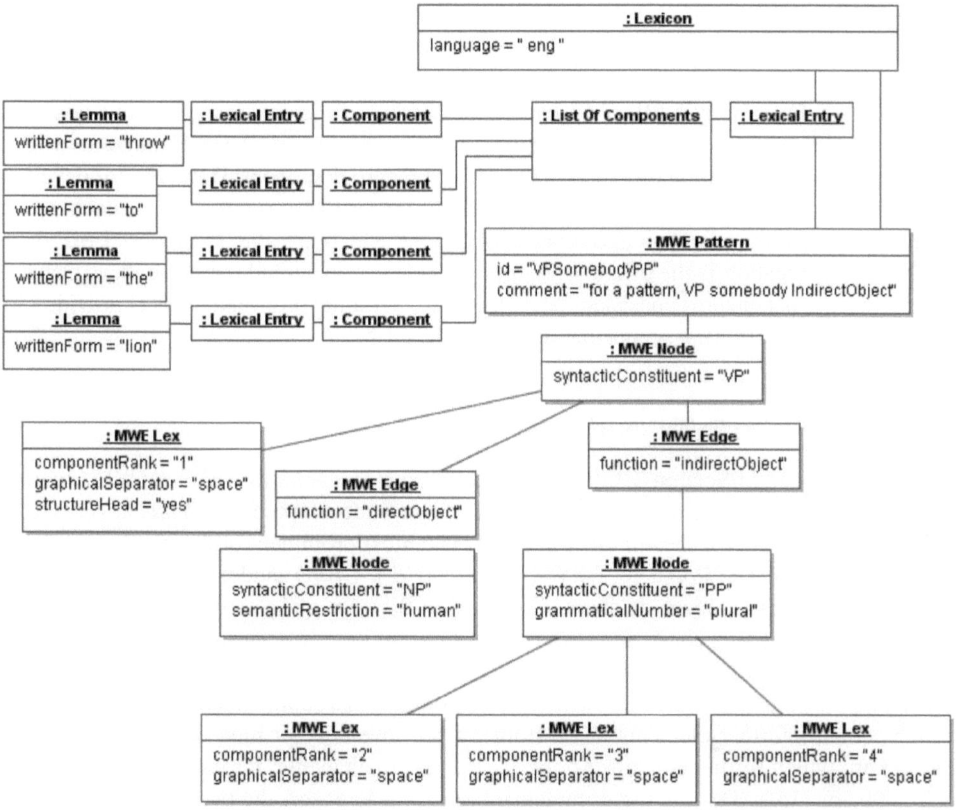

Figure 3.1: LMF representation of MWE patterns (taken from ISO/FDIS 24613, 2008: p. 66)

(3.5) `<MWELex att="componentRank" val="4"/>`

The problems with this representation are the following. Considering the possibility of defining `IDREF` attributes which would represent actual direct links between elements, it seems odd to make use of references that need to be established first. Moreover, these links are dependent on a particular ordering of the `Component` elements, and are in fact incorrect if this ordering is – maybe unintentionally – changed at one point. Finally, there is no inherent mechanism which could ensure that the number which is the value of the `val` attribute of the `MWELex` element is at most as high as the number of `Component` elements in the respective `ListOfComponents`. If an `IDREF` attribute had been used in order to link these elements, a validator would indicate links involving entities that do not exist. This is not the case with this representation, where the reference e. g. to a non-existent fifth component via `att="componentRank" val="5"` would not result in an ill-formed XML file. According to ISO/FDIS 24613 (2008), this has been done in order to »provide a generic representation of

MWE combinations within a given language« (*ibid.*, p. 64). Considering the disadvantages just presented, however, it seems questionable whether this has been the optimal choice.

In summary, it should be emphasised again that the objective of LMF is *not* to provide an XML format. Essentially, LMF is a *meta-standard* whose objective is to provide a common framework for specifying models for lexical resources by means of UML diagrams which conform to the specification provided in the LMF standard document. However, for developers of new or existing lexical resources who want to offer LMF as a format for exchanging data between their application and other applications which are able to process LMF data, the XML specification is the primary point of departure, and should therefore ideally be defined in a way that ensures consistent data exchange. With the informative DTD provided by ISO/FDIS 24613 (2008), it seems that this is not the case.

3.2.2.2 Lexical Systems and the Lexicon Graph

As was mentioned in Section 3.1.2.1, one of the requirements on the MLR model is to conceive of the lexicon as a graph. This view is a rather new development, and recent years have seen a number of approaches in this direction. The most prominent of these are the *Lexical Systems* approach (LS; Polguère, 2006) and the *Lexicon Graph* model (LG; Trippel, 2006), both of which view lexicons as directed graphs. In the case of LSs, these are implemented as flat Prolog databases consisting only of two different types of clauses, namely `entity()` and `link()`. In contrast to this, an LG is represented by means of a custom XML format consisting essentially of the three elements `lexitems`, `relations` and `knowledge`, each of which contains further elements taken from a fixed inventory of nine different types (e. g. `relation`, which further contains `source` and `target` elements; for more details see Trippel, 2006: p. 115f). Despite these implementational differences, the two approaches bear – as Polguère points out – »striking similarities« (Polguère, 2009: p. 43). This refers primarily to the fact that both approaches aim at the definition of flexible lexicon models which impose very little constraints on the data that can be represented.

Polguère (2009) criticises the fact that in lexical resources which are structured by means of predefined principles, developers have to »stretch« their models when adding further phenomena. In particular, this criticism is meant to apply to hierarchically structured resources, and Polguère emphasises that LSs are non-hierarchical structures which allow for the »injection« of a hierarchical organisation on demand (*ibid.*, p. 43). How this hierarchical interpretation comes about, however, remains rather unclear. In particular, if there is no inherent hierarchical organisation within an LS, it cannot be assumed that there is a built-in relation for representing inheritance, because if there was, then it would be hard to maintain a difference between hierarchical and non-hierarchical structures. Thus, there is no way to express that relations like »*is_a*« (as e. g. in DiCo; Polguère, 2000), »*inherits-from*« (as in FrameNet; Baker *et al.*, 1998) and »*subClassOf*« (as in any RDF-based resource) essentially refer to the same relation, since they are not mapped to a common relation in an LS. Therefore, if the mentioned resources were compiled into LSs, each of these relations would need their own interpretation function in order for the hierarchical organisation to be »injected«. Polguère mentions that for the compilation of the DiCo database, a hierarchy of semantic labels has been created by means of the Protégé ontology editor (Knublauch *et al.*, 2004), then exported to XML and finally inserted into the LS Prolog format. As this seems like a rather ad-hoc blend of different formalisms, and since this editor in particular has been developed primarily for ontology languages like OWL, it is not obvious why ontology formalisms have not been used in the first place. In contrast to this, the LG model tries to map different hierarchical relations to a common inheritance relation, rather than representing each of them individually (cf. Trippel, 2006: p. 108). This suggests a more principled and accurate treatment of hierarchical information in the LG model.

According to Polguère (2009), directed graphs are powerful representations »particularly suited for lexical knowledge«, which is emphasised by the author's claim that LSs are capable of representing »all information present in any form of dictionary and database« (*ibid.*, p. 49). While this may seem like a very advantageous property of LSs on the one hand, it somewhat summarises their major disadvantage on the other. In other words, the consequence of Polguère's claim is that *anything* can be modelled, including incorrect information. Although LSs offer a means for expressing a value of trust of a particular statement (see Polguère, 2009: p. 45) – with a value of '0' indicating that a certain piece of information ought to be incorrect – there is no inherent mechanism for determining under which circumstances a statement is incorrect. This would require a formal model that states e. g. that a lexeme which specifies two different parts-of-speech is incorrect. In addition to this, it seems difficult to detect missing information, since anything that is expressed as a Prolog clause using one of the two admitted predicates (see above) is a well-formed statement in an LS. Polguère seems to be aware of this, as he describes LSs as being »not too choosy«. In this respect, the LG model seems to be more restrictive, as it makes use of an XML document grammar. However, as Trippel (2006: p. 101f) indicates, this is limited to rather simple consistency issues.

In sum, it can be said that LSs are to be understood as highly flexible data structures rather than formal models for the representation of lexical information. The LG model provides a formal description to some extent, such as the constraint that the `relation` element consists of *at least* one `source` element and *exactly* one `target`. However, similar to the XML-based approaches discussed above, crucial aspects seem to be hidden mainly in `CDATA` values of elements and attributes, e. g. in the form of an unrestricted `type` attribute (Trippel, 2006: p. 116). Therefore, the provided formalisation refers to the data structure only, not to the actual linguistic content. For this, it would be necessary to add further definitions, e. g. for relations of a certain type, which are absent, however. While this is completely reasonable given its objective to define a generic and highly flexible lexicon model, it meets the requirements mentioned in the previous section only partly. In particular, given the need for a strongly typed formalism, and considering the benefits of widely used standard formalisms like RDF and OWL (see Section 4.3), both LSs and the LG model are regarded as being too unrestricted to serve as a formal basis for the definition of the multifunctional lexicon model, and thus, their overlap with the approach presented here is mainly restricted to the view of the lexicon as a graph.

3.2.2.3 The SALSA lexicon model

The SALSA lexicon model (Spohr *et al.*, 2007; Burchardt *et al.*, 2008a) is an approach to representing multi-layer corpus annotations in a form that enables flexible querying of the different layers. In particular, the approach has resulted in the definition of an OWL-based lexicon model, which has been done with the participation of the author. In addition to enabling flexible querying, the SALSA lexicon model aimed at the definition of mechanisms for checking the consistency and integrity of the manual annotations in the SALSA corpus (Burchardt *et al.*, 2006). In order to achieve this, the lexicon model provides a formalisation of FrameNet (Baker *et al.*, 1998), which has served as the framework for the lexical-semantic annotation layer, as well as the SALSA annotation scheme, which specifies e. g. the types of frames and semantic roles which can be annotated in a sentence. The lexicon model is thus not a generic one that generalises to other frameworks or annotation schemes, but rather the successful application of a general methodology for inducing a formal lexicon model from corpus annotations.

In addition to highlighting a number of benefits of modelling linguistic information in a logic-based formalism, the SALSA lexicon model has produced a useful workflow of the lexicon compilation process, covering the steps from the conversion of XML corpus annotations to OWL, the consistency and integrity checking of these annotations on the basis of description logic axioms and graph queries, as well as scalable storage in a relational database. Due to the close links with respect to the underlying formalism and the thus resulting overlap, several central aspects of the SALSA lexicon model will be discussed in the course of this book, primarily in Chapter 6.

3.2.2.4 Linguistic ontologies

While the previous subsections have presented different approaches to defining computational models which aim at the representation of lexical data, the current subsection deals with resources which describe linguistic information in general, without commitment to a particular model. In particular, we will briefly introduce the ISO 12620 *Data Category Registry* (DCR; ISO/FDIS 12620, 2009) and the *General Ontology for Linguistic Description* (GOLD; Farrar and Langendoen, 2003, 2010). These two resources are very relevant in the context of a lexicon model, as they provide inventories for linguistic description.

The DCR is an ISO standard aimed at the definition of »widely accepted linguistic concepts« (Windhouwer, 2009), whose latest version can be accessed via the ISOcat web interface[21]. Technically, the DCR is a flat list of categories that can be used for the description of linguistic entities. For each descriptive device, the DCR provides natural language definitions and examples, as well as names in different languages. For example, the data category entry of *partOfSpeech*[22] specifies that it is a »category assigned to a word based on its grammatical and semantic properties«, and that possible names are e. g. »pos« in English and »Wortklasse« in German. Finally, the valid values are specified (such as »adjective« or »commonNoun«), which can be used for modelling attribute-value pairs as mentioned above in the context of LMF (see page 24). However, as was further discussed there, no mechanism has been implemented yet which would ensure that the attributes make use of the admitted values only.

In contrast to this, the descriptions in GOLD are more formalised than the flat specifications in the DCR. According to Farrar and Langendoen (2010), GOLD is an ontological theory that specifies entities in the domain of linguistics, e. g. *InflectedUnit*, *TenseFeature* or *hasSubject*. Instead of a simple listing of the different types of linguistic entities, the OWL version[23] of

---

[21] See http://www.isocat.org/interface/index.html.
[22] See http://www.isocat.org/rest/dc/396.
[23] See http://www.linguistics-ontology.org/gold-2008.owl.

GOLD goes beyond the natural language definitions in ISO 12620 in that it further attempts to formalise general linguistic knowledge in the form of description logic axioms. Straightforward axioms specify e. g. that »verb« is a part of speech or »subject« is a syntactic role, while more complex ones like (3.6) (taken from Farrar and Langendoen, 2010) state that an inflected unit is a grammar unit that has an inflectional unit as constituent.

(3.6) $InflectedUnit \equiv GrammarUnit \sqcap \exists hasConstituent.InflectionalUnit$

These formalisations mean that GOLD can make use of the existing computational infrastructure of OWL, such as application programming interfaces and description logic reasoners for ensuring the use of valid attribute-value pairs. However, due to its emphasis on the ontological nature of linguistic entities, which focusses on giving definitions e. g. of what constitutes a phrase or a linguistic sign in general, GOLD provides a lot of information that is not relevant in the context of a lexicon model and is thus only indirectly usable. Compared to this, the objectives of ISO/FDIS 12620 (2009) are more closely related to the definition of a lexical resource. However, the implementation of ISO 12620 is still under development, which is shown e. g. by the fact that the current version of March 2010 contains two identical data categories for part-of-speech. Moreover, the DCR selection process as outlined in ISO/FDIS 12620 (2009) and ISO/FDIS 24613 (2008) has not been implemented yet. As a result, neither the DCR nor GOLD will be used directly in the MLR model presented here, in the sense that their specifications are not directly imported into the model. Nonetheless, as will be discussed in Chapter 5, both GOLD and the DCR have been very influential in the modelling of the descriptive devices in the MLR, and a number of data categories have in fact been taken from these resources.

3.2.2.5 Ontology lexicon models

The final type of lexicon model concerns models for so-called *ontology lexica*, which provide linguistic enrichment for the entities defined in an ontology. For example, a property like *capital* in a geographical ontology can be described by an entry in an ontology lexicon which specifies that it can be realised by means of »*is capital of*«, where the subject of the property *capital* is mapped to the subject of »*is capital of*«, and the object of the property to the complement of the preposition »*of*«. This information is then used for NLP tasks like natural language generation or question answering (see e. g. Unger *et al.*, 2010). The most prominent representatives of this category are LingInfo, LexOnto and LexInfo, with the latter being based on the former two models and LMF (see Cimiano *et al.* (2011) for a detailed discussion).

While being very closely related to the model presented here from a technological perspective – all of these models are based on Semantic Web formalisms –, they differ in terms of which purpose the model is to serve, as well as which kinds of linguistic information can be represented and how. On the one hand, they have been developed to represent lexicalisations of ontological concepts, not electronic dictionaries for computational and human use, and do thus not provide a rich classification of linguistic concepts as e. g. GOLD or the model developed in this work. On the other hand, as will become obvious in Sections 5.1 and 5.2 of this book, the representation of valence information and preference phenomena, in particular with respect to multi-word expressions, is rather different, as is the way in which these phenomena are interrelated in the model.

3.2.3 Interfaces to Electronic Dictionaries for Human Users

After having introduced a number of relevant models for computational lexical resources, we will now focus on a selection of electronic dictionaries for human use. This selection has been done on the basis of the requirements analysis presented above, as all of the dictionaries discussed in the following are considered to illustrate important aspects. Therefore, we will not reproduce the comprehensive discussions presented for example in Schall (2007), but rather highlight specific features which indicate the approach to multifunctionality taken in each dictionary. In general, it can be said that none of the mentioned dictionaries caters for NLP applications, which means that multifunctionality is restricted to »serving several types of human users«. Moreover, most of them are still in their development phase.

3.2.3.1 ADNW

The *Aktives Deutsch-Niedersorbisches Wörterbuch*[24] (ADNW; Bartels and Spieß, 2002) represents a very basic kind of multifunctional dictionary. It is being developed by the *Sorbisches Institut* in Saxony and is aimed at advanced learners as well as teachers and students of Lower Sorbian. Despite being explicitly under development, the ADNW displays a very clear tendency towards serving multiple functions. In particular, it offers for a selection of lexemes a »*Schulversion*« (»*school version*), which differs from the full version in the indications that are displayed in a dictionary entry as well as its general layout[25].

While the primary goal of the ADNW is to be published as a printed dictionary, the latest development steps are being released in electronic form on the dictionary's website[26]. Although this means that general benefits of the electronic medium, in particular advanced search functionalities, are not fully exploited and can therefore not be evaluated critically, the general attempt to approach multifunctionality by providing variable presentation modes for dictionary entries is without any doubt relevant in the context of this work.

3.2.3.2 Ordbogen over faste vendinger

The *Ordbogen over faste vendinger*[27] is a monolingual Danish idiom dictionary that provides a direct implementation of the key notions of function theory (see Section 2.2 above). It caters for different situation types by offering users different search options, such as »*I would like to have support in understanding an expression*«[28] for users in a text-receptive situation and »*... in writing a text*«[29] for text-productive situations. Moreover, it allows users to find

[24] »*Active Lower Sorbian Dictionary*«
[25] Compare the full entry of »*Ecke*« http://www.dolnoserbski.de/dnw/dnw/ecke.html with its school version, found at http://www.dolnoserbski.de/dnw/dnsw/ecke.html.
[26] See http://www.dolnoserbski.de/dnw/index.htm.
[27] »*Dictionary of fixed expressions*«; see http://www.ordbogen.com/opslag.php?dict=fvdd. As of September 2011, access to the dictionary is no longer free of charge. The following discussion is therefore based on Almind *et al.* (2006) and the examples in the instruction manual, which is – as the entire dictionary website – available in Danish only.
[28] »*Jeg vil have hjælp til at forstå en vending*«.
[29] »*... skrive en tekst*«.

expressions starting from a specific meaning[30] (onomasiological access) and further offers the option to learn more about an expression[31], which underlines its close connection to Tarp's concept of a leximat (cf. page 5 above).

Choosing one of these options has a direct impact on the way in which the dictionary entries are presented (see Almind *et al.*, 2006: p. 179). The instruction manual lists entries for *»have aben«* (*»to be in an undesirable situation«*; literally *»to have the monkey«*) as an example, whose text-receptive version contains only meaning indications, whereas the text-productive entry starts with the fixed expressions involving *»aben«*, followed by meaning indications, grammatical information, collocations, examples and synonyms. In other words, it contains those indications which correspond to Tarp's primary and secondary needs in text-productive situations.

Despite a very clear explanation of the fact that dictionary entries differ according to the selected situation, Almind *et al.* (2006) remain unclear as to how the actual process of selecting the relevant indications is carried out. More precisely, it is not explained explicitly if (i) there is a separate model that specifies which indications are relevant in a certain situation, or (ii) the relevance is represented as part of the dictionary itself, or even (iii) the dictionary entries themselves have been hard-coded. The chosen strategy is a very important factor in assessing the dictionary, as it has considerable effects on the adaptability of the dictionary to further communicative situations, as well as changes to the covered situations, e. g. if further indications are added at a later stage, or if existing indications are identified to be of less relevance than had been assumed. In addition to this, the *Ordbogen over faste vendinger* offers only very simple query access to the dictionary data. In particular, access by means of (partial) lemmata is the only search route offered, which means that it is not possible to query for more complex configurations, such as combinations of *»aben«* with a verb and/or an adjective. Finally, the fact that its interface exists in Danish only is a considerable obstacle for less advanced users, and therefore, the *Ordbogen over faste vendinger* is remarkable mainly for the multifunctional presentation of its dictionary entries.

3.2.3.3 BLF/DAFLES

Similar to the *Ordbogen over faste vendinger*, the interface to the *Base Lexicale du Français*[32] (BLF) is clearly oriented towards the notion of a leximat. According to Verlinde (2010), it is a lexicographic tool for learning French vocabulary that is entirely based on users' needs. The content of the BLF is based on the *Dictionnaire d'Apprentissage du Français Langue Étrangère ou Seconde*[33] (DAFLES; Selva *et al.*, 2002).

The general strategy of the interface to the BLF is to let users determine the kinds of information that they are given in response to a query. Here, the BLF makes use of Tarp's analysis of user needs in different communicative and cognitive situations (see above), and offers different entry points to the data. For example, a user can either get specific information on a particular word (such as the gender or orthography), verify the use of a word or a sequence of words, or learn how to express a certain idea. In general, a user's involvement starts with

30 *»... søge efter en vending ud fra en betydning«.*

31 *»... vide mere om en vending«.*

32 *»Lexical Resource of French«*, see http://ilt.kuleuven.be/blf/.

33 *»Learners' Dictionary of French as Foreign or Second Language«*

the specification of a lexical item, which is followed by selecting the desired output information. Once a query has been stated that way, users are given the desired answer, from where they have the chance to explore the respective item more, e. g. by clicking on it. Each of the queries and clicks of a user are recorded and stored in a database, from where they are available to further research into the consultation behaviour of dictionary users.

As the previous paragraph suggests, the considerations in the context of the BLF are very closely related to those presented in this work. The primary differences lie in the way in which the modelling of user needs is approached. As was mentioned in Section 3.1.3.1, the approach followed here is to devise a formal tool that specifies the pieces of information that are relevant in a certain situation – in contrast to the users specifying the output themselves. Primary reasons for doing so are to avoid overloading of the user with options (i. e. »information stress« or even »information death« in the sense of function-theoretic scholars like Henning Bergenholtz and Sven Tarp), and to make the consultation situation less dependent on the particular need. More precisely, the way in which users have access to the information they are looking for should not be fundamentally different depending on the type of the information. This dependence on particular needs and the resulting information stress has been attested in a recent usability study (Heid, 2011) and lead to a redesign of the BLF interface (cf. Verlinde, 2011). Further differences will become apparent in Sections 5.4 and 6.2.2.

3.2.3.4 ELDIT

The *Elektronisches Lernerwörterbuch Deutsch-Italienisch*[34] (ELDIT; Abel and Weber, 2000) is a freely available online platform aimed at Italian learners of German and German learners of Italian. While its initial conception focussed on learners in the area of South Tyrol, the system has been designed general enough as to serve learners of Italian and German in general. In addition to being multifunctional in the sense of serving different types of learners, the system further has a *user model* which allows for the customisation of the content e. g. according to proficiency, such as beginner vs. advanced, or e. g. according to domain, such as medical vs. technical. ELDIT does not, however, distinguish between receptive and productive situations within these user categories, and its multifunctionality is thus on a different axis than the one underlying e. g. the BLF interface.

In addition to the customisation features just mentioned, which can be set at the moment a user signs up to the ELDIT system, there is also a sophisticated adaptation system that observes user behaviour and presents the content appropriately. For example, if users are interested in the pronunciation of the words they look up – which can be detected by observing that they always click on the respective button in the dictionary entry – the system adapts its behaviour and automatically plays the sound file once a further word is looked up (Knapp, 2004: p. 99-103). Finally, ELDIT contains detailed valence descriptions which can be displayed to different users in different ways (Knapp, pers.comm.).

In sum, it can be said that ELDIT addresses a number of the requirements mentioned above. Similar to BLF, ELDIT even offers an advanced search functionality which allows users to search for a specific term within certain fields of the dictionary entries. However, the search is still restricted to the specification of a single query term, so there is no way to query for more complex configurations. Finally, due to its focus on language learners it has up to

---

[34] *»Electronic learners' dictionary German-Italian«*; http://www.eurac.edu/eldit

now not been tested in computational scenarios, although a systematic approach seems to be conceivable in general (cf. Knapp, 2004: p. 97).

3.2.3.5 elexiko/OWID

elexiko is part of the XML-based monolingual lexical information system OWID[35] developed at the *Institut für Deutsche Sprache* whose main target groups consists of German native speakers and learners of German. According to Haß (2005: p. 3), it is a »plurifunctional« dictionary which lets the users decide the function that it is to serve in a particular usage situation, by allowing them to display and hide certain indications once a dictionary entry is displayed (e. g. »for etymological information click here«). However, as Haß (2005) points out, the dictionary authors differentiate in the creation of the dictionary between information for laymen and information for expert linguists and model the information accordingly. As is shown in Müller-Spitzer (2005), this is achieved by means of XSLT stylesheets which display the indications that are relevant for a particular type of user. As of early 2010, it seems that this aspect is still under development, since it has not been made publicly available yet.

As with the other dictionaries discussed so far, the search functionality offered by *elexiko*[36] is rather limited. Its extended search allows to specify values for a small selection of indications, e. g. whether the part-of-speech is a verb or a noun. For other indications, however, it only offers the possibility to state if a certain indication should be there or not. Grammar indications, can e. g. be accessed only by means of selecting »any« or »with valence«.

In contrast to the recent developments in the field of computational lexicography, the model of *elexiko* is not at all graph-based. In fact, in can be taken as a prototypical example of a text-based dictionary in the sense of Polguère (2006). However, this is certainly true of the other dictionaries as well; it is just that *elexiko* allows us to gain detailed insights into its internal structure. As key multifunctional aspects are still under development, *elexiko* is only on its way to becoming a multifunctional lexical information system. Whether it is going to be multifunctional in the sense explained in Section 2.3 above by serving NLP applications as well, cannot be determined at this stage.

3.2.3.6 DWDS

The *Digitales Wörterbuch der Deutschen Sprache des 20. Jh.* (*»digital dictionary of 20th century German«*; DWDS[37]) is an ongoing project at the *Berlin-Brandenburgische Akademie der Wissenschaften*, aiming at the development of a freely available lexical database of German. While the DWDS is of limited interest from a user-oriented perspective on multifunctionality, in the sense of serving different types of users e. g. in text-receptive vs. text-productive situations, it is very relevant from the point of view of how lexical data can be presented to a user. Especially in its current development version 2.0beta, the DWDS has moved away from primarily displaying the entries from its printed predecessor, the *Wörterbuch der deutschen Gegenwartssprache* (*»dictionary of contemporary German«*; Klappenbach and Malige-Klappenbach, 1980) towards offering an interactive presentation.

---

35 *»Online-Wortschatz-Informationssystem Deutsch«*

36 See http://www.owid.de/suche/elex/erweitert.

37 See http://www.dwds.de/woerterbuch.

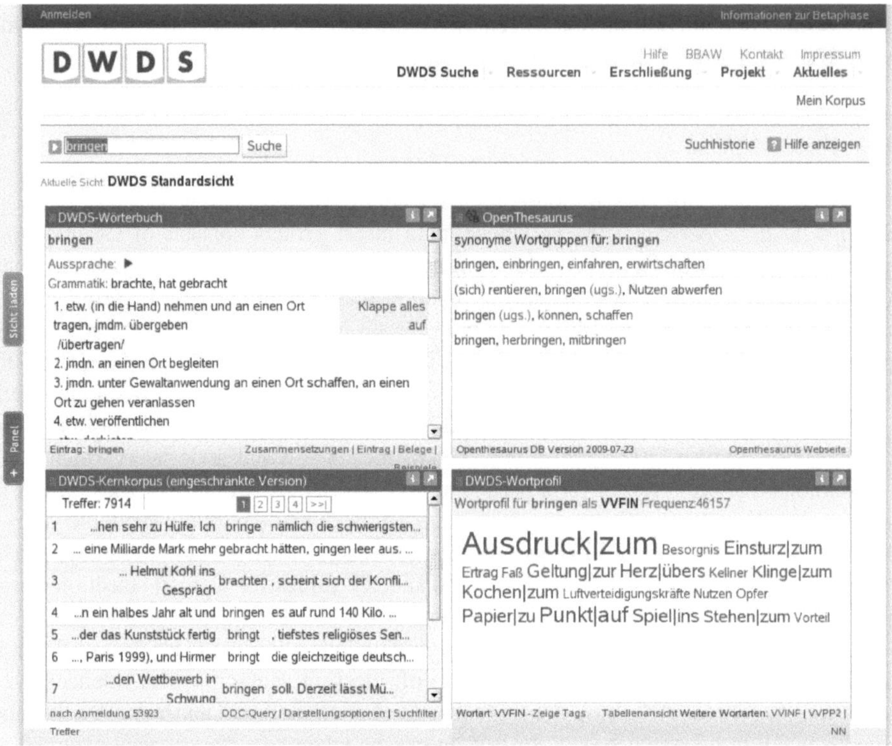

Figure 3.2: Screenshot of the DWDS view of *»bringen«* (*»to bring«*)

As can be seen in Figure 3.2, which shows a screenshot of the entry for *»bringen«*, the view contains four different panels which display information from the DWDS dictionary (top left), OpenThesaurus (top right) and the DWDS corpus (bottom left), as well as a word profile (bottom right). Further panels can be added by clicking on the blue button on the left-hand side of the screen, and each of these can be moved around freely on the screen. Within the DWDS dictionary panel, users can decide to be satisfied with the information displayed by default (namely grammatical information, sense definitions and style markings), or else click on specific items in the entry in order to get further information, mainly example sentences. Whether the selection of what is displayed is regulated by a formal model of user needs is not clear. However, there is no doubt that the contents of the dictionary panel could be adapted such that it serves different user types. In fact, the GUI has a button for changing between different views (see the brown button on the left-hand side of Figure 3.2), although this seems to affect only on the kinds of panels that are displayed, as well as where they are positioned on the screen. This mechanism could certainly be extended for the mentioned task. In sum, the DWDS is a very good example of how interoperability of different lexical resources can be achieved, by combining dictionary content, corpus access and access to external resources. Moreover, it aims at supporting the formulation of queries that go beyond the very simple ones seen on the previous pages. Although the query language used so far seems to be too complex for the average untrained user[38], the general idea of offering advanced options for stating complex queries is very positive. We will return to this aspect in the context of the following dictionary.

3.2.3.7 DiCouèbe

The last electronic lexical resource to be discussed here is the web interface to the *Dictionnaire de Combinatoire/Lexique actif du français* (DiCo/LAF[39]; Polguère, 2000; see also page 26 above), a monolingual French dictionary describing the combinatorial properties of lexical units based on Meaning-Text Theory (Mel'čuk and Žolkovskij, 1970). As with some of the dictionaries discussed so far, it is not explicitly targeted at a particular group of users, although its interface suggests that it is aimed at expert users rather than inexperienced learners (cf. Figure 3.3).

The web interface DiCouèbe is most remarkable for its query interface, which allows for the formulation of quite complex queries. As can be seen in Figure 3.3, the query interface provides a number of text fields for specifying values of particular properties, such as *»nom vocable«* (*»word«*), *»fonction lexicale«* (*»lexical function«*) or *»marque d'usage«* (*»usage marking«*). For most of these indications, more than one value can be specified. In addition to this, it is possible to specify the indications that should appear in the result, by ticking the boxes on the lefthand side of the query form. This way, users are shown only those indications that they have explicitly asked for. Although these features make the DiCouèbe interface – in terms of the complexity of the dictionary queries that can be formulated – the most advanced of the ones discussed in this section, it needs to be said that it is still very difficult for untrained users to pose queries. The main problem with the DiCouèbe interface is that for most indications the user needs to know the possible values. For example, it is necessary to know which usage markings exists and how they are spelt, before a felicitous query can be formulated. With possible values like *Caus1PredAble1Real1* for lexical functions, this is not a trivial task. Such problems can be overcome easily by offering drop-down lists instead of unconstrained text fields, which is the strategy that has been followed in this work (see Section 6.2.2.1).

3.2.4 Summary

Summing up what has been discussed on the previous pages, it can be safely said that none of the lexical resources – neither on the side of computational lexicons nor dictionaries for human users – has been conceptualised as a truly multifunctional lexical resource according to the definition in Section 2.3. Although some of them (e. g. the *Ordbogen over faste*

---

[38] One example provided in the online help is the query »`sein with $p=VVFIN #20 $p=VVPP #0 worden`«, which extracts phrases of the form *»sein Participle worden«*. Clearly, such queries are meant to be used for corpus look-up by expert users, rather than for mere dictionary consultation.

[39] See http://olst.ling.umontreal.ca/dicouebe/index.php.

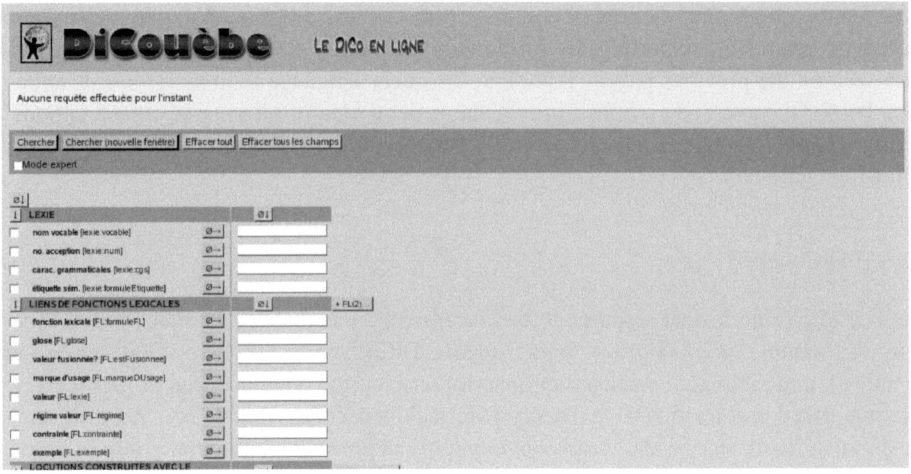

Figure 3.3: Screenshot of the DiCouèbe interface to the DiCo dictionary

vendinger) have been designed such that they can serve in different usage situations, they have not been prepared for access by or exchange with NLP applications. In addition to this, non-standard access as highlighted in Section 3.1.2.1 is possible only in *elexiko*, DWDS and DiCouèbe. While in the case of *elexiko* the offered means allow for the formulation of very simple queries only, the ones offered in the DWDS seem too complex as to be used by the average dictionary user[40]. The DiCouèbe interface seems to offer a very good balance between these two. As was mentioned above, however, it requires the user to have detailed knowledge of the names of the data categories in the resource in order to extract information. Moreover, as is the case for several of the monolingual dictionaries just discussed, they cater for one interface language only, namely the one that is identical to the object language (e. g. Danish for the *Ordbogen*, German for the DWDS or French for the DiCouèbe). As a result, their target groups are already restricted to users with advanced knowledge in these languages. Such issues certainly need to be overcome in order to make a dictionary interface useable for a wider audience, including learners at the beginner's level (cf. ELDIT).

Due to the fact that the focus of this study is on providing a *model* for a multifunctional lexical resource, the general steps towards the definition of an electronic dictionary for human users taken in this work – including ideas for user interfaces and query access – cannot be assumed to be able to »compete« with sophisticated user interfaces such as the one offered by the DWDS. Moreover, since most of the dictionaries discussed in the previous section allow only for very limited insight as to their underlying models, the major reference of this work is in the field of the models for computational lexicons (cf. Section 3.2.2). As was mentioned

[40] Again, linguistically untrained users are certainly not the target group of this feature of the DWDS, and this complexity of the query language is in line with the one of those used for other resources for computational lexicographic research.

there, comparisons with the LMF proposal will come up more often than not in the following chapters – in particular with respect to the types of linguistic description which have been identified in Section 3.1.1 as very relevant for both human users and NLP, e. g. valence and quantitative tendencies such as morpho-syntactic preferences.

As far as such models are concerned, XML is clearly the most widely used representation formalism. Some of the potential disadvantages of custom XML formats have been discussed above (such as the lack of sophisticated consistency control mechanisms). In the following chapter, we will further motivate the move to a more formalised representation language, by discussing advantages like the existence of built-in subsumption and inference mechanisms for the representation and extraction of underspecified information.

4 A Graph-based Formalism for Representing Lexical Information

As was mentioned in Chapter 3, a typed formalism is needed in order to meet the requirements that an MLR poses for example with respect to ensuring consistency and integrity of lexical data. A research activity that has put particular emphasis on the definition of such formalisms is the so-called *Semantic Web*, a project that builds on the already existing *World Wide Web* (see Section 4.1). Although the major aims of this project seem to have no direct connection to computational lexicography, they have nonetheless important side-effects that are very relevant to the requirements of an MLR. Of particular importance are the *knowledge representation* (KR) formalisms and tools that have been developed within the Semantic Web, and the fact that ISO specifications like LMF are planned to be implemented in one of these formalisms (Hayashi *et al.*, 2008) indicates their immediate relevance to computational lexicography.

After an outline of the history and basic ideas of the Semantic Web, its formalisms and tools will be discussed in Section 4.2. In addition to this, it will be shown how the formal properties of these formalisms can contribute to solving specific problems in computational lexicography (Section 4.3).

4.1 Brief History of the Semantic Web

> »The Semantic Web is not a separate Web but an extension of the current one, in which information is given well-defined meaning, better enabling computers and people to work in cooperation.« (Berners-Lee *et al.*, 2001)

4.1.1 The World Wide Web

In (Berners-Lee, 1989), the author described his vision of a web of entities that are interrelated by *typed links*, such as *»describes«* or *»wrote«*, which is widely accepted as representing the original proposal of the *World Wide Web* (WWW).

(4.1) *<Tim Berners-Lee> wrote <Information Management: A Proposal>*

The primary motivation at that time was to be able to keep track of the diverse projects and activities at the *European Organization for Nuclear Research* (*Conseil Européen pour la Recherche Nucléaire*; CERN[1]), and at the same time make the created documents and thus the gained knowledge and information easily accessible to the people working at CERN in a consistent way. The result of this proposal was a project based on the idea of combining *hypermedia* (i. e. hypertext as well as multimedia elements) with the internet, which was

[1] http://www.cern.ch

carried out at CERN and eventually evolved into the WWW. The main organisation coordinating further development of the WWW is the *World Wide Web Consortium* (W3C), whose main objective is »Web interoperability«, i. e. the development of protocols, standards and guidelines ensuring long-term growth for the WWW.[2]

4.1.2 Recent Developments

Despite the concept of *typed links* in the proposal, the WWW as we know it does not contain the degree of typing initially conceived by its creator. Instead, we mostly find information that remains implicit for a computer and is up for interpretation by the human user. For example, we find a hypertext reference from Tim Berners-Lee's W3C homepage[3] to the main W3C page devoted to the WWW. However, the nature of this relation, namely the information that the person is the inventor of the WWW, remains hidden – at least to the computer – and may only be inferred from the text immediately preceding the reference: <p>In 1989 he invented the <a href="/TheProject.html">World Wide Web,</a>.[4] In terms of the original proposal (Berners-Lee, 1989), this representation roughly corresponds to a statement like the following, where it is unknown what '⟶' means.

(4.2) <*Tim Berners-Lee*> ⟶ <*World Wide Web*>

It is only in recent years that there has been a particular focus on turning the WWW into what is commonly referred to as the *Semantic Web* (SW), i. e. a *web of data* and their relations among each other, as well as to objects in the real world.[5] Technically, the activity that is associated with creating the SW is about formats and languages, i. e. about providing the technical and formal equipment in order to express knowledge about resources on the web and their interrelationships. The main vision behind this is that one day it will be possible to have agents roaming the SW and performing complex tasks for their users (Hendler, 2001). As such, the SW is very closely connected to the field of *Artificial Intelligence* (AI), in the sense that the SW provides well-defined data that can be used by AI applications to perform tasks such as query answering, automated reasoning (i. e. the task of automatically deriving explicit knowledge from implicit statements) or automatic classification of data.

In this context, *ontologies* play an important role, as they attempt to model *world* or *domain knowledge* in a structured way, and thus provide the formal knowledge that is required to successfully complete tasks such as the ones just mentioned. Due to the importance of ontologies, a lot of research has gone into the definition of appropriate representation formalisms that are capable of modelling world and domain knowledge with varying expressivity, allowing for reasoning with different computational complexities.

Although the general motivation of the SW as well as the efforts made appear to be largely disjoint with the domain of computational lexicography at first sight, the formalisms and tools that have been developed within the SW are of immediate relevance. Among others, this is due to the amount of research that has been invested into their definition, which combines

---

2 http://www.w3.org/Consortium/

3 http://www.w3.org/People/Berners-Lee/

4 Note that it is moreover necessary to know that »he« in the preceding context refers to the person that is the topic of this webpage.

5 See http://www.w3.org/2001/sw/.

efforts from a variety of domains, such as computer science and formal logics. Therefore, the following subsections are dedicated to the explanation of these tools and formalisms, as well as to the languages that can be used to query resources defined in them.

4.2 Formalisms, Query Languages and Tools

The technologies developed within the SW, as well as their interrelationships, are commonly illustrated by means of the so-called *Semantic Web Stack* or *Layer Cake* (see Figure 4.1). The layers are organised from the bottom to the top, with URIs (*Uniform Resource Identifiers*) and IRIs (*Internationalised Resource Identifiers*) representing the most basic technology at the bottom of the diagram (Section 4.2.1). Located on top of the URI/IRI layer are the layers for XML (*eXtensible Markup Language*; Section 4.2.2) and RDF (*Resource Description Framework*; Section 4.2.3), which provide powerful means for representing and exchanging data on the web in a structured way. The fact that there is no direct connection between XML and the higher layers indicates that XML – contrary to RDF – is not an immediate prerequisite for these technologies.[6] Further on top is a group consisting of several components, with RDF Schema – a vocabulary for RDF – as well as the *Web Ontology Language* (OWL; Section 4.2.4) at its centre. The two vertical layers to the left and right of RDFS and OWL are those for rule languages (Section 4.2.5) and query languages (Section 4.2.6), which are represented in the figure by the *Rule Interchange Format* (RIF) and the SPARQL *Protocol and RDF Query Language* respectively.

In the following, the different technologies that enable the SW will be presented in greater detail. However, the discussion will be limited to those layers that have a direct impact on the definition of an ED model as carried out in this work, which includes the ones just mentioned as well as *Unifying Logic* and *Proof.* While these two layers will frequently be touched upon in the context of description logic reasoning (see Sections 4.2.4, 4.2.5 and 4.2.7), all other layers shown in the diagram can be considered irrelevant for the purpose of this study. These include the layers for *Crypto(graphy)* and *Trust*, as they are either concerned with the encryption of data that are exchanged over the web, or with actions carried out by agents, such as the verification that RDF statements originate from trusted sources. The *User Interface & Application* layer located at the very top of the figure will only be discussed at the level of relevant tools developed so far (Section 4.2.7), which should not be mixed up with interfaces to applications carrying out AI-oriented tasks on the web as outlined in Section 4.1.2 above.

4.2.1 URIs, IRIs and XML Namespaces

Uniform Resource Identifiers (URIs) and Internationalised Resource Identifiers (IRIs) are located at the basic layer of the diagram in Figure 4.1, and they provide a global dereferencing system of the WWW[7]. URIs and IRIs basically consist of a string of characters that identifies or names a resource on the internet. While URIs may only contain ASCII characters, IRIs

[6] See Section 4.2.8 for more details on this as well as possible misinterpretations of the layering.

[7] See http://www.w3.org/2004/Talks/0412-RDF-functions/.

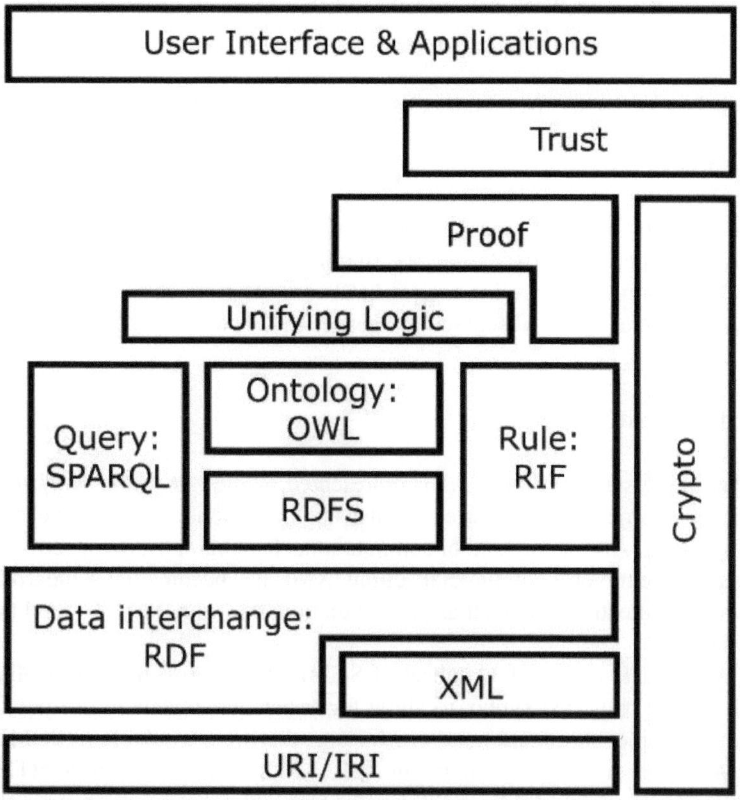

Figure 4.1: The Semantic Web layer cake (taken from http://www.w3.org/2001/sw/; version of January 2011)

may further contain Unicode characters (see Berners-Lee *et al.*, 2005; Duerst and Suignard, 2005). Example (4.2.1) is a valid instance of an URI, or more precisely, an *absolute* URI.

(4.3) `http://www.ietf.org/rfc/rfc3986.txt`

What is of particular relevance to this work is that URIs are used for declaring XML namespaces, where the respective namespace is identified by a URI reference (see Bray *et al.*, 2006). The following is an example of the beginning of an XML document containing the declaration of the namespace prefix `owl:` for the namespace dereferenced by the URI `http://www.w3.org/2002/07/owl#`.

(4.4)
```
<?xml version="1.0"?>
<rdf:RDF
    ...
    xmlns:owl="http://www.w3.org/2002/07/owl#">
    ...
</rdf:RDF>
```

In a file that contains this namespace declaration, elements that have been defined at the dereferenced URI, such as `http://www.w3.org/2002/07/owl#Class`, can be addressed with the declared namespace prefix, e. g. `owl:Class`. The benefits of namespaces in the context of an ED model will be discussed in Section 4.3.2 below.

4.2.2 XML, DTDs and XML Schema

The next layer of the stack in Figure 4.1 is represented by the *eXtensible Markup Language* (XML), which is a formalism that is used extensively throughout computer science and computational linguistics. Also in the field of computational lexicography, irrespective of whether it is done in an academic or a commercial setting, XML has become the standard formalism for the definition of electronic as well as printed dictionaries (e. g. ELDIT (Abel and Weber, 2000) or OED3[8]).

Historically, XML is a simplified subset of SGML (Standard Generalised Markup Language), with a more restricted syntax to allow for easier implementation of parsers for the language. For example, shorthand notations for tags that were available in SGML (such as `<A<B>` or `</A<B>`) are no longer available in XML.[9] Moreover, compared to HTML, which is an application language of SGML, XML has the restriction that every opening element tag also has an end tag, so elements like the line break element `<br>` commonly used in HTML would be disallowed in XML without a corresponding closing tag. Factors such as these have contributed to the wide acceptance of XML across disciplines – preferring it over SGML and older formalisms – and since 1998, XML has the status of a W3C recommendation, which means that it is a freely available de-facto standard.

The words »*markup language*« in the name of XML are slightly misleading, since XML as such cannot be considered a markup language sensu stricto. Rather, it provides a structural specification for defining custom formats, and is thus more accurately described as a *meta-language*. In designing custom formats based on XML, *Document Type Definitions* (DTDs) play a central role. They are one of the XML schema languages (next to e. g. RELAX NG[10] or W3C XML Schema[11]), which are used to define the permissible elements and attributes of a custom markup language, as well as the structure of documents defined in it (i. e. order and nesting of elements).

The *correctness* of an XML document is determined in two different respects. On the one hand, the XML language specification (Bray *et al.*, 2008) determines the *well-formedness* of XML documents, so that an XML document is only well-formed if it conforms to the

8 See http://www.oed.com/.

9 In XML, the examples just mentioned would be expressed as `<A><B>` and `</A><B>` respectively.

10 http://relaxng.org/

11 http://www.w3.org/XML/Schema#dev

language specification. On the other hand, there is the notion of *validity*, which refers to whether a document conforms to the structural definition in the XML schema assigned to it. How sophisticated this definition is crucially depends on the expressivity of the schema language used. Here, DTDs represent the least expressive schema language, whose most obvious drawback is the absence of datatypes. In a DTD, datatypes such as integers or strings are subsumed under the very general label `CDATA` (for *character data*) or `PCDATA` (*parsed character data*), without further distinction. As a result, it is not possible to restrict the content of an element like `<frequency>...</frequency>` to containing only numeric characters, and there is no inherent mechanism to ensure that this is the case.

In contrast to this, a schema language like W3C XML Schema is much more powerful, as it provides a rich system of datatypes, as well as a mechanism for defining more complex types. Moreover, whereas DTDs are syntactically based on SGML, XML Schema definitions are themselves XML documents. On the one hand, this makes it more homogeneous. On the other hand, however, this fact has also been noted as a disadvantage, due to the additional overhead that is required for processing the schema before the parsing of the actual XML document can take place.[12]

The general benefits of XML are manifold and have been discussed extensively and proven throughout the literature[13]. One of the most basic advantages over older alternatives (e. g. binary formats) is its suitability to serve as a common platform-independent formalism for exchanging data between applications, irrespective of which programming languages have been used for implementing the particular applications. A further benefit, which comes from its wide-spread use across disciplines, is that countless freely available and proprietary software applications have been developed that are capable of processing XML documents, in addition to the application programming interfaces needed for direct programmatic access. While many of these applications restrict themselves to merely displaying the structure of the document (cf. comments at the beginning of Section 4.2), there are also more specialised applications that focus on the needs of particular communities (see iLEX for an example of an XML-based application specifically designed for computational lexicography and dictionary publishing; Erlandsen, 2004). With XML-based formats reaching standard status (as is e. g. the case with the XML variants of RDF, RDFS and OWL), and with each format coming with its own formal specification in the form of an XML schema, the development of editing and processing software is enabled that is then likely to be widely used across communities.

The major criticism of XML, which has been pointed out e. g. by Champion (2004), is the huge overhead that is necessary to store and process XML data. However, with the considerable improvements that have been achieved with respect to hardware performance over the past years (e. g. increased storage bandwidth and central processing unit (CPU clock rate), for many tasks this issue has become less grave in comparison to the benefits of XML. In addition to this, there are scalable database solutions for storing and accessing XML data (e. g. Tamino XML Server; Schöning, 2001). Although an application-optimised binary format would undoubtedly still outperform any XML-based format, database back-ends for XML have enabled the transfer of at least some of the performance advantages of database management systems to XML technology.

The fact that XML can be used to derive custom formats makes it a very powerful formalism that can be adapted to one's particular needs. At the same time though, this characteristic

[12] Cf. http://www.sitepoint.com/xml-dtds-xml-schema/.

[13] For a more thorough overview, see e. g. Hunter *et al.* (2007).

also *encourages* to some extent the definition of custom formats for particular problems, frequently resulting in various competing XML-based formats essentially serving the same purpose[14]. On the other hand, as was mentioned above, some custom XML-based languages receive wide acceptance in a community, and in the following, we will discuss the SW languages and formats that can be expressed in XML, and that have reached the status of W3C recommendations.

4.2.3 RDF and RDF Schema

The *Resource Description Framework* (RDF) is a data model and specification for making statements about resources on the WWW (see Manola and Miller, 2004). The core of RDF is a model in which these statements as a whole are viewed as a set of directed labelled graphs, i. e. graphs whose edges carry labels and point *from* a node n_1 *to* a node n_2.[15] These consist of sets of subject-predicate-object triples, where for each triple the subject and object are interpreted as nodes, and the predicate as an arc between the two nodes (see Example (4.5) and Figure 4.2 below).

(4.5) subject: `<http://www.w3.org/History/1989/proposal.html>`
predicate: `<http://purl.org/dc/elements/1.1/creator>`
object: `<http://www.w3.org/People/Berners-Lee/card#i>`

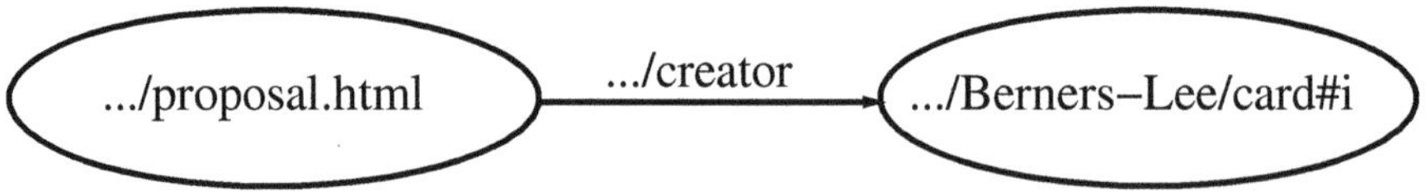

Figure 4.2: Graph representation of the triple in example (4.5)

Technically, subject and predicate represent resources that are dereferenced by URIs, and the object can represent either a resource or a literal value based on XML Schema datatypes. In example (4.5), the resource dereferenced by the subject URI is linked to the object URI using the typed predicate *creator*[16].

As can be seen in the example, which is a potential formalisation of example (4.1) above, RDF is very close to the initial conception of the WWW with typed links between resources. Moreover, it provides a very basic instantiation relation, *rdf:type*, which assigns to a resource i_1 the interpretation of an *instance* (or *object* or *individual*), and to a resource C that of a *class* (or *type* or *concept*) (see example (4.6)). In addition to this, predicates P which have i_1 as subject can be considered *properties* (or *relations* or *roles*) of i_1.

---

[14] Cf. the various XML-based tools and frameworks for linguistic annotation in corpora (see e. g. Bird *et al.*, 2000; Brants *et al.*, 2002), which may in the future be alleviated to some extent by initiatives to derive standards for linguistic annotation (see Ide *et al.*, 2003).

[15] See http://www.w3.org/TR/rdf-concepts/#section-data-model.

[16] The *creator* property is part of the Dublin Core metadata element set; for more information see http://dublincore.org/documents/dcq-rdf-xml/.

(4.6) i_1 *rdf:type* C
i_1 P i_2

As was mentioned in the introduction to Section 4.2, RDF can be expressed in a variety of syntax formats, of which the RDF/XML variant is probably the most widely used one. However, since RDF was originally conceived as a data model, it provides only a limited set of elements. More expressivity is supplied by RDF Schema (RDFS), a KR language located on the next layer of the SW stack in Figure 4.1 above. RDFS provides the basic vocabulary for defining type hierarchies in RDF – by means of the predicates *rdfs:subClassOf* and *rdfs:subPropertyOf* – and has, among others, the necessary means to express domain and range restrictions of a property.

(4.7) P *rdfs:domain* C_1
P *rdfs:range* C_2

The statements in example (4.7) express that resources in the domain of a property P (i. e. subjects of triples that have P as predicate) are instances of a class C_1, and resources in the range of P (i. e. objects of triples with predicate P) are instances of C_2 (see Brickley and Guha, 2004). This information is useful in a number of respects. On the one hand, it can be used for inferring the type of a subject or object of P, in the sense that a resource occurring as subject or object of P can automatically be classified as an instance of C_1 or C_2 respectively. On the other hand, editors such as Protégé (Knublauch *et al.*, 2004) use domain and range information in order to restrict the instances for which P is offered as property to those in its domain, and to suggest possible values for P based on the types in its range. Finally, this information can be used for error detection, to check e. g. whether the subjects (objects) of P are actually instances of C_1 (C_2) (cf. Sections 4.3.3 and 4.3.4 below).

As the above discussion shows, RDF and RDFS provide a formal graph-based framework for a weak formalisation of resources and their properties. Although the means are simple, however, RDFS can be used to define resources in a way that makes the resulting set of graphs very complex with respect to its computational properties, as there is no formal mechanism to restrict the use of the RDF and RDFS vocabulary. For example, it is possible in RDFS to define classes as instances of other classes, making the latter *classes of classes* or *metaclasses*. In formal terms, the resulting resources would be equivalent to higher order logics, with all the negative characteristics this entails, e. g. loss of the guarantee of computational decidability. Although this is not a crucial issue with respect to questions of computational lexicography, it is a rather critical behaviour for a formalism that is intended to serve as a basis for AI-oriented tasks, such as automated reasoning or classification of resources. Therefore, a further formalism has been proposed which is rather inspired by logics and has been developed with computational complexity in mind, namely the *Web Ontology Language*.

4.2.4 OWL

The *Web Ontology Language* (OWL) forms the next building block of SW technologies. As was just mentioned, OWL is a formalism based on RDF, though it is far more expressive than RDF's vocabulary RDFS. Most importantly, OWL provides further language constructs that enable an axiomatisation of resources in a way that is closely related to first-order logic

– like class disjointness, class equivalence or local property restrictions (e. g. cardinality restrictions) – and where classes and properties are interpreted as one-place and two-place predicates respectively. As with RDF, OWL can be expressed in XML syntax.

As the name already suggests, OWL is a KR language designed for modelling ontologies. In this context, the terms TBox and ABox are frequently used. While the TBox (*terminological component*), defines the intensional knowledge in an ontology, i. e. the concepts and their properties, the ABox (*assertional component*) contains extensional knowledge, by making statements about individual instances using the vocabulary defined in the TBox (cf. Nardi and Brachman, 2003: p. 16ff).

Being a declarative formalism based on first-order logic, OWL is complementary to frame-based alternatives (see e. g. Karp, 1992), which are based on prototypes and default values, and which resemble object-oriented programming languages in the way they are composed. In fact, OWL is the successor of a language combining the frame-based approach with a very expressive subset of first-order logic, namely DAML+OIL (DARPA[17] Agent Markup Language + Ontology Inference Layer; Horrocks, 2002). In contrast to frame-based formalisms, reasoning in OWL is *monotone*. Formally, an inference operation f is monotone if the following holds (see also Baader and Nutt, 2003).

(4.8) $\Gamma \subseteq \Delta \implies f(\Gamma) \subseteq f(\Delta)$

Monotonicity states that conclusions which have been derived on the basis of a set of premises Γ still hold after further statements have been added to Γ. For resources defined in OWL, this means e. g. that restrictions that have been defined for a class (such as the local property restrictions just mentioned) have to hold for its subclasses as well. In other words, a subclass *inherits* the restrictions of all its superclasses, which can be a single class or several ones (*multiple inheritance*). Closely related to this is the so-called *open world assumption*, which essentially means that failure to derive a fact does not imply its falsity. In the context of the SW, where it cannot be assumed that all information is explicitly stated somewhere, this is a crucial feature. To see this, assume a data set that does not contain the statement »*Barack Obama is the 44th president of the United States*«. In a closed world, the question »*Is Barack Obama the 44th president of the United States?*« would be answered with »*no*«, since the assumption is that there is no information beyond that which is represented explicitly. In contrast to this, an open world formalism like OWL would reply that the answer is »*unknown*«, since in case the above statement is added to the data set, OWL would have to rewrite its initial conclusion, thus conflicting with its property of being monotone. The same is true of the related *unique name assumption*, which states that each resource name uniquely denotes something else than any other resource name. OWL does not make this assumption, and thus two resources are not assumed to be different or equivalent unless explicitly stated so. Again, this is a very reasonable approach in a SW setting, where it is highly likely that different sources have more than one name for referring to a single resource (e. g. »*Barack Obama*«, »*Barack Hussein Obama II*« and »*the 44th president of the United States*«) and making the unique name assumption could require later cancellation of previous conclusions.

[17] Defense Advanced Research Projects Agency.

4.2.4.1 Three sublanguages of OWL

OWL comes in three language variants which differ with respect to their expressivity and thus also their formal properties. These variants are (i) OWL Full, which offers the unrestricted power of OWL, including full support for all RDFS constructs; (ii) OWL DL, a subset of OWL Full that is based on *Description Logic* (DL; see e. g. Baader *et al.*, 2003); and (iii) OWL Lite, a very light-weight and inexpressive subset of OWL DL. The decision as to which variant should be used crucially depends on the particular task at hand.

OWL Full provides full compatibility with RDFS and, as RDFS, does not impose strict disjointness of classes, properties, instances and datatypes (see Bechhofer *et al.*, 2004, Section 1.2). As a result, it is e. g. possible in OWL Full to define metaclasses, or to model entities that are properties and instances at the same time. While this can be a very desirable from a representational point of view (cf. the discussion in Section 4.3.5 below), such features have negative effects on the complexity of the modelled data, since formal qualities like decidability of entailment cannot be guaranteed.

Computational decidability is a crucial requirement in the context of the SW, since otherwise it cannot be guaranteed that agents finish their reasoning tasks in finite time. Therefore, OWL DL was designed which uses the same set of OWL language constructs as OWL Full, however, with restrictions on how this vocabulary can be used. One of these is the strict separation of classes, instances and properties and thus the lack of metaclasses. Formally, OWL DL is based on the fairly expressive description logic $\mathcal{SHOIN}$(D), a decidable fragment of first-order logic (Horrocks and Patel-Schneider, 2003).

The least expressive of the three sublanguages is OWL Lite, which does not only impose restrictions on how the language constructs are used (e. g. limiting the use of cardinality restrictions to cardinalities of 0 and 1), but also restricts the constructs that are available. For example, while OWL Full and OWL DL have operators for expressing class union and intersection, OWL Lite does not allow for such expressions. Due to its very limited expressivity, OWL Lite is only of interest to users who require a subsumption hierarchy and simple constraints. For other users, however, at least OWL DL should be considered. Therefore, we will focus on the features of OWL DL in more detail, and discuss the additional features of OWL Full whenever appropriate.

4.2.4.2 Main features of OWL Full and OWL DL

As was mentioned above, OWL DL is based on the $\mathcal{SHOIN}$(D) description logic, where the letters stand for the following available operations.

(4.9)	$\mathcal{S}$[18]	=	Concept negation and intersection, value restriction, existential quantification, transitive roles
	$\mathcal{H}$	=	Role inclusion
	$\mathcal{O}$	=	Nominals
	$\mathcal{I}$	=	Inverse roles
	$\mathcal{N}$	=	Number restriction
	(D)	=	Datatypes

Table 4.1 below summarises the main constructors and axioms available in OWL Full and OWL DL, with C and D denoting (atomic or complex) concepts, a and b individuals, and R and S roles.[19]

NAME	DESCRIPTION LOGIC SYNTAX	OWL CONSTRUCT
Concept intersection	$C \sqcap D$	*intersectionOf*
Concept union	$C \sqcup D$	*unionOf*
Concept negation	$\neg C$	*complementOf*
Value restriction	$\forall R.C$	*allValuesFrom*
Existential quantification	$\exists R.C$	*someValuesFrom*
Number restriction	$\geqslant n\, R$	*minCardinality*
	$\leqslant n\, R$	*maxCardinality*
	$= n\, R$	*cardinality*
Nominals	$\{a, b, \ldots\}$	*oneOf*
	$\exists R.\{a\}$	*hasValue*
Concept inclusion	$C \sqsubseteq D$	*rdfs:subClassOf*
Role inclusion	$R \sqsubseteq S$	*rdfs:subPropertyOf*
Concept equivalence	$C \equiv D$	*equivalentClass*
Role equivalence	$R \equiv S$	*equivalentProperty*
Individual equivalence	$a = b$	*sameAs*
Concept disjointness	$C \sqsubseteq \neg D$	*disjointWith*
Individual disjointness	$a \neq b$	*differentFrom*
Inverse roles	R^-	*inverseOf*
Functional roles	$\leqslant 1\, R$	*FunctionalProperty*
Inverse functional roles	$\leqslant 1\, R^-$	*InverseFunctionalProperty*
Symmetric roles	$R \equiv R^-$	*SymmetricProperty*
Transitive roles	$R^+ \sqsubseteq R$	*TransitiveProperty*

Table 4.1: Mapping from description logic expressions to constructors available in OWL Full and OWL DL

As can be seen in the table, OWL DL provides a set of constructors for formalising resources that goes far beyond the rather simple ones like *subClassOf*/*subPropertyOf* or *domain*/*range* available in RDFS. For example, OWL DL offers the possibility to refine the definitions of properties by assigning to them formal attributes like *symmetry* or *transitivity*. On the basis of such constructs, it is possible for a description logic reasoner to automatically infer further statements about resources. In the context of an ED, e. g., let us assume the synonymy relation as symmetric and transitive property, as well as the lexical items »*immer*«, »*stets*« and »*jederzeit*« (all meaning »*always*«). In this setting, it would suffice to define these three words as synonyms by simply stating that »*immer*« and »*stets*« are synonyms, as well as »*stets*« and »*jederzeit*« (see Figure 4.3). Further statements, e. g. that »*immer*« is also synonymous to »*jederzeit*«, would then be inferred by the appropriate reasoning software.

[18] In the description logic notational convention, $\mathcal{S}$ is used as an abbreviation for $\mathcal{ALC}_{\mathcal{R}^+}$, which stands for an attributive language with concept negation and transitive roles (see Baader and Nutt, 2003).

[19] Table 4.1 is a highly simplified account of the relevant tables in (Baader *et al.*, 2003, Appendix 1) and (Horrocks and Patel-Schneider, 2003).

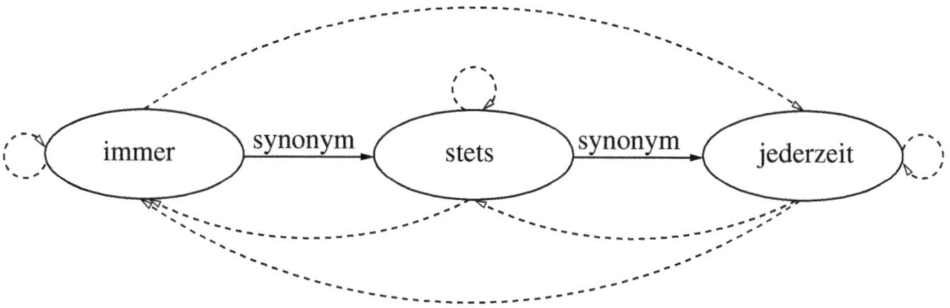

Figure 4.3: Synonymy as symmetric and transitive relation (with dashed arrows representing inferred statements)[20]

In addition to this, properties can be defined as being *functional* (in the sense of having exactly one value or none) or *inverse* to other properties. For example, a collocation can be said to have exactly one base, so a property like *hasBase* could be modelled as a functional property between a collocation and other lexical items. Moreover, any resource that is linked to a collocation via a property *hasBase* should automatically be assigned the property of being the base of that particular collocation. In other words, we could create a property *isBaseOf* that is the inverse of *hasBase*. As a consequence, a statement of the form *b isBaseOf a* would be automatically inferred from the statement *a hasBase b*.

On a more general level, OWL DL not only distinguishes between classes, individuals and properties, but also among properties between *object properties* that relate individuals with individuals, and *datatype properties* that relate individuals with XML Schema datatypes. In OWL Full, it is moreover possible to define *metaproperties*. Here, *object metaproperties* can be used to relate classes with classes, classes with individuals, or individuals with classes, while *datatype metaproperties* relate classes with datatypes. Whereas object and datatype properties are disjoint in OWL DL, they are not in OWL Full. In fact, the OWL class *DatatypeProperty* is formally a subclass of *ObjectProperty* in OWL Full, and therefore, it is possible to define a datatype property as subproperty of an object property in OWL Full, but not in OWL DL.

As was mentioned above, it is possible to add local property restrictions to a class definition. In an ED, one could e. g. want to state that transitive verbs have exactly two arguments, i. e. that the property *hasArgument* has exactly two values for instances of the class *TransitiveVerb*. This can be expressed using a *number* or *cardinality restriction*. On the one hand, this restriction could be formalised as a *necessary condition* of the class *TransitiveVerb*, in the sense that *TransitiveVerb* is a subclass of the (anonymous) class that consists of all entities that have exactly two arguments: $\mathit{TransitiveVerb} \sqsubseteq (= 2\ \mathit{hasArgument})$. However, in

[20] Reflexivity is a logical consequence of symmetry and transitivity, and thus a reasoner would also infer each item to be synonymous to itself. Although this is very reasonable from a logical point of view – since every lexical item could, in general, be considered to be synonymous to itself – it seems at least questionable from a lexicographer's point of view (cf. discussions in Section 4.3.3).

OWL DL it is also possible to model such restrictions as *necessary and sufficient conditions*, i. e. *TransitiveVerb* $\equiv$ *(= 2 hasArgument)*. The difference between the two formalisations is that in the latter case, where *TransitiveVerb* is a so-called *defined class*, a description logic reasoner can infer that any instance in the ED that has two arguments is a *TransitiveVerb*[21]. In the former case, where *TransitiveVerb* is a *primitive class*, the condition is not enough in order to be inferred as an instance of *TransitiveVerb*.

The cardinality restrictions just discussed are unspecified with respect to the type that should be the filler of the *hasArgument* property. However, OWL 2 provides support for so-called *qualified cardinality restrictions*. Using a qualified cardinality restriction, the necessary and sufficient condition from above can e. g. be formalised as *TransitiveVerb* $\equiv$ *(= 2 hasArgument.NounPhrase)*, stating that a transitive verb has exactly two noun phrases as arguments.

Commonly, local property restrictions like the ones discussed so far are defined for classes in the domain of the respective property, where the local restriction then refines the extension of the range of the property for that particular class. A conceivable example in an ED is again the relation between a collocation and its base, where the OWL constructor *allValuesFrom* can be used to restrict the range of the property *hasBase* – which would generally extend to all kinds of lexical entities – to entities of a specific kind. Here, a collocation of the type $V + N_{Obj}$, i. e. a collocation with nominal base that serves as direct object of the verbal collocate (see e. g. Heid and Gouws, 2006), could have the restriction $\forall hasBase.Noun$, which would express that for all instances of that collocational type, the values of the *hasBase* property have to be instances of the class *Noun*.

Restrictions such as the ones just discussed can be interpreted by editors like Protégé and thus contribute to the dictionary editing process in at least two respects. On the one hand, they minimise the chance of adding inappropriate property values for instances of a particular class, and on the other hand, the high degree of formalisation commits a dictionary editor to formal accuracy in designing the ED model. As a result, OWL has the expressivity to add another level of correctness to the ones mentioned above in the context of XML. In addition to syntactic wellformedness and validity with respect to a schema, OWL introduces the notion of *logical consistency*, where a resource is consistent only if it adheres to its logical definition (see more detailed discussion in Section 4.3).

With the core formalisms of the SW introduced, we will now turn to those components that are applied to them, namely *rule languages* in Section 4.2.5 and *query languages* in Section 4.2.6. As can be seen in the layer cake diagram on page 41, the blocks reserved for these components are situated to the left and to the right of RDFS and OWL. On the one hand, this indicates that both types of languages are not to be understood as layers in the sense of the ones discussed so far, but that they have a status of being *applied* to the representation formalisms. On the other hand, the colour scheme expresses that query languages are more closely linked to RDF and RDFS. Despite this, the way the blocks are arranged nonetheless captures the fact that rule languages and query languages are compatible with both RDFS and OWL.

---

[21] The condition would certainly be restricted to verbs that have two arguments, i. e. *TransitiveVerb* $\equiv$ *Verb* $\sqcap$ *(= 2 hasArgument)*.

4.2.5 Rule Languages

For applications which require additional expressivity that goes beyond the one offered by OWL DL, especially with respect to reasoning, the SW provides for rule-based extensions to OWL. In particular, the SW layer cake diagram mentions the *Rule Interchange Format* (RIF), an effort led by the W3C in order to produce recommendations for rule interchange that are compatible with previous W3C specifications[22]. As the work on specifying RIF is ongoing and has not progressed to the extent of releasing a standardised format yet, no application software that uses RIF has been developed. Thus, we will instead focus on the rule language that is currently the most widely used one, namely the *Semantic Web Rule Language* (SWRL; Horrocks *et al.*, 2004), which combines OWL with an XML-based rule language (RuleML[23]), and currently has the status of a W3C member submission. Syntactically, SWRL is compatible with the RDF/XML syntax of OWL, which ensures that the integration of SWRL rules into an OWL ontology poses only little extra representational requirements.

SWRL extends OWL DL with Horn clauses, i. e. disjunctions with at most one positive disjunct, which look like the one in example (4.10) below. Horn clauses are used especially in logic programming languages like Prolog, where procedures are expressed by means of Horn clauses, as in (4.11). In terms of SWRL, these two examples can be represented as in (4.12), where the antecedents of the implication are in the *rule body*; the consequent is called *rule head*, and variables are prefixed with '?'.

(4.10) $\neg P(x) \vee \neg Q(y) \vee R(x,y)$

(4.11) `R(X,Y) :- P(X), Q(Y).`

(4.12) $P(?x) \wedge Q(?y) \rightarrow R(?x,?y)$

Although the definition of Horn clauses states that they may only contain exactly one positive disjunct, i. e. one consequent, more complex consequents like the one shown in (4.13) are also possible, since these are nothing else than conjunctions of Horn clauses that share the same negative disjuncts, i. e. the antecedents (see (4.14)).

(4.13) $P(?x) \wedge Q(?y) \rightarrow R(?x,?y) \wedge S(?y,?x) \wedge T(?x,?y)$

(4.14) $P(?x) \wedge Q(?y) \rightarrow R(?x,?y)$
$P(?x) \wedge Q(?y) \rightarrow S(?y,?x)$
$P(?x) \wedge Q(?y) \rightarrow T(?x,?y)$

The rules are restricted in two respects. On the one hand, every variable that occurs in the rule head has to occur in the rule body as well. Thus, it is not possible to state something like $P(?x) \wedge Q(?y) \rightarrow R(?x,?z)$, since $?z$ does not occur in the antecedent. On the other hand, the vocabulary used in the rule has to be defined in the ontology. In our examples, P and Q would have to be classes in the ontology, and R, S and T properties.

---

[22] http://www.w3.org/2005/rules/wiki/RIF_Working_Group

[23] See http://ruleml.org/.

The necessity of rules in addition to OWL becomes clear when trying to model *property chains* like the classic *uncle* relationship, since OWL itself does not provide the formal vocabulary to express relations like this.[24]

(4.15) $hasParent(?x, ?y) \wedge hasBrother(?y, ?z) \rightarrow hasUncle(?x, ?z)$

In the context of computational lexicography, property chains are among others interesting for modelling the interplay between synonymy and antonymy, where it could be stated that the synonyms of an antonym *y* of *x* are also antonyms of *x* (see Section 4.3.3).

Within the Protégé ontology editor and the SWRL application programming interface (O'Connor *et al.*, 2008), SWRL is extended with a query language called SQWRL (*Semantic Query-Enhanced Web Rule Language*), which can be used to select data that match a certain configuration.

(4.16) $P(?x) \wedge Q(?y) \wedge R(?x, ?y) \rightarrow sqwrl{:}select(?x, ?y)$

While the possible uses of SWRL and SQWRL in the context of an ED are discussed in Sections 4.3.3 and 4.3.4 below, we will now turn to a more detailed discussion of more powerful SW query languages.

4.2.6 Query Languages

The query language that is mentioned explicitly in the diagram is the *SPARQL Protocol and RDF Query Language* (SPARQL; Prud'hommeaux and Seaborne, 2008), a rather recent development effort coordinated by the W3C. It combines features from a variety of query languages – most notably RDQL (Seaborne, 2004) and SeRQL (Broekstra and Kampman, 2003) – and is the only RDF query language so far to receive the status of a W3C recommendation. Due to the fact that SPARQL – unlike SeRQL – does not depend on a particular framework, and since the differences to other RDF query languages are mainly on a syntactic level, we will limit our discussion to presenting the main characteristics of SPARQL.

4.2.6.1 Main features of SPARQL

SPARQL is a graph-based query language in which queries are stated in the form of *graph patterns*. Coming back to our example (4.5) in Section 4.2.3, we could state a query like the one in example (4.17) in order to find out who created the original WWW proposal.

(4.17)
```
PREFIX dc: <http://purl.org/dc/elements/1.1/>
SELECT ?name
WHERE
 { <http://www.w3.org/History/1989/proposal.html> dc:creator ?name }
```

[24] Property chains are supported in OWL 2, where one can state that the chain of *hasParent* and *hasBrother* is a subproperty of the *hasUncle* property by means of the complex role inclusion axiom $(hasParent \circ hasBrother) \dot{\sqsubseteq} hasUncle$ (see e. g. Horrocks and Sattler, 2004).

The query starts with the definition of one or more namespace prefixes in order to avoid the use of absolute URI references in the query. The next line determines the type of the query form. In addition to the SELECT clause, which is used in the above query, SPARQL offers three further query forms, namely CONSTRUCT, DESCRIBE and ASK, which differ in their functionality and in the type of result they return. SELECT queries typically return variables and their bindings, so that the result of the query in (4.17) would be that the variable ?name would be bound to <http://www.w3.org/People/Berners-Lee/card#i>.

In contrast to SELECT queries, CONSTRUCT queries return an RDF graph. This graph is built up by means of a template that is provided in the CONSTRUCT clause. Among others, such templates can be used to create custom statements by reformulating triples from the original data set. For example, one could have a custom predicate *exa:created* that basically inverses the *dc:creator* relation, as in (4.18) below. The result of the query is given in (4.19)[25].

(4.18)
```
PREFIX dc:  <http://purl.org/dc/elements/1.1/>
PREFIX exa: <http://example.org/example/>
CONSTRUCT { ?x exa:created ?y }
WHERE { ?y dc:creator ?x }
```

(4.19)
```
@prefix exa: <http://example.org/example/> .

<http://www.w3.org/People/Berners-Lee/card#i>
  exa:created <http://www.w3.org/History/1989/proposal.html> .
```

Similar to CONSTRUCT, a DESCRIBE query returns an RDF graph as well. However, instead of providing a template of the result graph, it *describes* the resources provided in the DESCRIBE clause by returning their outgoing and – in some implementations – incoming arcs. In our simple example, this could look like in (4.20) and (4.21) below, although more complex configurations are possible as well by using variables and the WHERE clause.

(4.20)
```
PREFIX dc: <http://purl.org/dc/elements/1.1/>
DESCRIBE <http://www.w3.org/History/1989/proposal.html>
```

(4.21)
```
@prefix dc:  <http://purl.org/dc/elements/1.1/> .

<http://www.w3.org/History/1989/proposal.html>
  dc:creator <http://www.w3.org/People/Berners-Lee/card#i> .
```

The last form offered in SPARQL is the ASK query, which is a boolean query that returns *yes* or *no* to the question whether there is a graph in the RDF data that matches with a specified graph pattern. In the following query, the question is whether there is something that has the *dc:creator* with the specified URI, to which the answer would be *yes* in the case at hand.

(4.22)
```
PREFIX dc: <http://purl.org/dc/elements/1.1/>
ASK { ?x dc:creator <http://www.w3.org/People/Berners-Lee/card#i> }
```

[25] Following the notation in the SPARQL language reference (Prud'hommeaux and Seaborne, 2008), the query results are given in the Turtle syntax. See http://www.w3.org/TeamSubmission/turtle/ for details.

SELECT and ASK queries can be serialised in the SPARQL Query Results XML Format (Beckett and Broekstra, 2008), again a recommendation of the W3C. For the graph query forms CONSTRUCT and DESCRIBE, the standard RDF/XML format can be used (Beckett and McBride, 2004), as in (4.23), which is the RDF/XML version of (4.21). However, specific query engines also offer direct access to all query result types via application programming interfaces, which can be used to directly post-process the result data programmatically and thus circumvene the serialisation.

(4.23)

```
<?xml version="1.0"?>
<rdf:RDF
    xmlns:rdf="http://www.w3.org/1999/02/22-rdf-syntax-ns#"
    xmlns:dc="http://purl.org/dc/elements/1.1/">
  <rdf:Description
      rdf:about="http://www.w3.org/History/1989/proposal.html">
    <dc:creator
        rdf:resource="http://www.w3.org/People/Berners-Lee/card#i"/>
  </rdf:Description>
</rdf:RDF>
```

Finally, in addition to the clauses illustrated in examples (4.17) to (4.22), SPARQL also offers a set operator for matching alternatives ({ } UNION { }), an optionality operator for specifying optional parts of a graph pattern (OPTIONAL { }), filters for restricting the solutions of a graph pattern match (FILTER ( )), and several solution modifiers (e. g. ORDER BY for ordering results or DISTINCT for removing duplicates from the result set). As these represent more advanced features and will be an integral part of Chapter 6, we have omitted them from this general introduction to SPARQL and instead refer the reader to the relevant discussions in Section 6.2.2.

4.2.7 Tools

The use of SW formalisms crucially depends on the development of appropriate tools that are able to interpret the vocabulary of the respective formalism. For RDFS and OWL, considerable effort has gone into the development of ontology editing tools, description logic reasoners and rule engines, as well as scalable storage solutions. In the following paragraphs, we will briefly introduce those that are most widely used in the community, and that have also been considered in this study.

4.2.7.1 Ontology editors

With more than 160,000 registered users[26], the freely-available *Protégé Ontology Editor* (Knublauch *et al.*, 2004) is the most widely used ontology editor in the SW community. It is an open source framework implemented in Java that offers full support for OWL 1.0 as well as (from Protégé 4.1 on) OWL 2 constructs, such as qualified cardinality restrictions. Moreover, Protégé has built-in reasoning support in the form of the Pellet OWL DL reasoner

[26] As of January 2011 (see http://protege.stanford.edu/).

(see below) and provides interfaces to other description logic reasoners and rule engines in order to complete reasoning tasks like taxonomy classification, consistency checking or type inference. In addition to this, Protégé offers the possibility to automatically generate a Java application programming interface for the entities defined in an OWL ontology. For example, if the model contains a class *Collocation* with a property *hasBase* with range *LexicalItem*, then the automatically generated Java class `Collocation` contains methods for adding a base to a collocation (e. g. `void addHasBase(LexicalItem base)`) or for retrieving the base of a collocation (e. g. `LexicalItem getHasBase()`). Finally, Protégé maintains a very active OWL mailing list that has almost 2,000 users and provides very good technical support.

The basic tools in Protégé consist of tabs for editing the definitions of OWL classes, properties and individuals, in addition to a tab for managing SWRL rules. As was mentioned in sections 4.2.3 and 4.2.4, Protégé directly interprets domain and range information as well as many of the necessary and necessary and sufficient conditions, and is thus also useful for editing the data in an ED as well as its model. In addition to this, Protégé can also be accessed through a Java application programming interface that allows for programmatic processing of the lexicon model and data.

The only real alternative aside from Protégé is the *TopBraid Composer*™, although its user base is already considerably smaller, having roughly 500 registered mailing list users.[27] For this reason, and since it is only commercially available, it was not considered within this study.

4.2.7.2 Description logic reasoners and rule engines

In contrast to the rather monopolistic situation for ontology editors, there is a much broader range of freely and commercially available description logic reasoners. Among the most widely used ones are *FaCT++* (Tsarkov and Horrocks, 2006), *KAON2* (Motik and Studer, 2005), *Pellet* (Sirin *et al.*, 2007) and *RacerPro* (Haarslev *et al.*, 2007), most of which fully support the OWL DL constructs. Within an ontology editor like Protégé, these reasoners can be plugged in and accessed through a standard interchange format specified by the *Description logic Implementation Group* (DIG[28]), the so-called DIG interface. Here, implementational details are hidden to the user and only the result of the reasoning task (e. g. the inferred subclass tree) is returned to Protégé. For this reason, and since the reasoners do not differ so much with respect to performance, it is of minor importance to most applications which particular reasoner is used, as long as it can be accessed through the DIG interface.

Reasoning is performed by transforming an OWL ontology into a knowledge base (KB) consisting of description logic axioms, and checking whether this KB is satisfiable. For most of the reasoners just mentioned, this is done by means of the *tableau calculus*, according to which a KB is satisfiable if it is possible for an algorithm to construct a clash-free semantic tableau for it (see e. g. Baader and Nutt, 2003)[29]. Since OWL entailment has been shown to be reducable to description logic satisfiability (cf. Horrocks and Patel-Schneider, 2003), description logic reasoners are also frequently called *theorem provers* in the literature. For

[27] http://www.topquadrant.com/products/TB_Composer.html

[28] See http://dl.kr.org/dig/.

[29] KAON2 is an exception, as it performs reasoning based on disjunctive datalog (cf. Hustadt *et al.*, 2007)

example, in order to find out whether $C \sqsubseteq D$ (i. e. $\neg C \sqcup D$), one can assume $C \sqcap \neg D$ (i. e. $\neg(\neg C \sqcup D)$) and prove that the resulting tableau contains a clash, i. e. a contradiction.

As of today, the probably biggest problem with respect to description logic reasoners is scalability, as all of the current implementations seem to perform rather poorly on large data sets (see Bock *et al.*, 2008). This is, of course, largely due to the very high worst-case complexity of OWL DL, which can require exponential time for some reasoning tasks. Therefore, reasoning solutions based on a reduced set of RDFS and OWL Lite constructs in combination with scalable storage backends have been developed, such as OWLIM for the Sesame framework (see below).

As for rule-based reasoning, KAON2 and Pellet provide limited support for SWRL rules. For complete and efficient SWRL reasoning, the *Java Expert System Shell* (Jess®; Friedman-Hill, 2003) can be used, which uses the RETE algorithm to perform rule processing (Forgy, 1982). Although the rule engine has its own rule language, it is possible to translate SWRL rules into this format in order to make them processable. As with description logic reasoners, the Jess® rule engine can be easily plugged into Protégé (Golbreich and Imai, 2004).

4.2.7.3 RDF triplestores

Scalability has been mentioned above as one of the current drawbacks of SW applications. However, there have been significant developments with respect to combining RDFS and OWL reasoners with efficient query engines and scalable storage architectures. These are commonly referred to as *RDF triplestores*, as they are optimised for storing RDFS and OWL data in the form of RDF triples (cf. Section 4.2.3 above). An RDF triplestore typically offers several storage backends (e. g. in-memory, native and database storage) and may scale up to several billion statements[30]. Triplestores can typically be accessed by a variety of query languages, with the current standard query language SPARQL being supported by most architectures, though with implementational differences. For example, while the *AllegroGraph RDFStore*™ (Franz Inc., 2006) extracts only outgoing arcs for a SPARQL `DESCRIBE` query, the *Sesame* framework (Broekstra *et al.*, 2002) extracts incoming arcs as well. As Prud'hommeaux and Seaborne (2008) put it, the data returned by a `DESCRIBE` query are »not prescribed by a SPARQL query, [...] but, instead, [are] determined by the SPARQL query processor«, and thus the choice of the triplestore may to a certain extent depend on the characteristics of the query processor. In addition to this, the section devoted to `DESCRIBE` in the SPARQL specification does not have normative status, which might also have an influence on implementational differences between architectures.

As was mentioned in the previous section, it is also possible to reason with triplestore data. Some architectures provide built-in RDFS reasoning or custom inferences like direct type inference. Other triplestores allow for OWL-based reasoning layers on top, such as the OWLIM storage and inference layer for the Sesame framework (Kiryakov *et al.*, 2005). What these approaches share is that they perform reasoning by means of *forward chaining* of inference rules, i. e. statements are inferred beforehand, when the data are added to the triplestore. This way, all information is stored explicitly in the triplestore and no further reasoning is required at the time of accessing the data (see Section 6.1.1.2 for more details).

---

[30] See http://www.w3.org/wiki/LargeTripleStores for a recent overview.

4.2.8 Criticism of the Layer Cake Diagram

While the organisation of the layers in Figure 4.1 is under heavy discussion and has changed more than once over the years, even the illustration of SW technologies as layer cake itself is not uncontroversial, mainly due to the potential misinterpretations it gives rise to. Some of these equal the relation between the layers with the relation of *dependency* or *increasing power*. For example, it might be tempting to assume that RDF *depends* on XML, or that OWL is *more powerful* than XML, since they are located on higher layers respectively. However, the former case is incorrect since RDF has – next to its XML serialisation RDF/XML (cf. 4.2.3) – also serialisations in Turtle and N-Triples[31] and is thus completely independent of XML. The latter case is incorrect since everything that can be expressed in OWL can also be expressed in XML, which is e. g. shown by the fact that XML is a possible serialisation for OWL. However, it is the more restricted and thus more standardised vocabulary that makes OWL more *expressive* or *meaningful*, since there are tools that understand the semantics of this vocabulary. Thus, given random files in OWL and in XML that adhere to the respective functional specifications, the former will always be assigned an interpretation that goes beyond that of the XML file, due to the fact that the software *understands* the OWL termini. In contrast to this, in common XML applications (e. g. Altova XMLSpy®) only the structure of the XML document will be understood, and the assignment of meaning to the content has to be achieved by devising custom interpretation software.

After this discussion, it becomes obvious that the different technologies depicted in the figure originate from different motivations and serve different purposes. While dependency might in some cases be involved (e. g. RDF Schema definitely depends on the RDF model and syntax), other cases suggest a relation of the kind *»is applied to«*, such as the one between SPARQL and RDFS or OWL. Therefore, a safer interpretation of the diagram is that the layers form the building blocks of the SW, where higher layers use capabilities introduced on lower layers. In general, all layers represent important achievements for realising the vision of the SW as anticipated by the people who have conceptualised it.

4.3 Benefits of Semantic Web Formalisms for Computational Lexicography

Using a formalism that is located on a higher layer in the SW stack – such as RDFS or OWL – brings with it a number of benefits, some of which have already been mentioned in the sections above. The present section is devoted to a more detailed discussion of the most relevant ones on the basis of previous work with OWL in computational lexicography. In particular, we base our assumptions on work done on a model for a dictionary of collocations (Spohr and Heid, 2006; Heid *et al.*, 2007), on suggested OWL models for GermaNet (Lüngen and Storrer, 2007), and on a lexicon model for lexical-semantic corpus data (Spohr *et al.*, 2007; Burchardt *et al.*, 2008a), as well as more general remarks from an AI-based perspective (Görz, in prep). Most of the issues discussed below apply to both OWL DL and OWL Full, and the differences between the two are only of little relevance. However, since OWL DL is

[31] http://www.w3.org/TR/rdf-testcases/#ntriples

suggested as the first choice for the definition of electronic lexical resources (Görz, in prep) and has been successfully used to implement models for linguistic annotation (cf. Chiarcos, 2008), we will assume OWL DL as the underlying language in the following subsections, and discuss possible reasons for going beyond the scope of description logics in Section 4.3.5.

4.3.1 Types and Restrictions

As was mentioned in Chapter 3.1 above, types and typed links are crucial requirements in an ED. RDFS and OWL not only provide a convenient way of expressing types and typed links, but also to organise them hierarchically. In addition to this, they allow for the unambiguous identification of different kinds of indications, in the sense of explicitly (as opposed to implicitly) organised lexical resources (see Heid, 1997: p. 12f). Finally, they provide the formal means necessary to refine their definitions in the form of domain and range restrictions as well as more sophisticated necessary (and necessary and sufficient) conditions formalised using description logics. Therefore, these formalisms provide the ideal formal devices for defining the appropriate properties and relations for a lexical item, in addition to restricting their values to the relevant data categories or lexical items.

In this respect, RDFS and OWL are reminiscent of constraint-based formalisms like the *Typed Feature Structure* (TFS) representation formalism (see Heid, 1997; Emele, 1994), which aim at providing a balance between feature structures, KR formalisms and logic programming. A combination of RDFS, OWL and SWRL with description logic reasoning is thus very closely linked to the TFS approach, which has already been applied in the context of computational lexicography (Heid, 1997). However, SW formalisms go beyond TFS in that their formal restrictions are directly interpreted by editors like Protégé and thus already contribute during the dictionary editing process – on the one hand by allowing for a very high degree of formalisation of the data in the lexical resource as well as its formal correctness, and on the other hand by easing the editing of data by minimising the chance of adding inappropriate property values (cf. Section 4.2.4). Moreover, the availability of scalable storage and retrieval software for RDFS and OWL, which primarily stems from their wide-spread use and interest to industrial partners, enable their usage on a much larger scale. Nonetheless, it is certainly the case that the two approaches are very similar in spirit.

4.3.2 Graph Interpretation and Modularity

Through its underlying graph model RDF and the existence of links between entities, RDFS and OWL allow for a graph-based view on the lexicon, which among others enables non-standard access to the data (Spohr and Heid, 2006) and is in line with the most recent developments in the field (cf. Trippel, 2006; Polguère, 2006). In addition to this, with N-Triples and Turtle, RDF offers formats that encode the data in the form of triples, and thus the lexical resource directly receives its graph interpretation without much markup overhead. Still, the advantages of XML – such as efficient processing with XSLT – are also available for RDF in the form of its XML-based serialisation format RDF/XML. Therefore, the benefits of the two can be combined, with storage in an RDF triple store that allows for a direct interpretation as graph, and with XSLT processing of the RDF results in RDF/XML. Without any doubt,

»plain« XML-based formats can also be used to model lexical data in the form of a graph, as has been successfully shown e. g. by Trippel (2006). However, in RDF the graph is directly reflected in the triple representation format, which can be achieved in XML only by means of the appropriate interpretation software.[32]

In addition to the graph-based view, OWL allows for a very modular organisation of the data in an ED as well as its components. More precisely, modularity is achieved in two different respects. On the one hand, through its distinction between classes, properties and instances, OWL enables a strict separation of metalanguage and object language that essentially comes for free (see e. g. Burchardt *et al.*, 2008a). On the other hand, modularity is achieved by means of the namespace mechanism (cf. Section 4.2.1), that can be used to distinguish between different components of an ED. This has for example been shown by Spohr and Heid (2006), where the namespace mechanism has been used to dereference lexical data and relations in a bilingual dictionary that consists of a combination of two monolingual ones. In particular, the added value was to be able to define a symmetric translation relation that has German lexical entities in its domain (e. g. *de:LexicalEntity*) and English lexical entities in its range (e. g. *en:LexicalEntity*). This way, it was only possible to link German lexical entities to English ones and vice versa, but not to link e. g. German lexical entities to German ones.

4.3.3 Underspecification and Inference

As was mentioned above, RDFS and OWL allow for a hierarchical organisation of types and relations by means of the built-in predicates *rdfs:subClassOf* and *rdfs:subPropertyOf*, and thus provide the core prerequisites for basic *subsumption* and *inheritance* inference. In a formalism like XML, the modelling of hierarchical information is of course possible as well, which is trivially shown by the fact that RDF and OWL have XML-based serialisations. However, it is important to understand that in a »plain« XML setting that involves the definition of a custom format, the semantics of the elements is completely open a priori, and the hierarchical interpretation has to be accomplished by devising format-specific software[33]. In a way, this is directly linked to the *Lexical Systems* approach (Polguère, 2006; cf. Section 3.2.2.2 above), according to which lexical models should not be designed according to principles that impose a hierarchisation on the data, but rather the hierarchical structure »should be projected 'on demand' onto lexical models« (Polguère, 2006, p. 51). However, this »projection« of course implies the implementation of the relevant mechanisms.

In contrast to this, due to the fact that the vocabularies of RDFS and OWL have become web standards, the necessity of custom interpretation software is reduced, since a wide range of software is available already and the inheritance mechanism is practically built-in. Although there have been several XML-based standardisation efforts as well (cf. Section 3.2.2.1

[32] Cf. the remarks on inheritance in Section 4.3.3 below.

[33] The implicit assumption here is that a straightforward hierarchical format, such as `<A><B><C/></B></A>`, which would receive an appropriate interpretation by very basic XML editors, can be disregarded among others due to the fact that – although being hierarchical – it would not automatically express inheritance as well, let alone multiple inheritance. For this to happen, again additional interpretation software would be required, and thus increased implementational effort is required as well.

above), many have restricted themselves to the formal specification of a format, without providing the necessary software (yet). Therefore, it cannot be claimed that any one of these formats has reached standard status in a wider community, and thus the number of custom formats and software keeps rising as new XML-based projects are initiated.

An immediate benefit of the built-in inheritance mechanism of RDFS and OWL is the possibility to use underspecified information in retrieving data from the ED. Among others, this has been shown in (Spohr, 2005) and (Spohr and Heid, 2006), where underspecification is enabled via the *rdfs:subPropertyOf* construct. In a query presented there, the general property *hasSemanticRelationTo* is used to extract entities that have semantic relations to each other, such as synonymy or antonymy. While the actual links between the entities in the dictionary have been stated by means of relations like *isSynonymOf* and *isAntonymOf*, the fact that these are more specific subproperties subsumed by the general *hasSemanticRelationTo* suffices to identify them as statements that are relevant to the query (cf. Spohr and Heid, 2006, p. 68).

Very closely related to the underspecified retrieval of data, though with slightly more focus on the representational side, is the possibility to express generalisations in a hierarchy. In the context of electronic lexical resources, this has been discussed e. g. in Burchardt *et al.* (2008a). Their approach combines linguistic corpus annotations on multiple layers (i. e. syntax, lexical semantics and morphology) with FrameNet (Baker *et al.*, 1998) on the one hand and a formalisation of the corpus annotation scheme on the other. There, the class hierarchy is used in order to generalise and thus to abstract over particular kinds of annotations. For example, different kinds of frame annotations (e. g. simple, metaphorical and underspecified ones) are grouped under a common label *FrameAnnotation* in order to be able to express annotation requirements that hold for all frame annotations irrespective of their particular type. In addition to this, it provides a convenient way of extracting the different kinds of frame annotations, again based on the basic subsumption inference.

A further kind of inference has already been introduced in Section 4.2.4 above, where synonymy was defined as a symmetric and transitive relation. As the combination of these two properties logically results in reflexivity, their use seems questionable from a representational point of view. However, since synonymy in the sense of a real equivalence relation does exist in the literature (see e. g. Edmundson and Epstein, 1969), and since the WordNet practice of grouping synonyms in so-called *synsets* is nothing else than the partitioning of an equivalence relation, we maintain the claim that transitivity is a necessary formal concept in an ED and thus a formal benefit of using OWL. Far less controversial is the benefit of symmetric and inverse properties, since inferences based on these formal attributes are more common in an ED. For example, it is without doubt desirable to automatically derive a statement like *b hasSemanticRelationTo a* on the basis of *a hasSemanticRelationTo b*.

In addition to the inferences just mentioned, there are two more types, namely inferences based on description logic axioms, as well as rule-based inferences (cf. sections 4.2.4 and 4.2.5). There, a class *TransitiveVerb* could be defined by means of the necessary and sufficient condition $TransitiveVerb \equiv Verb \sqcap (= 2\ hasArgument)$, and thus all entities that are instances of the class *Verb* and have exactly two arguments would be inferred as instances of the class *TransitiveVerb*. These conditions can be used to define *value partitions*[34] that provide views on the data. For example, if parts of speech are modelled as values of a property *hasPartOfSpeech*, one could define a class *NOUN* that is equivalent to the set of all entities

[34] See e. g. http://www.w3.org/TR/swbp-specified-values/.

that have the part-of-speech *Noun*, so e. g. $NOUN \equiv \exists hasPartOfSpeech.\{Noun\}$, and the instances that satisfy the condition are inferred as instances of *Noun*.

As for rule-based inferences, a language like SWRL can be used in order to infer more distant relations between lexical items as in the example below.

(4.24) $isAntonymOf(?x, ?y) \wedge isSynonymOf(?y, ?z) \rightarrow isAntonymOf(?x, ?z)$

On the one hand, a rule like the one in (4.24) is certainly an inference rule, in the sense that the synonyms z of an antonym y of x are also antonyms of x, and thus the corresponding inferred statements are added to the lexicon. On the other hand, one could argue that the lexicographers should have been aware of this circumstance in the first place, i. e. they should have already inserted the antonym relation between x and z. In other words, the rule in (4.24) could also be considered a formalisation of a what was called an *integrity constraint* in Section 3.1.2.2 – i. e. a constraint checking whether the descriptions of the lexical items are complete –, which brings us to the next set of benefits of SW formalisms for computational lexicography.

4.3.4 Consistency Checking and Data Integrity

Checking the consistency of the model as well as the integrity of the data has been identified as one of the most crucial requirements of an ED. It is in this area that SW formalisms have considerable advantages over other formalisms, adding these further notions to the more basic forms of correctness, namely *well-formedness* and *validity*. Since the main benefits rely on the fact that OWL is a logic-based formalism, this task is closely related to the inferencing capabilities mentioned in the previous section.

As was discussed in Section 4.2.4, the vocabulary of OWL DL allows for a very fine-grained and formally rich formalisation of the entities in a lexical resource, on the level of both data categories and types of lexical items. While it may be tempting to use only those constructs that enable the definition of a straightforward taxonomy, it should be noted that the main advantages of OWL lie in its tight link to description logic and logic programming, as it is exactly this link which commits the lexicographer to formal consistency in designing the ED model. In addition to the rule-based encoding of integrity constraints that has been presented in the previous section, there is also the formalisation using description logics. Here, the necessary as well as the necessary and sufficient conditions, which are understood and processed by editing and reasoning software, minimise the chance of errors being inserted into the ED. However, they do not completely eliminate the chance of errors. For example, let us assume a case in which a collocation like »*to do the dishes*«, which should belong to the collocation type $V + N_Obj$, was accidentally defined as being of the type $N + Adj$. Moreover, we assume that the type $N + Adj$ has at least the following necessary and sufficient conditions.

(4.25)
$$
\begin{aligned}
N + Adj \equiv\ & \exists hasBase.Noun \\
& \forall hasBase.Noun \\
& \exists hasCollocate.Adjective \\
& \forall hasCollocate.Adjective
\end{aligned}
$$

These conditions state that (i) the collocation has a base of the type *Noun*, (ii) all bases of the collocation are of the type *Noun*[35], (iii) the collocation has a collocate of the type *Adjective*, and (iv) all collocates of the collocation are of the type *Adjective*. If, for example, the base (»*dish*«) and the collocate (»*do*«) are added to the collocation before its exact type has been specified, i. e. before the conditions in (4.25) apply, the editing software has no way of restricting the set of possible entities that may be added as values of the respective property. However, it is still possible to identify this mistake at a later stage. In order to achieve this, it is possible to have a description logic reasoner check the consistency of the ED. Since the definition of the type $N + Adj$ states that all values of the *hasCollocate* property are adjectives, and since »*do*« is stated to be the collocate of »*to do the dishes*«, »*do*« is inferred to be of the type *Adjective*. However, »*do*« has already been stated as being of the type *Verb*. In this context it is important to note that if the classes *Verb* and *Adjective* are not defined as being mutually disjoint, then there is no inconsistency, since nothing would prevent an entity from being an adjective and a verb at the same time. However, if we assume that verbs and adjectives are mutually disjoint, i. e. the statements $Verb \sqsubseteq \neg\ Adjective$ and $Adjective \sqsubseteq \neg\ Verb$ are part of the model, then *Verb* and *Adjective* cannot share instances. Therefore, the fact $Verb(do) \wedge Adjective(do)$ causes the reasoner to report an inconsistency in the ED, which shows that fully exploiting the expressivity of OWL DL allows for a homogeneous method to ensure consistency and integrity.

While the previous cases dealt with the integrity of the lexical data, there are also cases of model inconsistencies. These represent mistakes that occur most often in the process of defining the model, e. g. when new classes or properties are added whose definitions conflict with the ones already contained in the model. Although it is more complex to construct a possible scenario for a model inconsistency, it is certainly helpful to do so and to discuss this example case in more detail. Therefore, consider the following sample class and property hierarchies, as well as the statements in (4.26).

CLASS HIERARCHY	PROPERTY HIERARCHY
LexicalItem	*hasCollocationalRelationTo*
SingleWordEntity	*hasBase*
MultiWordEntity	*hasCollocate*
Collocation	

Table 4.2: Sample class and property hierarchy

(4.26) $MultiWordEntity \sqsubseteq \neg SingleWordEntity$
$SingleWordEntity \sqsubseteq \neg MultiWordEntity$
$hasCollocationalRelationTo \sqsubseteq Collocation \times LexicalItem$

The first two statements in (4.26) express that *MultiWordEntity* and *SingleWordEntity* are mutually disjoint, while the third line states that *hasCollocationalRelationTo* is a relation from collocations to lexical items (in general). As explained in Section 4.2.4, these statements are passed on through the hierarchy and also hold for the subclasses and subproperties respectively. In the process of refining the model, one could now decide to define inverse properties

[35] This condition as well as condition (iv) can be omitted if *hasBase* and *hasCollocate* have been defined as functional properties.

to *hasBase* and *hasCollocate*, e. g. *isBaseOf* and *isCollocateOf*, both of which would – since they are inverses of the respective properties – have *LexicalItem* in their domain and *Collocation* in their range (e. g. $isBaseOf \sqsubseteq LexicalItem \times Collocation$). The resulting situation is that *hasCollocationalRelationTo* has *Collocation* in its domain, while its subproperties have *LexicalItem* in their domains. The effect of this is that *LexicalItem* and *Collocation* are inferred as being equivalent, since otherwise the newly added subproperties would conflict with the monotonicity of OWL DL. However, if *LexicalItem* is equivalent to *Collocation*, and *Collocation* is disjoint with *SingleWordEntity*, then *LexicalItem* is also disjoint with *SingleWordEntity*. This is, of course, an obvious contradiction, since a class cannot be disjoint with its subclass, and therefore the model is inconsistent.

This example illustrates that, although cases of model inconsistency are rather complex in their origin, they are nevertheless likely to occur in the actual model creation process, especially if more than one person is contributing to the formalisation of the ED. Therefore, it is again vital to have the formal means to identify such inconsistencies, such as the ones offered by OWL DL.

4.3.5 OWL DL and Beyond

As was mentioned in Section 4.2.4 above, staying within the scope of OWL DL guarantees computational decidability of entailment. However, this does not mean that leaving the realms of OWL DL inevitably results in undecidability. Motik (2005) has been able to show isolated features of OWL Full that lead to undecidability, such as the *unconstrained* use of the metamodelling facility, which allows among others to state axioms about the built-in OWL vocabulary. In addition to this, Motik has proven the decidability of a formalism based on description logics extended with metamodelling. It is hence not the case that every OWL Full ontology is undecidable per se, but rather that decidability cannot be guaranteed in the same way as for OWL DL. Still, although some OWL DL-based software is able to simply ignore OWL Full constructs and still deliver correct results (e. g. the Pellet OWL DL reasoner; cf. Section 4.2.7.2), others fail at the attempt to classify a knowledge base that goes beyond the scope of OWL DL. For these reasons, and since it offers the best trade-off between expressivity, decidability, complexity, and efficiency of processing (cf. Görz, in prep), OWL DL should be the first choice for the definition of an ED model.

However, one cannot deny the fact that metamodelling has a very strong attractivity especially with respect to questions of computational lexicography (see e. g. Lüngen and Storrer, 2007). For example, one might want to include metainformation about source or authorship of concepts in an ED, to indicate e. g. who created or modified a particular concept, or which source a specific concept has been taken from. Although RDFS provides a limited set of so-called *annotation properties* like *rdfs:label* or *rdfs:comment* that can be used to capture this information in OWL DL – albeit in a suboptimal way –, adding a custom annotation property like *source* inevitably classifies the ED model as being in OWL Full.

Issues like these represent no problems to an »unconstrained« formalism like XML, and a lexicographer using OWL DL has to face the justified criticism that the added semantics in the higher layers of the SW actually comes at a very high cost. In favour of OWL Full, it can be argued that computational decidability, despite being a desirable formal characteristic, is of minor importance in a field where the primary focus is on the representational aspects of a formalism and thus its expressivity. However, if we follow this line of argumentation, then the additional layer of correctness that has been discussed in Section 4.3.4, namely logical consistency, becomes void since suddenly no software is available that is able to reliably perform consistency checking in finite time. Therefore, a valid strategy is to separate OWL DL data from OWL Full constructs, in analogy to the common practice in conceptual modelling according to which *conceptual knowledge* is separated from *data knowledge* (see e. g. Motik, 2005). This way, it is still possible to perform consistency checks on the isolated data knowledge, while the »critical« conceptual information is sourced out until the data have passed the consistency checks. Once these have been performed, conceptual and data knowledge are combined again in the triplestore, and hence all information is available again.[36] In this manner, it is possible to combine the expressivity and metamodelling facilities of OWL Full with the computationally favourable properties of OWL DL, and it is thus the strategy that has been adopted for the definition of the MLR model (see Chapter 5, especially Section 5.4.5).

[36] As was mentioned in Section 4.3.2, this separation can be conveniently achieved using namespaces and OWL's import mechanism.

5 Components of the Multifunctional Lexicon Model

The present chapter deals with a graph-based model for a multifunctional lexical resource (MLR). In particular, this chapter provides details on the different components of MLR model, their formalisation in OWL, as well as the relations between them. The core component is the *linguistic model*, which consists of a lexical part and a descriptive part. Figure 5.1 displays the very simple division at the highest level of the class hierarchy, where both *LexicalEntity* and *DescriptiveEntity* are subclasses of the predefined top-level class *owl:Thing*.[1] Similar to this distinction in the class hierarchy, the object property hierarchy is divided into *lexical relations* (i. e. relations between lexical entities) and *descriptive relations* (i. e. relations between descriptive entities or between a lexical and a descriptive entity). For easier readability of the statements, these relations are termed *hasLexicalRelationTo* and *hasDescriptiveRelationTo* respectively. In total, we say that the subclasses of *LexicalEntity* and the subproperties of *hasLexicalRelationTo* constitute the *lexical part* of the linguistic model, while *DescriptiveEntity* and the subproperties of *hasDescriptiveRelationTo* – in addition to the datatype properties – constitute the *descriptive part*.

While the lexical part of the linguistic model provides the classes and relations that are necessary to organise the lexical entities in a lexicon, the descriptive part provides the formal tools necessary to describe those lexical entities. Therefore, although the descriptive entities will be discussed mainly in Section 5.2, they will already be part of the discussion of lexical entities in Section 5.1, as they are reflected in their descriptive properties and relations.

The distinction between these two parts of the linguistic model reflects, to some extent, the distinction between the *object language*, i. e. the language that is described, and the *metalanguage*, i. e. the language that is used in order to make statements about the object language. Strictly speaking, however, the classes and relations defined in the lexical part pertain to the metalanguage as well. Therefore, using description logic terminology, it is more accurate to say that in the descriptive part, both the terminological component (TBox) and the assertional component (ABox) provide metalanguage vocabulary, whereas the complete ABox of the lexical part consists of instances of the object language.[2] Section 5.3 provides details on the formalisation of the classes in the MLR model by means of description logic axioms.

In addition to the distinction between metalanguage and object language, the MLR model foresees an independent layer for the *interface language(s)*, i. e. the language(s) in which the metalanguage vocabulary is presented to users of the lexical resource. This layer, which

---

[1] Throughout this chapter, several UML diagrams are used to illustrate relations between classes and instances. In these diagrams, classes are represented as white rectangles, whereas instances are represented as grey rectangles. Datatype properties – if considered relevant – are displayed as attributes in those rectangles, and object properties as links between them. In diagrams that contain black and grey links, the former are meant to be more important with respect to the subject that is to be illustrated, while the latter refer to links that are less relevant in the discussion at hand. The same is true of rectangles that have been drawn in grey lines. Other figures, such as those illustrating the class and property hierarchies or higher-level relationships between components of the MLR model, are not represented in the form of UML diagrams.

[2] See Section 4.2.4 or Nardi and Brachman (2003) for the definition of the terminological and assertional components.

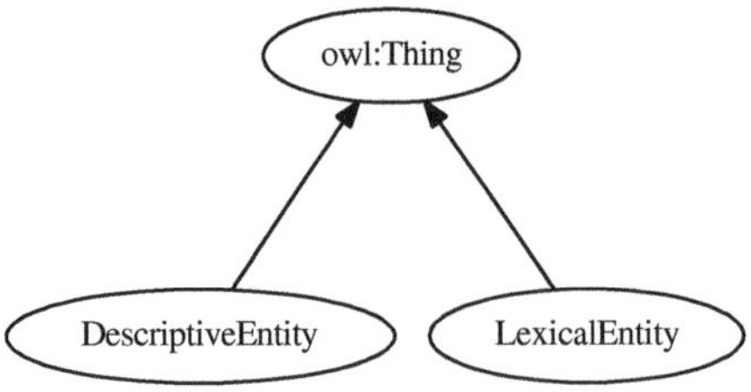

Figure 5.1: Lexical entities vs. descriptive entities

further provides a formalisation of user needs based on the classification in Tarp (2008), is discussed in Section 5.4. Finally, Section 5.5 shows how the components of the MLR model are interrelated. Examples of representations of lexical entities are provided in the appendix.[3]

5.1 Lexical Entities

5.1.1 Lexemes, Forms and Senses

The *LexicalEntity* class is a means for representing different aspects of lexical items as well as of their description. In line with general lexicographic practice, we assume that a lexical entity has a *form component* and a *sense component* (see e. g. ISO/FDIS 24613, 2008: p. 8f). For example, while some aspects of the description of a lexical entity refer to its form (e. g. orthography and pronunciation), others are only applicable in the context of senses, such as lexical-semantic relations. Even others refer to the lexical unit itself as an abstract morphological unit – such as the part-of-speech or whether the lexical unit is e. g. a nominalisation or a collocation – which are shared by all of its forms and senses. Similar to the *General Ontology for Linguistic Description* (GOLD; Farrar and Langendoen, 2003; cf. Section 3.2.2.4), we therefore distinguish between three subtypes of lexical entities: *lexemes*, *forms* and *senses*, where lexemes represent abstract entities for associating forms with senses.[4] More precisely, by linking instances of *Form* and *Sense* to instances of *Lexeme*, we do not need to associate forms with senses directly, which would – if one wants to express that each sense can be

[3] Throughout this chapter, the discussion of details of formal aspects of the MLR model will be limited to those points which are either considered necessary for the understanding of this work, or interesting from a theoretical or practical perspective. For example, we will only discuss the details of lexical relations, such as their domain and range as well as other formal characteristics, not of every single property that has been defined in the MLR model. Readers interested in those aspects of this work are referred to the appendix. Moreover, the appendix provides examples of representations of lexical entities.

[4] In GOLD, these are labelled *grammar unit*, *form unit* and *sense unit* respectively.

expressed by each form – result in $|Form| \times |Sense|$ links. By means of a *Lexeme* class, $|Form| + |Sense|$ links suffice, and statements that are true of all forms and senses, such as the ones mentioned above, need to be encoded only once.

Among forms, two types are distinguished, namely *InflectedForm* and *UninflectedForm*. While a lexeme may be linked to zero or more word forms via *hasWordForm*, it may only designate one of its word forms as its *lemma* by means of *hasLemma*. Whether this is an inflected or uninflected word form should not be predetermined by the MLR model, since it is well-known that this may vary from dictionary to dictionary (see e. g. Stowasser *et al.* (1994), where verbs are listed in their »*first person singular present indicative active*« form). In the traditional lexicographic sense, as well as to some extent in Tarp (2008), the term *lemma* refers to the form of a lexeme under which it can be found in a dictionary, i. e. its *citation form*. However, in the context of an electronic lexical resource, this sense of the term is rather obsolete, since the access structure is completely different and lexical entries should also be found on the basis of word forms (as well as various other features). Therefore, we rather use the property *hasLemma* here in order to designate the form that is considered most appropriate for presenting a lexeme to the user. Instances that are values of *hasWordForm*, on the other hand, are meant as forms which enable access to a lexical entry as well, but that are not necessarily presented to the user.

Whether word forms should be part of the lexical resource at all is a separate question, and one whose answer should not be determined by the fact that the model is too restrictive as to allow for a variety of solutions. In particular, rather than storing all word forms in the lexicon, it may be more appropriate to use a morphological analyser that processes the input provided by a user (e. g. a query for an inflected word form) and returns in its result set the entries of the relevant lexemes. The same could be done for the presentation of a lexical entry, where inflected forms could be generated by a morphological generation tool in case they are needed or requested. In contrast to this, however, the major advantage of a *full-form lexicon*, i. e. one that specifies all word forms in the data, is that one can make statements about the word forms. For example, one might want to express that, in case of variant forms, one variant is more common than the other variant. This can only be done if the respective word forms are part of the lexicon. However, storing all word forms for all lexical items inflates the lexicon enormously. Therefore, we propose to deal with this by foreseeing a morphological tool that is capable of analysing and generating inflected word forms, and by providing the means for storing individual word forms for which there is the need to make e. g. quantitative statements. This way, we should be able to benefit from the advantages of each approach.

Figure 5.2 shows how *Lexeme*, *Sense* and *Form* are interlinked. Each instance of *Lexeme* is linked to at least one *Sense* instance and one *Lemma* instance, both of which are only linked to this *Lexeme* instance. While this configuration suggests that lexemes are the core entities in the MLR model, it should be noted that this is rather a necessity than a desideratum. Ideally, we would like senses to be the primary lexical entities, as all kinds of lexical relations seem to be defined between senses. For example, besides the obviously sense-related lexical-semantic relations, also collocational relations need to be defined between senses. On the one hand, this is due to the fact that e. g. a collocation like »*Gegner + ausschalten*« (»*eliminate + opponent*«) consists of a particular sense of »*ausschalten*«, which is different from the one in »*Licht + ausschalten*« (»*switch off + light*«), for example. On the other hand, however, collocations may also have several senses themselves. Siepmann (2005) lists the French collocation »*heures creuses*« (»*hollow hours*«) as an example of a polysemous col-

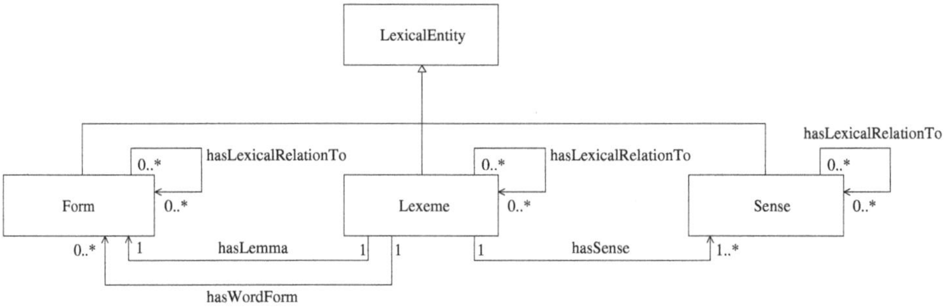

Figure 5.2: Interrelationships between a lexeme and its forms and senses

location that has e. g. in its "telephony" reading the antonym *»heures pleines«*, whereas in its "road transport" reading it is in opposition to *»heures de pointe«*. The same is true for morphological relations, where the compound *»Ausschaltknopf«* (*»OFF button«*) consists of the second sense of *»ausschalten«* mentioned above, as well as a sense of *»Knopf«*, which is different from the one in *»Hemdknopf«* (*»shirt button«*), for example.

In sum, a model which defines such relations on the basis of lexemes cannot do justice to these observations. However, due to the fact that knowledge in that detail is rarely available, let alone in a setting were data are acquired (semi-)automatically from corpora, lexical relations cannot be defined for senses only either – unless one wants to include "phantom senses" in the lexicon, as done for example in the SALSA project (Burchardt *et al.*, 2006). Here, support verb constructions are annotated with an underspecified SUPPORT frame, where the collocate is the frame-evoking element and assigns to the base the SUPPORTED role. In order not to exclude any of these possibilities, the MLR model foresees lexical relations for both lexemes and senses. In contrast to lexemes and senses, instances of *Form* are limited to descriptive relations. Finally, *LexicalEntity* is a common superclass in order to provide a means to commonly address instances of *Lexeme*, *Form* and *Sense*, and to have a straightforward distinction to descriptive entities.

While *Sense* has no further subclasses, a rich taxonomy of lexical entities is defined below *Lexeme*. The main reason for defining this taxonomy underneath *Lexeme* is to avoid a large amount of redundancy. As was mentioned above, types such as *Compound* or *Collocation* do not change from sense to sense or from form to form, and therefore, defining this taxonomy below *Sense* or *Form* would unnecessarily inflate the lexicon. Moreover, one would have to ensure that all senses of a lexeme actually belong to the same class – which would be possible, but an unnecessary complication. However, this decision does not come without its drawbacks either. The biggest one comes from the fact that this way, relations like *hasBase* or *isCompoundOf* are defined, on the lexeme side, for collocations and compounds respectively, and on the sense side for any kind of sense. In other words, we undermine the benefit of OWL to restrict the domain of a property, since now any kind of sense can make use of these properties. In addition to the inflation of the model, the choice to do it like this can be

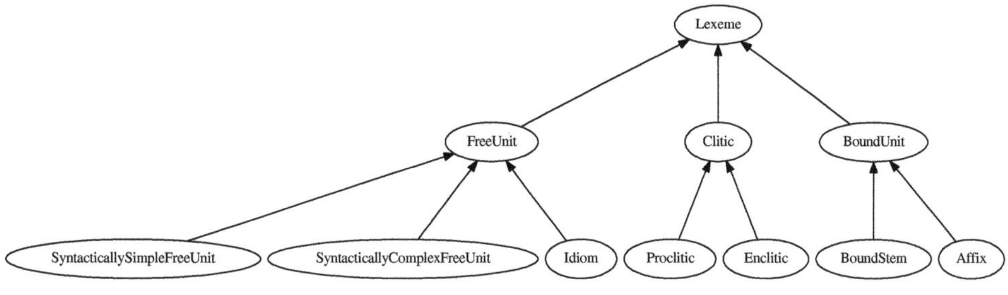

Figure 5.3: Top level of the *Lexeme* hierarchy

motivated as follows. The process of creating a new lexical item by means of an application programming interface (API) will typically start at the level of the lexeme, rather than at the level of specific senses. Therefore, if for example the type *Collocation* is chosen for the lexeme to be created, and if one then wants to add a specific sense to this lexeme, the constraints can simply be transferred to the sense in the API. In particular, when adding the sense, the API can check internally if the relevant property has been defined for the respective lexeme. Moreover, one can define description logic axioms which ensure that a sense makes use of only those properties that are defined for the corresponding lexeme. The discussion of such axioms is deferred to Section 5.3, as it is necessary to introduce the different types of lexemes as well as lexical relations (Section 5.1.3) first.

5.1.2 Types of Lexemes

In this subsection, we will provide details on the typology of lexemes. This typology is partly inspired by GOLD, though it deviates in the respects which are explained below. Figure 5.3 displays the top-level classes defined below *Lexeme*, namely *BoundUnit*, *FreeUnit* and *Clitic*. Here, free units are lexical entites »that can exist on their own without being a constituent of another morphological unit«[5], whereas bound units cannot exits on their own (e. g. affixes). While this corresponds to the general morphological notion of free and bound morphemes, we have extended the definition of free units to cover syntactic units as well (see below).

The reason for defining clitics alongside bound and free units is that they may occur both as bound affixes and as independent words (see e. g. Cocchi, 2001). Therefore, a hard classification as either bound or free can never be uncontroversial, and thus, clitics have been defined next to bound and free units.

In the following discussion, we will focus on different subtypes of *FreeUnit*, since free units represent the main types of lexical entities in the MLR model, and since a thorough discussion of the other subclasses is not considered relevant for the objectives of this work. A complete overview of the subtaxnomies below *Lexeme* is provided in the appendix.

5 See http://linguistics-ontology.org/gold/2008/FreeUnit.

5.1.2.1 Free units

Among free units, three types are distinguished, namely *syntactically simple free units*, *syntactically complex free units* and *idioms* (see Figure 5.4). Syntactically simple free units cover abbreviations (e. g. »*H of C*«; for »*House of Commons*«), *morphologically complex* free units[6] like derivations (e. g. »*housing*«) and compounds (»*guesthouse*«), and *morphologically simple* free units like »*house*«. Syntactically complex free units subsume collocations (e. g. »*to bring the house down*«) and proverbs (»*a house is not a home*«). The definition of the class for idioms next to syntactically simple and syntactically complex free units is to account for the fact that compounds, collocations and proverbs can be idiomatic as well. Therefore, we allow for instances of the other two types of free units to be instances of the *Idiom* class as well. More precisely, we do not define these classes as disjoint with *Idiom* and thus allow for multiple inheritance.[7]

This classification is in contrast to GOLD, where morphological and syntactic units are separated at a higher level in the taxonomy by defining two classes *MorphologicalUnit* and *SyntacticUnit* underneath a class *GrammarUnit*. Although this may suggest that these types of units are distinct, the definition of the class *FreeUnit*, which is located underneath *MorphologicalUnit*, indicates that this is not necessarily the case, as it states that »free units can also be syntactic units«[8]. Therefore, for the organisation of lexemes in the MLR model, we consider the distinction between morphological and syntactic types of lexemes as such of minor relevance, and instead refer to their syntactic complexity.

The distinction between syntactically complex and simple free units replaces to some extent a distinction between multi-word units and single-word units. However, the terminology based on the syntactic complexity has been preferred due to the fact that compounds, which are morphologically complex in any language, have the status of single-word units in German (e. g. »*Baustelle*«, »*Grundschule*«), whereas many of them are multi-word units in English (e. g. »*construction site*«, »*elementary school*«; see also the definition of MWE in ISO/FDIS 24613, 2008: p. 12). Therefore, they cannot be classified as either multi-word or single-word unit, and a classification relying on this terminology would run into problems here. Although compounds may reflect internal syntactic structure (e. g. »*Geldgeber*«, »*investor*«; literally »*money giver*«), this structure is not available at the surface level. Therefore, we classify compounds as syntactically simple free units, irrespective of whether particular instances are written as multi-words or single-words. More specific classes can be defined under *Compound*, such as classes for *noun-noun compounds* like »*construction site*« or *noun-verb compounds* like »*breastfeed*«. In addition to this, the MLR model provides more specific classes for *derived units*, such as adjectivisations or nominalisations. For the purposes of presenting the lexical part of the MLR model, this granularity suffices, and it is possible to add further subclasses to any these types if desired.

Due to the central role of collocations in lexicography as well as the requirements their representation imposes on the model (see Heid and Gouws, 2006; see also Section 3.1.1

[6] More precisely, we should be referring to "morphologically complex, but syntactically simple free units".

[7] Although the classification of an instance as an *idiom* has to do with its semantic compositionality, it is nonetheless the case that every instance of an idiom is a free unit. Therefore, we include them underneath this class.

[8] See http://linguistics-ontology.org/gold/2008/FreeUnit.

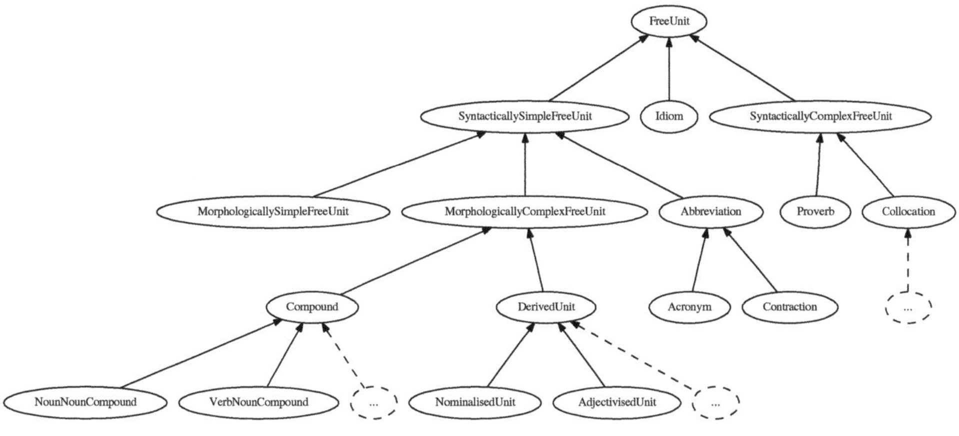

Figure 5.4: Types of free units

above), we have applied a very high level of granularity to the modelling of their typology. The following subsection is devoted to the explication of this typology of collocations as well as the definitions of the different types.

5.1.2.2 Collocations

The typology of collocations contained in the MLR model is based on the one presented in Spohr (2005), which was in turn based on Heid and Gouws (2006). The underlying definition of collocations is that of Hausmann (2004), according to which a collocation consists of an *autosemantic* base which brings its semantic content into the collocation, and a *synsemantic* collocate which is semantically weak and receives its interpretation only in the collocation. As Tutin (2008) has pointed out, the view of collocations as binary combinations is too narrow, and her definition allows for more than one collocate so that collocations can be decomposed into three or more components (e. g. »*in other words*«). Moreover, she has refined the definition of what we will call *complex collocations* below, namely collocations which consist of at least one collocation themselves. This has led to a reworking of the hierarchy presented in Spohr (2005) in order to cover the types of collocations discussed by Tutin (2008). Figure 5.5 displays the complete hierarchy.

The top-level distinction of collocations is between *simple* and *complex collocations*. While simple collocations may only consist of what we have called *syntactically simple* free units above (e. g. derivations or morphologically simple free units), complex collocations involve at least one other collocation. While the typology of simple collocations has remained essentially unchanged from the one presented in Spohr (2005), the typology of complex collocations has undergone several changes and extensions. As Figure 5.5 shows, the MLR model distinguishes among complex collocations between *merged* and *recursive* collocations. The

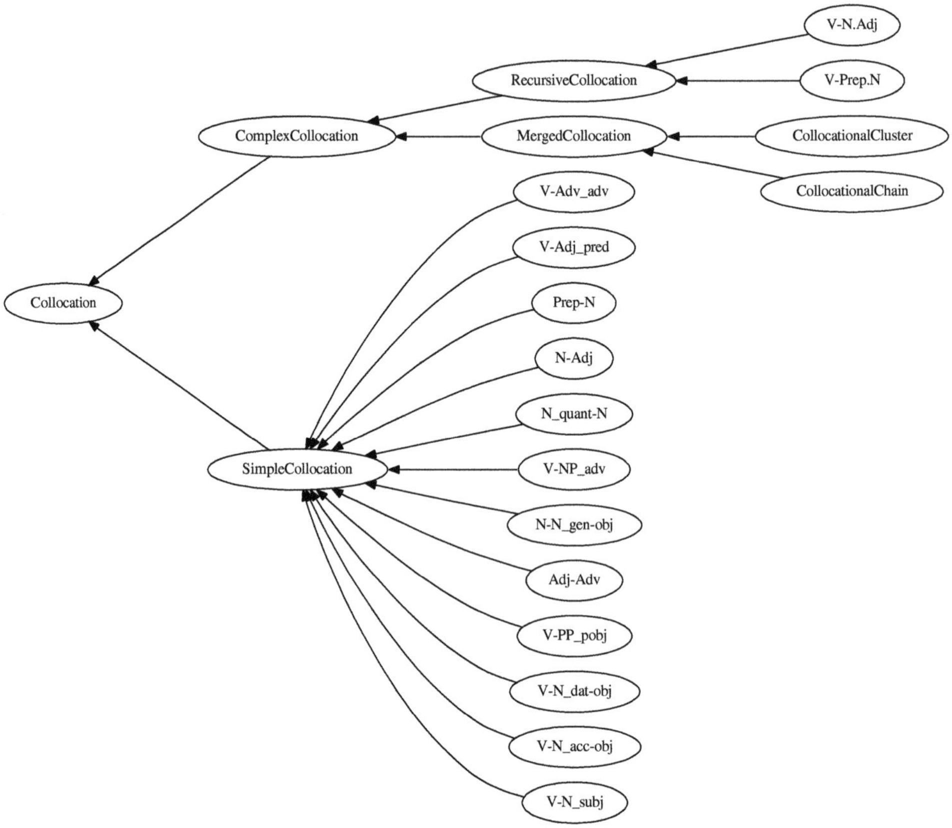

Figure 5.5: Types of collocations

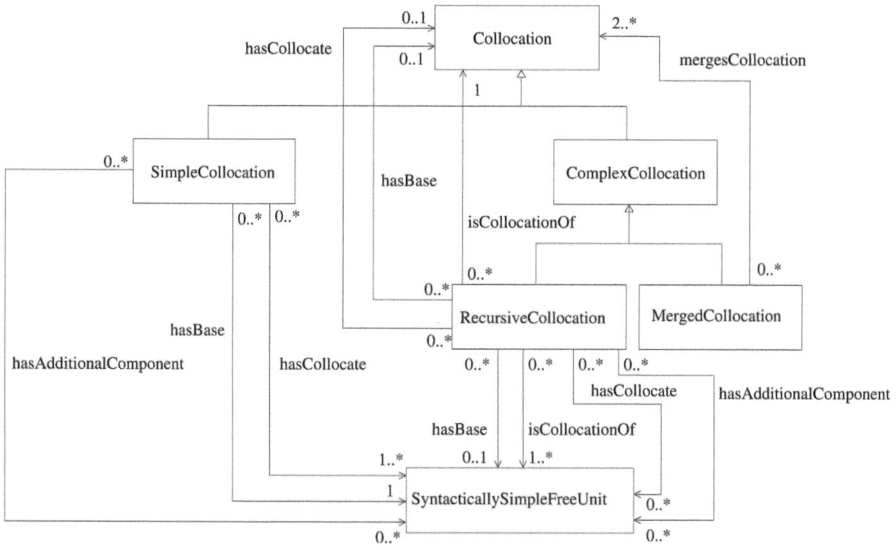

Figure 5.6: Relations of Collocations

class *MergedCollocation* refers to collocations which merge two collocations, in the sense described by Tutin (2008). However, in contrast to Tutin (2008), we distinguish between two different types of merged collocations, namely *collocational clusters*, i. e. collocations where the two collocations which are merged share the same base (e. g. »*pay close attention*«, which merges »$pay_{collocate}$ + $attention_{base}$« and »$close_{collocate}$ + $attention_{base}$«), and *collocational chains*, where the base of one of the collocations that are merged is the collocate of the other one (e. g. »*strongly recommended book*«, which merges »$strongly_{collocate}$ + $recommended_{base}$« and »$recommended_{collocate}$ + $book_{base}$«). In contrast to merged collocations, *recursive collocations* are cases where a collocation serves as base or collocate. In other words, not a merging of two collocations has taken place, but rather the combination of a collocation with a *non-collocational* component. Tutin (2008) gives »*fall + (in + love)*« as an example of a recursive collocation. Here, the component »*in + love*« is a collocation itself and serves as the base of the complex collocation, which has »*fall*« as collocate.

Figure 5.6 illustrates the relations that have been defined between a collocation and its components. As was mentioned in Section 5.1.1 above, since collocations are made up of particular senses of other lexical items (e. g. »*Gegner + ausschalten*« vs. »*Licht + ausschalten*«) and may be polysemous themselves (e. g. »*heures creuses*« or »*donner exemple*«; cf. Siepmann, 2005: p. 436f), these relations ideally link the senses of a collocation with the senses of its components.

Figure 5.6 shows that a *SimpleCollocation* can only have instances of *SyntacticallySimpleFreeUnit* as values of the *hasBase* and *hasCollocate* relations. While only one value is allowed for *hasBase*, *hasCollocate* may specify more than one value. In contrast to this, a

RecursiveCollocation may also have instances of *Collocation* as values of these relations. Moreover, while a *RecursiveCollocation* may have any number of collocates, it may contain at most one *Collocation*. This is achieved by means of the *isCollocationOf* relation, a superproperty of both *hasBase* and *hasCollocate* (cf. Section 5.1.3), for which we specify that it can refer to at most one *Collocation*. A further subproperty of *isCollocationOf*, namely *hasAdditionalComponent*, can be used to specify additional components of the collocation, such as function words (e. g. »*zu*« in »*zu Protokoll geben*«, »*to have something recorded*«). Finally, instances of *MergedCollocation* are linked to at least two instances of *Collocation* via the *mergesCollocation* relation. As will be shown in Section 5.1.3, each of the relations mentioned so far, as well as all other lexical relations in the MLR model, either specifies an inverse or has been defined as symmetric, so that links between lexical entities can be traversed easily in both directions.

This modelling of collocations as shown in the figure above is rather different from the approach taken in LMF. There, no difference is made between the status of the components of a collocation as base, collocate or additional component. In LMF, components of an MWE are simply referenced by means of a *ListOfComponents*, and thus, it is not possible to process them individually. For example, while the MLR model specifies that a collocation has exactly one base but potentially more than one collocate, no such statement seems to be possible in LMF. In addition to this, it may be desired to have a link from »*Gespräch*« and »*kommen*« to the collocation »*ins Gespräch kommen*«, whereas it is questionable whether the same should be done for »*in*«. It is not obvious how this could be achieved in LMF, as it seems that information about the status of the components cannot be expressed. Therefore, if LMF is to be used as an exchange format, features like the ones just mentioned would get lost in the conversion, since they cannot be represented.

A further difference with LMF is that the MLR model does not represent the constituent structure of a collocation. On the one hand, this is due to the fact that we consider it to be of minor interest to human users. On the other hand, however, we believe that it can also be considered as negligible for NLP applications, as long as the MWE as such is identifiable. In our opinion, constituent structure is part of the grammar, not of the lexicon, and thus, if it is of interest, it should be generated or analysed by a grammar component. Therefore, representing the constituent structure of collocations which adhere to the grammar rules of a language is not necessary. For MWEs which do not adhere to these rules, e. g. fixed expression like »*by and large*«, the constituent structure does not provide necessary input to an NLP tool either. What is important is that the MWE can be recognised as such – which is given by the fact that it is stored as a lexical entity of its own in the lexicon – as well as the functional structure. In other words, from an NLP perspective it is more relevant to get information e. g. on which argument slot one component fills with respect to the valence frames of the main predicate in the MWE, or which arguments are subcategorised by the MWE as a whole. These kinds of information, as well as the issues that we have identified in this respect in the LMF model, are discussed in the context of valence descriptions in Section 5.2.4.6.

Besides the representational differences with LMF, the modelling of collocations as presented in this section further differs from the one underlying the *meaning-text theory* of Mel'čuk and Žolkovskij (1970), which forms the basis of electronic dictionaries like DiCouèbe (cf. Section 3.2.3.7 above). For example, the meaning-text theory uses the lexical function »*Magn*« to state that the adjective »*scharf*« *magnifies* »*Kritik*«, as in (5.1).

(5.1) *Magn(Kritik) = scharf*

As is obvious from this example, collocations are modelled by means of lexical functions projecting from the lexical entry of one of the components to the lexical entry of another component. In other words, the collocation itself is not represented as an entity in the lexicon, but rather as part of the entry of its base. This approach makes it hard to attach further properties like morpho-syntactic preferences to a collocation, and has therefore not been chosen as the way to illustrate the representation of collocational information in our model here. That said, the model is not tied to a specific theory of collocations, and as such it would also be possible to accommodate an representation based on the meaning-text theory in the model, in case e. g. an NLP application depends on the meaning-text theory. Here, lexical functions could simply be represented as subproperties of *hasCollocationalRelationTo*, e. g. *Magn* $\sqsubseteq$ *hasCollocationalRelationTo*, linking the entries of the collocational components.

5.1.3 Lexical Relations

In this section, we will discuss the various relations that the MLR model provides for relating lexical entities with each other, i. e. the relations between instances of the subclasses of *Lexeme*, as well as between instances of *Sense*. While lexical relations between instances of *Form* are limited to a single "catch-all" relation *hasRelatedForm*, the lexical relations defined for instances of *Lexeme* and *Sense* are more diverse and have a more complex structure. As the following subsections will show, the organisation of classes and relations in typed hierarchies that is offered by OWL (and RDFS) enables a very structured modelling of the relations between lexical entities in a lexicon. Moreover, it allows for the expression of domain and range restrictions, as well as for inferences by means of symmetric, transitive and underspecified relations.

After a brief discussion of the interrelations between instances of *Lexeme*, *Form* and *Sense*, the following subsections will focus on the different kinds of lexical relations between lexemes and senses respectively.

5.1.3.1 Relations between *Lexeme*, *Sense* and *Form*

As was already shown in Figure 5.2 on page 68 above, instances of *Lexeme*, *Sense* and *Form* are interlinked by means of the object properties *hasSense*, *hasLemma* and *hasWordForm*. Each of these properties has an inverse – *isSenseOf*, *isLemmaOf* and *isWordFormOf* respectively – which allows for easy traversal of the links in both directions and facilitates the formulation of query paths (cf. Section 6.2.2). Moreover, in order to be able to extract all interrelations between a particular lexeme and its senses and forms in a straightforward way, we subsume these relations under a common superproperty *hasSenseOrFormRelationTo*, which we define as a symmetric and transitive property. This way, a single SPARQL query like the one in (5.2) suffices to extract all the senses and forms that a lexeme is connected to – irrespective of whether the particular type of ?a and ?b is *Lexeme*, *Sense* or *Form*.[9]

[9] As these relations should rather be hidden from the user, a query like the one in (5.2) is primarily of use for internal process such as query generation (see Section 6.2.2).

NAME	DOMAIN	RANGE	FORMAL ATTRIBUTES
hasSenseOrFormRelationTo	*LexicalEntity*	*LexicalEntity*	symmetric, transitive
hasSense	*Lexeme*	*Sense*	*isSenseOf*⁻
isSenseOf	*Sense*	*Lexeme*	functional, *hasSense*⁻
hasLemma	*Lexeme*	*Form*	functional, *isLemmaOf*⁻
isLemmaOf	*Form*	*Lexeme*	functional, *hasLemma*⁻
hasWordForm	*Lexeme*	*InflectedForm*	*isWordFormOf*⁻
hasRegularWordForm	*Lexeme*	*InflectedForm*	*isRegularWordFormOf*⁻
hasIrregularWordForm	*Lexeme*	*InflectedForm*	*isIrregularWordFormOf*⁻
isWordFormOf	*InflectedForm*	*Lexeme*	functional, *hasWordForm*⁻
isRegularWordFormOf	*InflectedForm*	*Lexeme*	functional, *hasRegularWordForm*⁻
isIrregularWordFormOf	*InflectedForm*	*Lexeme*	functional, *hasIrregularWordForm*⁻

Table 5.1: Hierarchy and formal attributes of relations between lexemes, forms and senses

(5.2)
```
SELECT ?b
WHERE {?a :hasSenseOrFormRelationTo ?b}
```

In addition to the relations just mentioned, *hasWordForm* and *isWordFormOf* have further subproperties, namely *has(Ir)RegularWordForm* and *is(Ir)RegularWordFormOf*. This has been done in order to mark irregular inflection forms, which are of special importance to language learners (see e. g. Tarp, 2008), so that they can be treated in a special way if desired. Table 5.1 summarises the relations between a lexeme and its forms and senses, along with their formal attributes.

5.1.3.2 Collocational relations

While the relations introduced in the previous subsection are used to interlink lexemes with their senses and forms, the relations discussed in the following subsections are used to link lexemes with other lexemes, as well as senses with senses of other lexemes. All of them are subproperties of the object property *hasLexicalRelationTo*, which has been defined as a symmetric relation between instances of *LexicalEntity*.

The first direct subproperty of *hasLexicalRelationTo* that is to be discussed is the very general property *hasCollocationalRelationTo* (see Table 5.2). It subsumes relations like *hasBase* and *hasCollocate*, which are meant to relate instances of the various subclasses of *Collocation* with their components. While *hasCollocationalRelationTo* has been defined as a symmetric property, each of its subproperties specifies an inverse. For example, the inverse of *hasBase* is the property *isBaseOf*, and accordingly their domain and range are inverse as well. While a lexeme can be the base of more than one simple or recursive collocation, the opposite is not the case; both simple and recursive collocation have exactly one base. Therefore, *has-*

NAME	DOMAIN	RANGE	FORMAL ATTRIBUTES
hasCollocationalRelationTo	*Lexeme, Sense*	*Lexeme, Sense*	symmetric
hasCollocation	*Lexeme, Sense*	*Collocation, Sense*	*isCollocationOf*$^-$
isBaseOf	*Lexeme, Sense*	*Recursive-Collocation, Simple-Collocation, Sense*	*hasBase*$^-$
isCollocateOf	*Lexeme, Sense*	*Recursive-Collocation, Simple-Collocation, Sense*	*hasCollocate*$^-$
isAdditionalComponentOf	*Lexeme, Sense*	*Collocation, Sense*	*hasAdditional-Component*$^-$
isMergedIn	*Collocation, Sense*	*Merged-Collocation, Sense*	*mergesCollocation*$^-$
isCollocationOf	*Collocation, Sense*	*Lexeme, Sense*	*hasCollocation*$^-$
hasBase	*Recursive-Collocation, Simple-Collocation, Sense*	*Lexeme, Sense*	functional, *isBaseOf*$^-$
hasCollocate	*Recursive-Collocation, Simple-Collocation, Sense*	*Lexeme, Sense*	*isCollocateOf*$^-$
hasAdditionalComponent	*Collocation, Sense*	*Lexeme, Sense*	*isAdditional-ComponentOf*$^-$
mergesCollocation	*Merged-Collocation, Sense*	*Collocation, Sense*	*isMergedIn*$^-$

Table 5.2: Hierarchy and formal attributes of collocational relations

Base has been defined as functional, whereas *isBaseOf* is not. Following Tutin (2008), we allow for more than one collocate for a simple or recursive collocation, which is why *hasCollocate* is not a functional property. However, this can be restricted for particular types of collocations. For example, collocations of type *V + N (obj-acc)* (e. g. »*to accept an offer*«) can have only one collocate, and therefore, the definition of the class *V-N_obj-acc* contains a cardinality restriction on the *hasCollocate* property (cf. (5.11) on page 107). The remaining collocational properties have been discussed in Section 5.1.2.2 above already, namely *hasAdditionalComponent/isAdditionalComponentOf* and *mergesCollocation/isMergedIn*.

In order to assign more structure to the various collocational relations, we include further intermediate properties *isCollocationOf* and *hasCollocation*. This enables us to query for components of a collocation without knowing the actual status of the component. For example, one could query for collocations that have »*recommend*« as one of their components, irrespective of whether it serves as base (as in »*strongly recommend*«) or as collocate (as in »*to recommend a book*«).

5.1.3.3 Lexical-semantic relations

As can be seen in Table 5.3, the definition of lexical-semantic relations between lexical entities is less complex than that of collocational relations. This is due to the fact that, unlike collocational relations, lexical-semantic relations are only defined between instances of *Senses*, not between instances of *Lexeme* as well. On the other hand, lexical-semantic relations make use of *transitive* properties. For example, the *hasSynonym* relation has been defined as a symmetric and transitive property, so that $hasSynonym(a,b) \wedge hasSynonym(b,c) \rightarrow hasSynonym(a,c)$ (see Section 4.2.4.2 above; cf. Spohr, 2005: p. 32). However, since "real" synonymy in the sense of an equivalence relation is rather rare, we define a weaker form of synonymy, *hasQuasiSynonym*, as symmetric only. Both of these relations are subsumed under the relation *hasSynonymicRelationTo*, in order to be able address them collectively. For antonyms, the situation is slightly different. Here, both *hasAntonym* and *hasQuasiAntonym* have been defined as symmetric only, since otherwise each sense would be inferred as being an antonym of itself[10]. In contrast to synonymy and antonymy, *hasHyperonym* and its inverse *hasHyponym* are both defined as transitive only. Table 5.3 summarises the definition of lexical-semantic relations, which can further be extended e. g. with meronymy or troponymy (see e. g. Fellbaum, 1998).

5.1.3.4 Morphological relations

Similar to collocational relations, morphological relations are defined between instances of *Lexeme* and instances of *Sense* respectively. As was mentioned in Section 5.1.1, this is due to the fact that a compound like »*Ausschaltknopf*« is made up of specific senses of »*ausschalten*« and »*Knopf*«. The immediate subproperties of *hasMorphologicalRelationTo* are *hasMorphologicalComponent* – for links from (senses of) a *MorphologicallyComplexFreeUnit* to (the senses of) its components – and its inverse *isMorphologicalComponentOf*, for the links in the opposite direction. Both of these properties have been defined as transitive

[10] Recall that reflexivity is a logical consequence of symmetry and transitivity.

NAME	DOMAIN	RANGE	FORMAL ATTRIBUTES
hasLexicalSemanticRelationTo	*Sense*	*Sense*	symmetric
hasAntonymicRelationTo	*Sense*	*Sense*	symmetric
hasAntonym	*Sense*	*Sense*	symmetric
hasQuasiAntonym	*Sense*	*Sense*	symmetric
hasSynonymicRelationTo	*Sense*	*Sense*	symmetric
hasSynonym	*Sense*	*Sense*	symmetric, transitive
hasQuasiSynonym	*Sense*	*Sense*	symmetric
hasHyperonym	*Sense*	*Sense*	transitive, *hasHyponym*$^{-}$
hasHyponym	*Sense*	*Sense*	transitive, *hasHyperonym*$^{-}$

Table 5.3: Hierarchy and formal attributes of lexical-semantic relations

relations, as they reflect the transitive part-whole relation[11]. Below these relations are more specific morphological relations, such as *isCompoundOf* or *isNominalisationOf*, with their respective inverses *hasCompound* and *hasNominalisation* (see Table 5.4).

5.1.3.5 Meronymic relations

As can be seen in the various tables above, the model distinguishes between different meronymic relations, such as *hasMorphologicalComponent*/*isMorphologicalComponentOf* or *hasBase*/*isBaseOf*. Up to now, these relations do not have anything in common except for sharing the superproperty *hasLexicalRelationTo*. Intuitively, however, these relations are very closely related, as they are used to link a whole to its parts and vice versa. Therefore, a general relation *hasComponentRelationTo* has been defined, with subproperties *hasComponent* and *isComponentOf*. Relations like *isMorphologicalComponentOf* and *isBaseOf* are then defined as subrelations of *isComponentOf*, and *hasMorphologicalComponent* and *hasBase* as subrelations of *hasComponent* respectively. This way, they can be queried very generally, such as »*x has some component y*«, irrespective of whether »*x*« is a collocation and »*y*« its base, or »*x*« a compound and »*y*« its head, or »*x*« an abbreviation of »*y*«, and so on. As each component relation is still a subrelation of its respective other superrelation (e. g. *hasBase* of *isCollocationOf*), this illustrates how the lexicon model can benefit from the definition of a multiple inheritance hierarchy for lexical relations.

5.1.3.6 Further lexical relations

The remaining lexical properties that have been defined are used to link instances of *FreeUnit* (or their senses) to instances of *Idiom*, *Proverb* and *Abbreviation*, as well as in the opposite direction. The respective properties are *hasIdiomaticRelationTo*, *hasProverbialRelationTo* and *hasAbbreviationalRelationTo*, and in line with the relations discussed above, all

[11] See e. g. http://www.w3.org/2001/sw/BestPractices/OEP/SimplePartWhole/.

NAME	DOMAIN	RANGE	FORMAL ATTRIBUTES
hasMorphologicalRelationTo	*Sense, Lexeme*	*Sense, Lexeme*	symmetric
hasMorphologicalComponent	*Sense, MorphologicallyComplexFreeUnit*	*Sense, SyntacticallySimpleFreeUnit*	transitive, *isMorphologicalComponentOf*$^-$
isCompoundOf	*Sense, Compound*	*Sense, SyntacticallySimpleFreeUnit*	transitive, *hasCompound*$^-$
hasCompoundHead	*Sense, Compound*	*Sense, SyntacticallySimpleFreeUnit*	*isHeadOfCompound*$^-$
isDerivationOf	*Sense, DerivedUnit*	*Sense, SyntacticallySimpleFreeUnit*	transitive, *hasDerivation*$^-$
isNominalisationOf	*Sense, NominalisedUnit*	*Sense, SyntacticallySimpleFreeUnit*	*hasNominalisation*$^-$
isMorphologicalComponentOf	*Sense, SyntacticallySimpleFreeUnit*	*Sense, MorphologicallyComplexFreeUnit*	transitive, *hasMorphologicalComponent*$^-$
hasCompound	*Sense, SyntacticallySimpleFreeUnit*	*Sense, Compound*	transitive, *isCompoundOf*$^-$
isHeadOfCompound	*Sense, SyntacticallySimpleFreeUnit*	*Sense, Compound*	*hasCompoundHead*$^-$
hasDerivation	*Sense, SyntacticallySimpleFreeUnit*	*Sense, DerivedUnit*	transitive, *isDerivationOf*$^-$
hasNominalisation	*Sense, SyntacticallySimpleFreeUnit*	*Sense, NominalisedUnit*	*isNominalisationOf*$^-$

Table 5.4: Hierarchy and formal attributes of morphological relations

NAME	DOMAIN	RANGE	FORMAL ATTRIBUTES
hasAbbreviationalRelationTo	*Sense, FreeUnit*	*Sense, FreeUnit*	symmetric
hasAbbreviation	*Sense, FreeUnit*	*Sense, Abbreviation*	*isAbbreviationOf*$^{-}$
hasAcronym	*Sense, FreeUnit*	*Sense, Acronym*	*isAcronymOf*$^{-}$
hasContraction	*Sense, FreeUnit*	*Sense, Contraction*	*isContractionOf*$^{-}$
isAbbreviationOf	*Sense, Abbreviation*	*Sense, FreeUnit*	functional, *hasAbbreviation*$^{-}$
isAcronymOf	*Sense, Acronym*	*Sense, FreeUnit*	functional, *hasAcronym*$^{-}$
isContractionOf	*Sense, Contraction*	*Sense, FreeUnit*	functional, *hasContraction*$^{-}$
hasIdiomaticRelationTo	*Sense, FreeUnit*	*Sense, FreeUnit*	symmetric
hasIdiom	*Sense, FreeUnit*	*Sense, Idiom*	*isIdiomOf*$^{-}$
isIdiomOf	*Sense, Idiom*	*Sense, FreeUnit*	*hasIdiom*$^{-}$
hasProverbialRelationTo	*Sense, FreeUnit*	*Sense, FreeUnit*	symmetric
hasProverb	*Sense, FreeUnit*	*Sense, Proverb*	*isProverbOf*$^{-}$
isProverbOf	*Sense, Proverb*	*Sense, FreeUnit*	*hasProverb*$^{-}$

Table 5.5: Hierarchy and formal attributes of abbreviational, idiomatic and proverbial relations

of them have been defined in order to be able to query for their more specific subproperties at the same time. While idiomatic and proverbial relations only subsume the relations *hasIdiom/isIdiomOf* and *hasProverb/isProverbOf* respectively, further subproperties have been defined underneath *hasAbbreviation* which correspond to the subclasses of *Abbreviation* in the class hierarchy, i. e. *hasAcronym/isAcronymOf* and *hasContraction/isContractionOf*. The remaining features are summarised in Table 5.5.

5.2 Descriptive Entities

In the previous section, we have introduced the *lexical* part of the MLR model, i. e. the different types of lexical entities as well as the lexical relations between them. In the following subsections, we will discuss in detail the *descriptive* part of the linguistic model, namely the entities that are needed in order to describe the lexical entities in an MLR. These *descriptive entities* cover straightforward indications like gender or part-of-speech, but also more complex descriptions like valence descriptions or morpho-syntactic preferences. Very frequently, these more complex descriptions have their own descriptions as well, e. g. when one wants to quantify the use of a certain valence frame with respect to a particular sense. Such configurations will be discussed in more detail in the subsections below and, if this is the case, the drawbacks that current proposals like LMF have with respect to these issues will be pointed out.

Naturally, there is always more than one way of modelling a particular kind of description, and in the context of OWL, typical choices involve questions as to which entities in the lexical resource should be represented as instances, datatypes, classes or properties, as well as how long the path from an entity to its description should (or needs to) be. Therefore, in the following subsection, we will try to motivate the most fundamental modelling decisions that have been made. The subsequent subsections will introduce a large part of the so-called *data categories* (ISO/FDIS 12620, 2009), i. e. the descriptive inventory of the MLR model, as well as the sources they have been taken from.

5.2.1 Basic Modelling Decisions

In the context of the decisions that have been made, it is necessary to recall some of the major requirements that have been identified in the context of an MLR model. One of the crucial requirements refers to the *multifunctionality* of the model, and here in particular to its ability to serve the needs of several kinds of users. As has been discussed in Chapter 3.1.3 above, and as will become apparent in Section 5.4, this requirement involves the need to be able to assign specific treatments to specific kinds of indications, so that they can be presented to a user in an appropriate way, depending on the situation that the user is in. On the one hand, this includes that different indications are treated differently within one group of users, but also that the same indication may have to be treated differently across different groups of users.

A further requirement that is relevant in this context comes from the objective not to be more complex than necessary, i. e. only as complex as a particular description demands. This is very important, on the one hand, in order to be able to access and retrieve the information in the lexicon with a reasonable amount of effort. On the other hand, however, it is also important for the support that the model can provide with respect to the definition of user interfaces and presentation modules (see Section 6.2.2).

These requirements have a direct impact on the modelling decisions. For example, the modelling of an indication like *part of speech* could be approached – similar to the different types of lexical entities – by creating a hierarchy of classes like *Noun*, *Verb* etc., underneath *Lexeme*, and to have lexical entities instantiate these classes directly. This way, a noun like

»house« would be an instance of the class *Noun* or, in more technical terms, the instance representing *»house«* would be linked to the *Noun* class via an *rdf:type* link. If one now wanted to assign a specific treatment to the part-of-speech indication, e. g. if one wanted it to be emphasised and displayed with a certain label in the lexical entry, then this would mean having to assign this treatment to *rdf:type*. On the one hand, this would mean that the part-of-speech indication is to some extent hidden behind *rdf:type*. On the other hand, however, *rdf:type* is like the "backbone property" of RDF and ubiquitous in any resource defined in OWL or RDFS, and setting a uniform label for *rdf:type* is not possible beyond a rather unspecific label "type", let alone applying a uniform treatment across the whole resource.

In contrast to this, if the part-of-speech indication is modelled by means of a property like *hasPartOfSpeech*, it is directly obvious how to assign a specific treatment and label to this property, across different groups of users and situations.[12]

For these reasons, the general strategy underlying the definition of the descriptive part of the model is to have properties which correspond to typical indications in a dictionary, such as part-of-speech or grammatical gender, and which link a lexical entity to an instance that represents the value of the corresponding data category. More precisely, the descriptive part of the model consists of a number of classes which correspond to types of data categories – e. g. *GrammaticalGender*, *GrammaticalNumber* or *DiastraticMarking*, as defined by resources like GOLD (Farrar and Langendoen, 2003), ISO/FDIS 12620 (2009)[13] and Wikipedia[14] –, and whose instances represent the possible values (e. g. *feminine*, *plural* or *colloquial*).

This way, a descriptive relation like *hasGender* has the class *GrammaticalGender* in its range, which means that the set of possible values that *hasGender* can have is determined and restricted by the instances of the respective class. However, this straightforward way of modelling indications does not work in the same way for more complex descriptions, since these typically consist of more than one property (e. g. example sentences, which should specify – next to the actual sentence – the corpus or any other source that the respective sentence has been taken from). Therefore, the hierarchy of descriptive entities is divided, as shown in Figure 5.7, into *features* and *descriptions*. Here, the class *Feature* refers to "simple" data categories like the ones mentioned above (e. g. grammatical gender, number, etc.), whereas the subclasses of *Description* represent more complex descriptions. Features will be discussed in Section 5.2.2, and specific cases of more complex descriptions – namely orthography, valence, illustrative descriptions (e. g. example sentences or images) and preference descriptions – will be the subject of Sections 5.2.3 to 5.2.6.

---

[12] This seems to be a strategy that has been followed in (ISO/FDIS 12620, 2009) as well, where the data category *noun class*, which had been part of an earlier version of the standard, has become dispreferred and »part of speech noun« should be used instead (see http://www.ttt.org/clsframe/datcats02.html). However, all this does not mean that it is not possible to model part-of-speech in terms of classes, and in fact, as was suggested on page 60, the different approaches can be combined. It should be pointed out, though, that an approach that assigns special treatment to specific indications can operate more easily and in a more uniform way if these indications do not rely too much on a single property, but if they are distinguished in a rather fine-grained way instead. It seems that in an instantiation-based (i. e. *rdf:type*) approach, more exceptions would need to be paid attention to.

[13] See http://www.isocat.org/.

[14] See http://www.wikipedia.org/.

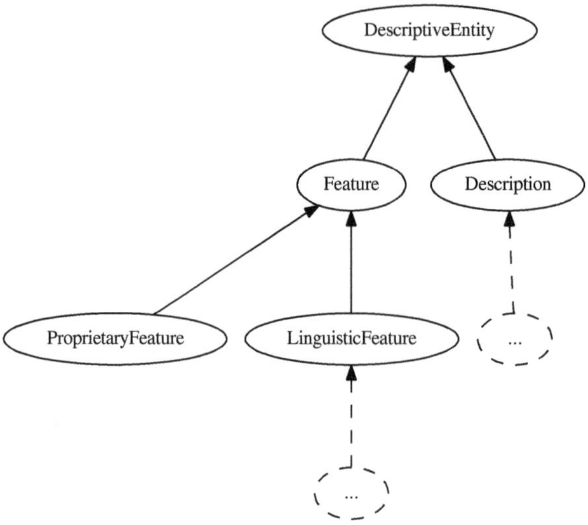

Figure 5.7: Types of descriptive entities

5.2.2 Simple Data Categories

Among features, the MLR model distinguishes between *LinguisticFeature* and *ProprietaryFeature* (cf. Figure 5.7). The direct instances of *ProprietaryFeature* represent the possible values for the *hasProprietaryRestriction* property, such as *TradeMark* or *TradeName*, which specifies any proprietary restriction that a lexical entity may have (e. g. »*Game Boy*®«). In contrast to this simple feature, the second type of features, i. e. *LinguisticFeature*, subsumes a rich hierarchy providing different linguistic features which are used to describe different aspects of a lexical entity as well as of more complex descriptions. As is illustrated in Figure 5.8, the subclasses of *LinguisticFeature* cover the different linguistic subdisciplines, such as morphology, morpho-syntax and semantics. Each of these classes in turn subsumes more specific types of features, e. g. *SyntacticCategory* in the case of *SyntacticFeature*. As was mentioned above, the instances of these classes represent the admissible values for descriptive properties. For example, the property *hasTense* has *Form* in its domain and *Tense* in its range, among whose instances are e. g. *FutureTense*, *PastTense*, *PresentTense* and *PastInFutureTense*. This way, an instance representing a particular word form like »*gets*« can be linked to *PresentTense*, *ThirdPerson* and *SingularNumber* by means of the properties *hasTense*, *hasPerson* and *hasNumber* respectively. A comprehensive list of the linguistic features and descriptive properties covered by the MLR model can be found in the appendix, although it should be noted that any of these can be extended by adding further subclasses, instances and properties.

As was mentioned in the previous subsection, more complex descriptions cannot be dealt with in this straightforward way, by means of an immediate link between a lexical entity and a feature value. These descriptions will be discussed in the following subsections.

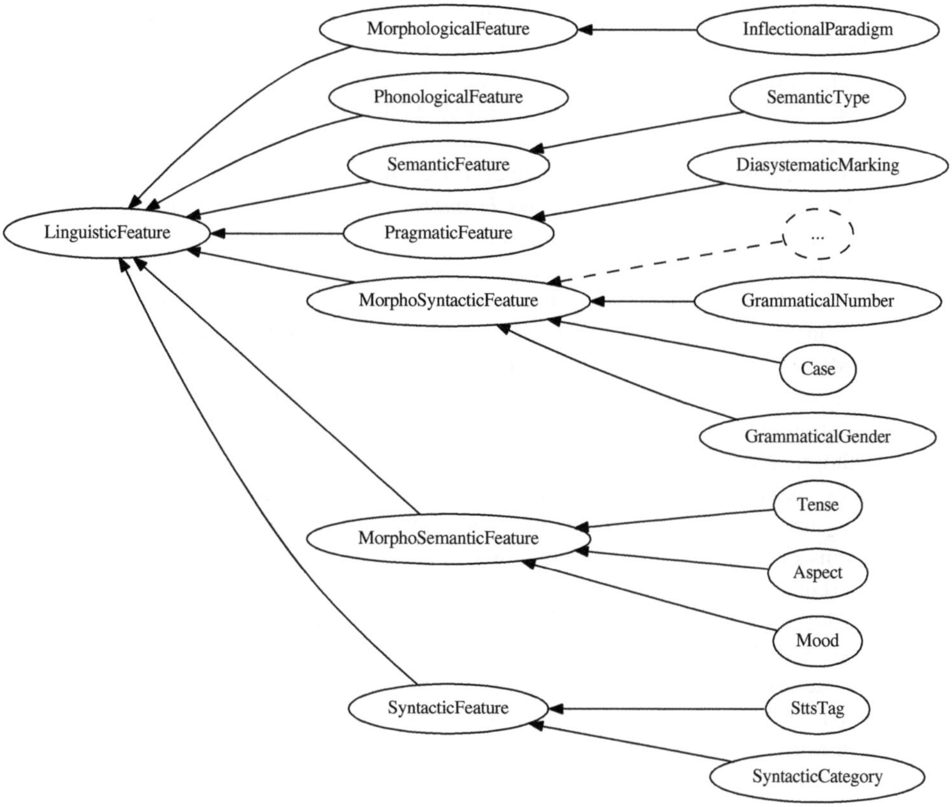

Figure 5.8: Types of linguistic features

5.2.3 Form Description

Form descriptions are the most basic kind of description in the MLR model. Here, the major source of complexity comes from the fact that a lexeme can have more than one orthographic form in one or more writing systems. Moreover, each orthographic form frequently has its own syllabification as well as its own pronunciation that distinguishes it from the other orthographic variants. For example, the German word *»gabelig«* (*»forked«*), which can also be written as *»gablig«*, has two different syllabifications and pronunciations, namely *»ga|be|lig«*, [ˈgaːbəlɪç] vs. *»gab|lig«*, [ˈgaːplɪç], both of which depend on the orthographic difference. Due to this dependency, it is advisable to keep orthography, syllabification and pronunciation together. Moreover, in order to be able to model information on the regional distribution of a specific orthographic variant as well as to quantify its occurrence, each orthographic form needs to be kept separate from the other orthographic forms. Otherwise, it would not be possible to express e. g. that *»gabelig«* is the more common way of writing the lexeme.

Instead of creating a new *Lemma* instance for each orthographic variant, we propose to model orthography in instances of a class *FormDescription*. This way, it is also possible to express that the two female forms *»gabelige«* and *»gablige«* are both linked to a single *WordForm* instance. Finally, we consider orthography, syllabification and pronunciation to be properties of *forms*, which is why instances of *FormDescription* are linked to instances of *Form* by means of the properties *hasFormDescription* and *isFormDescriptionOf*.

This modelling is largely compatible with the LMF-based model, where a *FormRepresentation* class contains the details of a specific orthographic variant. However, LMF seems to follow this strategy only for forms where there are several scripts or orthographies, whereas simple orthographies are specified directly in the respective *Lemma* or *WordForm* instance by means of the attribute *writtenForm* (cf. Figures B.2 and B.4 in ISO/FDIS 24613, 2008: p. 17f). On the one hand, this means that there is more than one way of specifying orthographic forms of a lexical item in LMF – which is not necessarily a disadvantage as such. More importantly, however, this also means that in case e. g. a second orthographic form is added to a formerly simple orthographic description at a later stage, the "old" description needs to be re-modelled and moved to a *FormRepresentation* instance, in order to account for the new description. In contrast to this, orthography is dealt with uniformly in the MLR model, and all orthographic forms – single or multiple – are modelled in terms of a *FormDescription* instance, and thus, whenever an orthographic form needs to be added, only another *FormDescription* instance containing the description needs to be created.

Figure A.7 on page 204 illustrates the modelling of orthographic information. The figure displays the fact that *»Dekor«* (*»decor, decoration«*) has two valid orthographies for the nominative plural word form, i. e. *»Dekors«* and *»Dekore«*, as well as masculine and neuter gender. More details can be found on page 197.

5.2.4 Valence Description

As was mentioned in Section 3.1.1, a detailed valence description is among the core requirements in designing a model for an MLR. On a lexicographic level, this is due to its immediate relevance to both human users and NLP applications, and thus its importance in the context of multifunctionality. On a more technical level, however, providing an adequate internal representation of valence is among the most intricate aspects of designing a multifunctional lexical resource model, as it poses high demands on the formalism as well as the actual model. This complexity has various different sources, which refer to the questions as to (i) which are the entities that receive a valence description, (ii) what are the kinds of information that are to be represented, and (iii) how are the descriptions represented. These different aspects will be discussed in detail on the following pages.

5.2.4.1 Lexical type of the described entity

The most basic question is the one referring to the types of entities that receive a valence description in the lexicon, i. e. abstract *lexemes*, specific *senses* of lexemes, or possibly both. When examining valence information in resources like VDE (Herbst *et al.*, 2005) or FrameNet (Baker *et al.*, 1998), it becomes apparent that a model of valence description needs to be able to represent that different senses of a lexeme very frequently subcategorise different types of arguments and thus have different valence frames. According to VDE, for example, the valence frame $N + V\text{-}ing_P$ (i. e. a nominal subject with a passivisable gerund complement phrase, as in »*he stopped worrying*«) is only assigned to a sense of »*to stop*« that roughly means »*no longer do*«, while the frame »$N + N + V\text{-}ing_P$« (nominal subject and object with gerund complement phrase, as in »*he stopped her writing*«) is only used by the sense of »*to stop*« that means »*to prevent*« (cf. Herbst *et al.*, 2005: p. 811). Therefore, it seems vital to encode syntactic valence information at the level of individual senses.

However, it is important to note that the descriptions contained in resources like FrameNet or VDE have been compiled with huge amounts of manual labour. Moreover, the current state in computational lexicography is such that it seems unrealistic to assume a similar degree of detail for most languages other than English. Especially if semi-automatic or even fully automatic procedures are used in order to extract valence patterns from corpora, the resulting data are not as accurate as to contain a reliable mapping between individual senses and occurrences of a word-form with a valence pattern. Therefore, one needs to be able to model valence information not only at the level of individual senses, but at the level of more abstract lexemes as well. In contrast to this, we consider semantic valence information to be useful only on the level of individual senses, and thus semantic valence descriptions are not foreseen for lexemes.

In order to accommodate both options in the model, we propose to first link syntactic valence frames to a lexeme, thus providing a sort of *inventory* of valence frames for all the senses of a particular lexeme. Specific senses of a lexeme can then be related to those frames that they use. If these links cannot be established at the time the data are added to the lexicon, they can also be created manually by a lexicographer. In other words, it is possible to add refined, sense-specific syntactic valence descriptions at a later stage, without further need to adapt the model.

A simplified summary of the resulting picture is illustrated in Figure 5.9, ignoring specific details on the structure of the valence frames. In the figure, we see that the black links relate the lexeme »*stop*« with two (and possibly more) syntactic frames. As was mentioned above, these represent the syntactic frames that are available to the senses of »*stop*«, of which the $N + V\text{-}ing_P$ frame is attached to »$stop_1$«, and the $N + N + V\text{-}ing_P$ frame to »$stop_2$«. In addition to this, »$stop_1$« and »$stop_2$« may be linked to semantic frame instances. In the

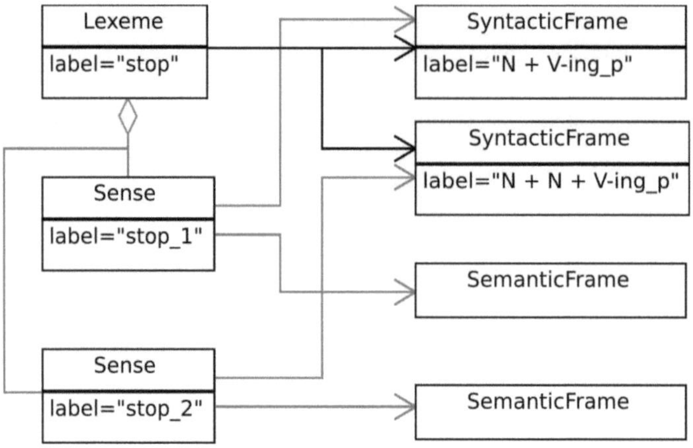

Figure 5.9: The relation of a lexeme and its senses to their syntactic valence frames

following paragraphs, we will now turn in more detail to the actual kinds of information that are represented, and how they relate to each other.

5.2.4.2 Syntactic description

As was mentioned above, the most basic kind of valence description concerns the syntactic properties of the arguments. Here, it is not only necessary to specify the syntactic category of an argument, such as »*noun phrase*« or »*wh-clause*«, but also the syntactic function it realises, e. g. »*subject*« or »*prepositional object*«. Especially the latter information is required in order to make the resource useful for NLP applications. For example, making the valence descriptions in VDE usable for an LFG grammar (cf. Kaplan and Bresnan, 1982) proved to be a non-trivial task, as VDE provides only information about the syntactic categories of the arguments. The necessary manual "construction" of functional information proved to be a very tedious and time-consuming task (Spohr, 2004). Therefore, in addition to information on the syntactic category of the arguments, we propose to include information on the functional argument structure of a predicate, in a format that allows for easy extraction of LFG-style subcategorisation information. Figure 5.10 shows how this information is represented in the model.

The left-hand side of the figure shows that instances of *Lexeme* and instances of *Sense* are linked to instances of *SyntacticFrame* via a relation *hasSyntacticValenceFrame*. In turn, a syntactic frame has a direct *predicate* link to the lexeme it belongs to. Although this link is to some degree redundant, given that the syntactic frame is already indirectly linked to the respective lexeme, it eases the extraction of LFG-style subcategorisation descriptions considerably, and is thus considered useful. In addition to the *predicate* link, the syntactic frame has at least one *ValenceArgument*, which is related to an instance of *SyntacticCategory*.

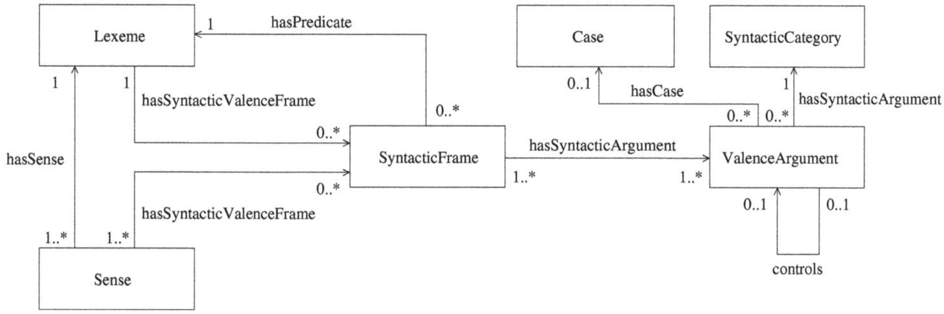

Figure 5.10: Syntactic valence description

In order to be able to model the relation between the arguments of *control constructions*, we further allow a *controls* relation between individual valence arguments. This is needed to express the difference between frames which share all syntactic functions as well as syntactic categories of their arguments, but which differ with respect to the control relation. For example, in a sentence like »*Mary promised Peter to write a book*«, the subject of the main predicate »*promise*« is also the subject of the predicate in the embedded clause, whereas in a sentence like »*Mary convinced Peter to write a book*«, the object of the main predicate controls the subject of the embedded clause (see e. g. Bresnan, 1982).

In contrast to syntactic categories, we do not model syntactic functions as instances, but as object properties (i. e. *relations*) between instances of *SyntacticFrame* and instances of *ValenceArgument*. The decision to do so has various reasons. On a formal level, we would like to capture that they are *functions*, i. e. two-place predicates, rather than one-place predicates. From a more technical perspective, however, representing syntactic functions as object properties also gives us a nice way to model different types of subcategorisation frames, where e. g. the *object* function is not available to intransitive frames, whereas it has to be present in transitive frames (see following subsection). In addition to this, we can e. g. state that a governable grammatical function like *subject* is functional, i. e. having only one value, whereas a non-governable function like *adjunct* allows for several values. Figure 5.11 displays the complete property hierarchy of syntactic functions, inspired by Kaplan and Bresnan (1982).

5.2.4.3 Typology of syntactic valence frames

As was just mentioned, modelling syntactic functions as relations supports the definition of different types of syntactic valence frames, with certain argument relations being available only to certain types of syntactic frames. Figure 5.12 displays some of the types of syntactic frames that have been defined in the MLR model.[15]

[15] We do not claim the following list to be exhaustive, nor the list of types that have been defined in the model. It is rather intended to serve the purpose of illustrating how different types of frames can be

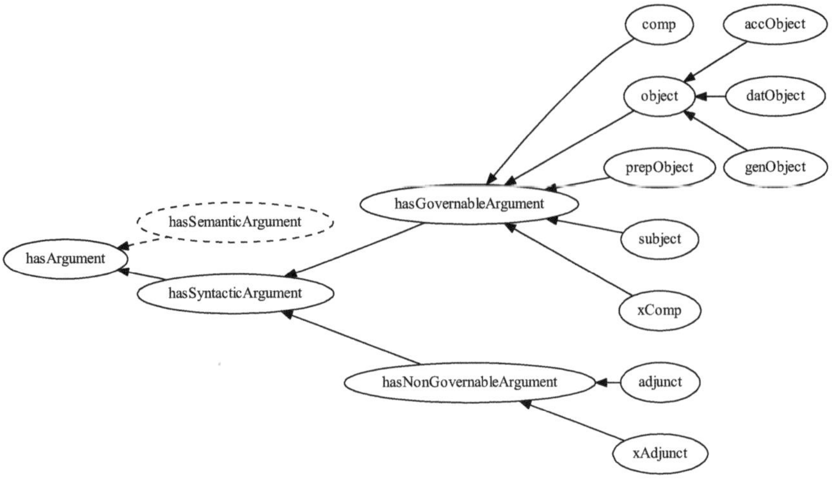

Figure 5.11: Property hierarchy of syntactic functions

One immediate benefit of defining different types of syntactic frames is the generalisation that can be expressed. As was mentioned above, it is e. g. possible to express that the syntactic frames in the sentences »*Mary promised Peter to write a book*« and »*Mary convinced Peter to write a book*« are essentially of the same type (i. e. *SubjectObjectXCompFrame*), differing only in the nature of their control relation. Therefore, although the frames would correspond to two different instances in the resource, they would be connected through their belonging to the same type of syntactic frame.

This methodology of assigning syntactic frames to different instances is not only applied to frames that differ with respect to their syntactic properties, but also to frames that are syntactically identical. Thus, a syntactic frame for »*force*« (as in »*Mary forced Peter to write a book*«) would be an instance of its own, although its syntactic properties are the same as the ones for »*convince*« in the sentence above. As a result, each lexeme has its own set of syntactic frame instances. On the one hand, this is already implicitly suggested by the fact that each syntactic frame instance specifies its own predicate, and thus there are – strictly speaking – never two completely identical syntactic frames across different lexical items. Irrespective of this, however, this approach has also been chosen due to its benefits, which will be discussed below in the context of MWEs (see page 95).

In addition to the types of syntactic frames shown in Figure 5.12, it is also possible to define types which generalise over other aspects of the syntactic valence description. For example, one could define types such as *ObjectControlFrame* and *SubjectControlFrame*, or

defined and organised, with the possibility to add further types to the list at a later stage.

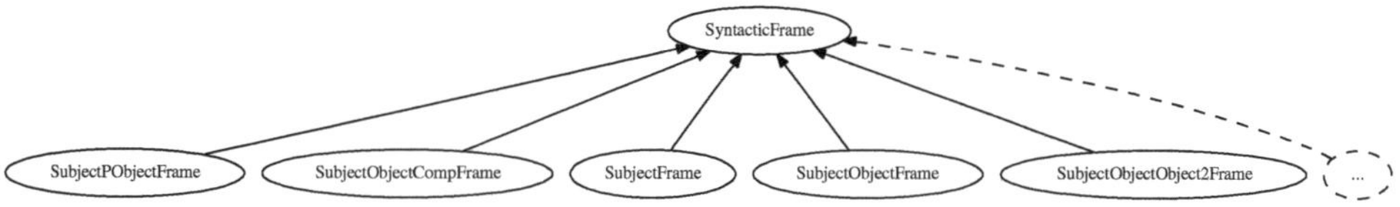

Figure 5.12: Type hierarchy of syntactic valence frames

types like *MonotransitiveFrame*, *DitransitiveFrame* etc. as in VDE (Herbst *et al.*, 2005), ignoring details about the particular arguments in the frame. This way of generalising over specific syntactic valence information is in direct contrast to the representationally more compact approach foreseen e. g. in LMF, where the idea is that there is only one frame instance per syntactic construction (see ISO/FDIS 24613, 2008: p. 25). Therefore, the two predicates *»promise«* and *»convince«* would be linked to two different syntactic frames, since they are not completely identical, while *»force«* would be linked to the same frame instance as *»convince«*. The problem with this approach is that now the generalisation that the two frame instances have essentially the same arguments is lost, for there is no common type – except for the type *SubcategorizationFrame* – that is shared by them.[16] Therefore, the connection between the two frame instances can only be established by iterative comparison of the arguments. Moreover, this approach poses high demands on the transparency of the names that are assigned to instances representing particular syntactic constructions. This transparency can only be achieved by means of strict terminological guidelines across languages. However, the fact that LMF mixes e. g. different variants of English in the definition of its vocabulary (cf. BE *SyntacticBehaviour* vs. AE *SubcategorizationFrame*) already shows the detail that would need to be paid attention to in the compilation of such guidelines. Nonetheless, the transparency is needed in order to be able to determine, e. g. when incrementally adding data, whether an instance has already been created for a specific syntactic configuration.[17] If this is not possible in a computationally straightforward way, it would represent a non-trivial problem that may – in the worst case – involve iteration over all frame instances.[18]

---

[16] LMF mentions the possibility of a »reflexive link« between frame instances in order to »integrate a hierarchical structure of Subcategorization Frame instances« (ISO/FDIS 24613, 2008: p. 25). However, the nature of this relation is left unspecified in the standard, and it is thus not clear if it would be used to capture such cases.

[17] This is, of course, unless one assumes that an *exhaustive* list of possible syntactic constructions has been compiled in advance and the creation of further instances for syntactic constructions is not necessary at a later stage. However, we consider the creation of such a list not feasible.

[18] The descriptive comment foreseen in LMF that specifies which syntactic construction is dealt with by a particular frame instance is of course only useful for humans and cannot be considered for the automatic addition of data.

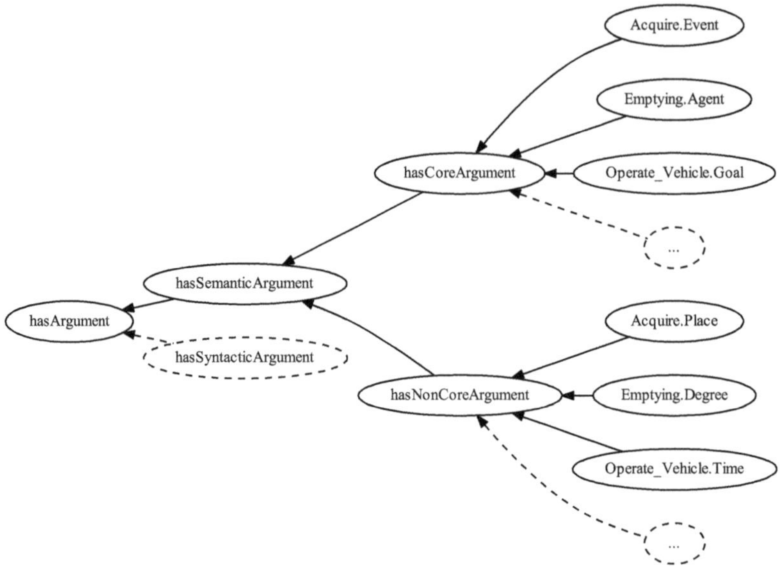

Figure 5.13: Part of the property hierarchy of semantic roles

5.2.4.4 Semantic description

In addition to information on the syntactic properties of a lexical item, it is highly desirable – especially from an NLP perspective – to model information on the semantic roles that are filled by the arguments, whenever this information is available. However, also from the perspective of a human user semantic information is extremely useful, though not necessarily in its fully explicit detail. In particular, semantic role information has been successfully used to capture the mapping relation between arguments e. g. of morphologically or semantically related lexical items – as well as of translation equivalents across languages – in a convenient way (see e. g. Heid, 2006; Burchardt *et al.*, 2008a; Subirats, 2009). It is thus a lexicographically relevant aspect of description that needs to be covered. In a sense, this information is implicit, as the arguments are only linked by virtue of denoting the same semantic role. Still, as the mapping relation can be reconstructed easily, there is no need to define an explicit mapping relation between arguments.

Similar to syntactic functions, we suggest to model semantic roles as relations between a semantic frame instance and a valence argument. The reasons for doing so are also closely related to the ones mentioned in the context of the syntactic valence description, namely that – like syntactic functions – roles are two-place predicates. Moreover, it is again possible to define particular semantic roles for particular types of semantic frames only, such that roles

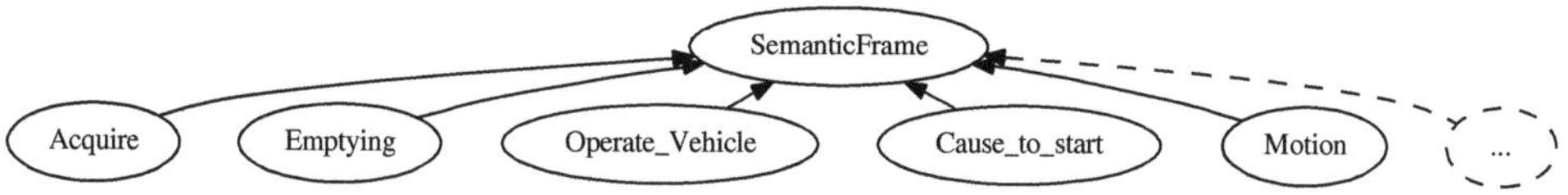

Figure 5.14: Type hierarchy of semantic valence frames

like COMMERCE_SELL.BUYER and COMMERCE_SELL.SELLER only have COMMERCE_SELL in their domain. Finally, it provides a compact means of defining the mapping between syntactic and semantic arguments, which will be discussed in the next subsection. Figure 5.13 shows a part of the property hierarchy of semantic roles.

As the figure suggests, the semantic roles that have been defined are based on the FrameNet inventory of *frame elements* (Baker *et al.*, 1998)[19], as well as its distinction between *core* and *non-core roles*. On the one hand, this choice of semantic roles is due to the large amount of data that have been annotated with FrameNet frames (see e. g. Burchardt *et al.*, 2006), and which are thus available for representation in the model. On the other hand, the frames defined in FrameNet and SALSA can be directly used as types of semantic valence frames, which gives us a clear typology of semantic valence frames along with their set of semantic roles (see Figure 5.14). Moreover, due to the wide usage of FrameNet data in various fields of NLP (such as machine translation or textual entailment recognition; cf. Boas, 2002; Burchardt and Frank, 2006), the data in the resource can be of use to a wide range of applications.

Despite the present choice of framework for the semantic description, it is important to note that neither the resource nor the methodology rely on FrameNet, and as such it is not attempted to provide a model of FrameNet and its inter-relations between frames and roles. In particular, even the fundamental inheritance relation that organises frames and roles into hierarchies has been deliberately excluded from this model – for a number of reasons. First of all, a hierarchisation of the semantic roles can have a negative impact on the extraction of argument mapping information between related lexical items. This is because a role like *Operate_Vehicle.Vehicle* inherits from *Operating_a_System.System*, *Using.Instrument*, up to roles like *Objective_influence.Dependent_entity*. This means that if one wants to extract e. g. arguments that realise the *Objective_influence.Dependent_entity* role, as in »*The Beatles have influenced [many music groups$_{Dependent_entity}$].*«, one would also extract arguments like »*Yesterday, Mary drove [my car$_{Vehicle}$].*«, which realise the *Operate_Vehicle.Vehicle* role, since every *Operate_Vehicle.Vehicle* is also an *Objective_influence.Dependent_entity*. The question whether such inherited roles should be considered as related in a way that is relevant to human users or NLP applications is a question of its own and will not be discussed here. For the purposes at hand, we have decided to represent this kind of semantic information *explicitly*, and to leave inferences up to applications that access the resource, and that may have a formalisation of FrameNet in the background (cf. Burchardt *et al.*, 2008a). In addition

[19] More precisely, the used inventory has been defined in the SALSA project (Burchardt *et al.*, 2006), which extends the frames defined in FrameNet with frames that have been identified as missing in FrameNet.

to the previous issue, there are formal inaccuracies in FrameNet's inheritance relation, with core roles in one frame inheriting from non-core roles in other frames. The effect of this is that the distinction between core and non-core roles – which we consider a useful distinction – would be softened by a hierarchical organisation of the roles.

These issues are not to say that a hierarchical organisation of frames and roles is in general not possible. Moreover, it is without any problems possible to define ones own set of semantic roles and work with them. Therefore, the choice to use the SALSA/FrameNet inventory should be considered, among others, as based on illustrative purposes.

Finally, we offer the possibility to specify the *semantic type* of a particular argument. For example, the direct object of »*über's Ohr hauen*« (»*to fool*«) is typically filled by a human entity. In order to specify this, we can link the respective frame instance – syntactic or semantic, depending on the kind of information that is available – to an instance of *SemanticTypeDescription*, which in turn specifies the semantic type of an argument by means of the relations *semanticType* and *argument*. One might ask why the semantic type of an argument is not specified in the same way as e. g. the control relation, i. e. to state the semantic type directly: *ValenceArgument hasSemanticType SemanticType*. The reason for dealing with this description separately is that semantic types, unlike the control relation between arguments, may need to be *quantified*. For example, it might be desired to specify that a certain argument only shows a *preference* for a specific semantic type, without absolutely restricting its argument to that semantic type. For such cases, it is possible to specify a value for the *hasQuantification* property of the *SemanticTypeDescription* instance.

5.2.4.5 Syntax-semantics mapping

As was mentioned in the previous subsection, the decision to model syntactic functions and semantic roles as relations between instances of (syntactic and semantic) valence frames and instances of valence arguments provides an straightforward and intuitive way of modelling the syntax-semantics mapping. In particular, the representation that has been chosen is that a semantic role that is realised by some argument with a certain syntactic function points to the same argument instance as the syntactic function. For example, in a sentence like »*Mary saw Peter.*«, we would say that the NP »*Mary*« realises the *subject* function and – following the FrameNet terminology – the *Perception_experience.Perceiver_passive* role, while »*Peter*« realises the *direct object* function and the *Perception_experience.Phenomenon* role. The respective valence frame of the corresponding sense of »*see*«, i. e. <*Subject|NP|Perception_experience.Perceiver_passive, Object|NP|Perception_experience.Phenomenon*>, would be represented in the model as in Figure 5.15.

This approach to modelling valence information also offers a straightforward representation of incomplete valence information, in case e. g. the semantic part of the description is missing. In the current example, the instance representing »*see*$_1$« would only be linked to the *SubjectObjectFrame* instance. If semantic information is available at a later stage and needs to be added, then it suffices to create a corresponding semantic frame instance, and to assign the semantic role relations to the valence argument instances accordingly.

Our way of representing valence information is in contrast to the one presented in LMF, where the syntax-semantics mapping is dealt with by means of a *SynSemArgMap* class, which is intended to represent »the links between a semantic argument and a syntactic argument«

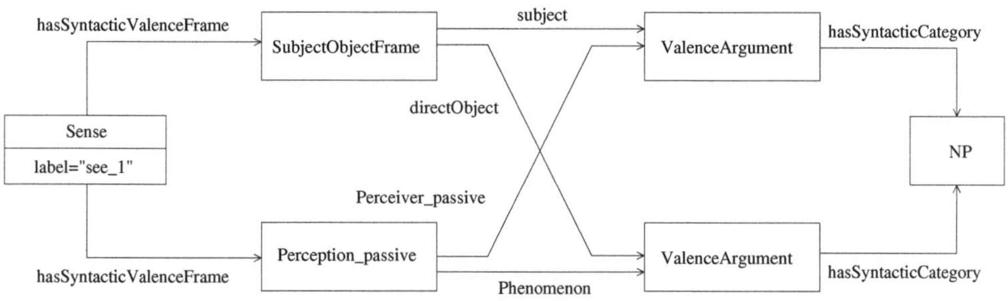

Figure 5.15: Representation of syntax-semantics mapping

(ISO/FDIS 24613, 2008: p. 31). Moreover, LMF's *SynSemCorrespondence* class is to represent »a set of *SynSemArgMap* instances for a given *Subcategorization Frame* instance« (ibid.). Although LMF offers an apparently transparent and extensible way of dealing with the mapping between syntactic and semantic arguments, it seems that neither of these "links" is to be represented explicitly in LMF-encoded data, as the current LMF DTD (cf. ISO/FDIS 24613, 2008: pp. 72-75) does not provide the attributes that are necessary for expressing cross-references between the respective elements (i. e. XML `IDREF` attributes). This is in line with LMF's general tendency to use implicit links that need to be constructed by dedicated external software, e. g. by parsing the `CDATA` values of XML attributes rather than following clearly defined `IDREF`s (cf. the discussions in the following subsection). We believe that our way of representation is more intuitive and can also be queried more easily, although empirical comparisons are not possible at the current stage due to missing implementations of LMF.

5.2.4.6 Valence description of multi-word expressions

As was mentioned before, valence behaviour of MWEs is a lexicographic phenomenon that is generally underrepresented in current dictionaries, and is believed to be covered inadequately by current lexicon models. Although one could argue that valence information is rarely ever available in this detail for a given MWE, recent corpus linguistic work has shown that it is to some extent possible to acquire such information automatically from text corpora (see e. g. Weller and Heid (2010)). Moreover, given that information on the valence behaviour of the components of an MWE is likely to be available, one could use this information in order to make predictions as to the valence behaviour and argument mappings of the MWE itself, and try to verify whether these predictions are actually true for a given MWE. For these reasons, providing satisfactory solutions to crucial representational issues like (i) the relation between the valence frames of the MWE and those of the components of the MWE, and (ii) the relation between the valence frames of the MWE and the components themselves (i. e. the actual lexical items) is a central modelling aspect that may greatly enhance the capabilities of the lexical resource as a tool for lexicographic research.

With respect to (i), we have created a *usesFrame* relation that links valence frames of the MWE to those valence frames of its components that are used by the MWE. The idea is that the MWE thus states *explicitly* how the valence behaviour of its components is reflected in the MWE. In principle, there are five possible configurations for one MWE valence pattern:

(1.) the MWE valence pattern uses only frames that have been defined for its components, and that is it; an example would be the collocation »*Kritik üben*«, where the collocate »*üben*« subcategorises a *subject* and a *direct object*, and the base »*Kritik*« subcategorises a *prepositional object* with »*an*«; the »*direct object*« slot is filled by the base itself, and thus the collocation as a whole subcategorises the prepositional object;

(2.) like (1.), but adding further arguments that are not contained in the frames of the components;

(3.) the MWE valence pattern uses only a frame of one of its components, and that is it;

(4.) like (3.), but adding further arguments; e. g. the collocation »*Unterstützung finden*«, where »*finden*« subcategorises a *subject* and an *object*, the *object* slot is filled by »*Unterstützung*«, and the MWE as a whole subcategorises a *bei-PP* that none of its components subcategorises;

(5.) the MWE valence pattern does not use any of the valence frames of its components.

In case (1.), the syntactic frame instance of the MWE has a *usesFrame* link to the syntactic frame instance representing the *'üben <Subject|NP, Object|NP>'* frame in the description of »*üben*«, as well as a *usesFrame* link to the instance representing *'Kritik <Prep-Object|an-PP>'* in the description of »*Kritik*«. Case (2.) is very similar, the difference being that in addition to the two *usesFrame* relations, the MWE valence frame instance has further links to the other arguments it subcategorises. Cases (3.) to (5.) are not very different from (1.) and (2.) with respect to their representations, except for the fact that either one or both *usesFrame* links are missing. Nonetheless, their representations *are* different and can thus be extracted separately. Therefore, we consider this way of modelling the relation between valence frames of MWEs and valence frames of their components more fine-grained and more transparent than the LMF-based representation, as it is e. g. not clear how the extraction of such phenomena could be accomplished in LMF in a straightforward way. This is because a syntactic valence frame that results from combining frames of one or more components will most likely be different than any of the frames of the individual components (cf. all of the above cases except for (3.)), and thus, the LMF strategy to express generalisation by reference to a single shared instance that represents a particular syntactic construction will, in our opinion, run into problems when trying to reconstruct a link between the frames of the MWE components and their composition (see ISO/FDIS 24613, 2008: pp. 24-28 and 63-66).[20]

[20] In this paragraph, we have deliberately stated that the extraction should be *straightforward* since – as was previously mentioned in this work – anything that can be expressed in XML can also be extracted by XQuery, due to its property of being Turing complete (Kepser, 2004). However, the XQuery expression that is necessary for extracting such phenomena should not resemble a program rather than a query, and thus we would like to emphasise that the extraction should be achievable with an appropriate amount of effort.

While the discussion about the relation between valence frames of MWEs and those of their components has up to now focussed solely on syntactic valence frames, the relation between their semantic valence frames needs to be addressed as well. In fact, the semantic aspect of this relation is more intricate than the rather straightforward configurations mentioned above. This is due to the fact that different types of MWEs differ with respect to the extent to which the meaning of their components is reflected in the MWE. For example, while (Hausmann, 2004) states that collocations typically contain a base which keeps its semantic content also in the collocation, idiomatic MWEs typically have a new, uncompositional meaning of their own. For example, while the collocation »*Kritik üben*« as a whole could be assigned a semantic valence frame of the type *Judgment_communication*, i. e. the frame of its base »*Kritik*«, it is not obvious from the components which frame needs to be assigned to »*an den Tag legen*« (»*to display*«).

In our opinion, this should also be reflected in the representation. For non-idiomatic collocations, we therefore propose to create a semantic valence frame of the type denoted by the base, and to have a *usesFrame* link between that frame and a corresponding semantic frame in the description of the base. Since the *synsemantic* collocate (cf. Hausmann, 2004) does not contribute semantically, we propose not to link the semantic frame of the MWE with any semantic frame of the collocate. One could in fact assume that the collocate has a *support (verb) reading* that does not have any semantic frames. This would roughly correspond to the approach followed in SALSA, although the assumption there is that a support verb evokes a – semantically unspecified – *Support* frame, that assigns to the base the semantic role *Supported* (Burchardt *et al.*, 2006). Unfortunately, however, the semantic contribution of the base also remains semantically unspecified. In contrast to this, we propose to assign to the *syntactic* arguments of the collocate semantic roles according to the semantic frame of MWE and base. For example, the combination of »*Kritik*« and »*üben*« as respective base and collocate of »*Kritik üben*« have the effect that the subject of »*üben*« is assigned the semantic role of a *Judgment_communication.Communicator*, as the base – and thus the MWE – evokes the *Judgment_communication* frame (see Figure 5.16 on page 100 for an illustration of this representation in the model).

In contrast to this, the meaning of idiomatic MWEs is typically non-compositional, in the sense that the components do not retain their original meaning in the MWE. Therefore, we propose not to link the idiomatic MWE with any of the semantic frames of its components via the *usesFrame* relation, but instead to create a semantic frame instance for the MWE itself, and to assign its semantic roles to the arguments of the respective syntactic frames that the MWE uses of its components. This way, we are able to capture the fact that an idiomatic MWE is semantically non-compositional, while potentially reflecting some of the syntactic properties of its components.

Point (ii) mentioned above, i. e. the relation between the valence frames of the MWE to the actual lexical items that constitute the MWE, refers to how the components relate to each other syntactically, e. g. which syntactic function is realised by one of the components with respect to the other components. In other words, it refers to aspects of the internal syntactic structure of the MWE. An example of relevant information in this context is the embedding of one component in the functional structure of the other component, making the latter the main predicate of the MWE, and the former an argument of this predicate. In contrast to LMF, where the constituent structure is also represented in the MWE, we focus only on the functional syntactic structure, since we believe that the constituent structure should not be encoded at the level of lexemes or senses, but should instead come from grammar rules. If the internal syntactic constituent structure cannot be generated from the rules of the grammar, however, we propose to leave the MWE as one unanalysed chunk. Irrespective of this strategy, the syntactic categories of the components are specified and can be extracted (e. g. if somebody wants to extract MWEs that consist of a verb and a prepositional phrase), and thus, we do not think that further information, such as the hard-coding of a fixed internal constituent structure, is relevant to NLP or to human users (cf. Section 5.1.2.2 above).

The way we represent this functional embedding in our model is to have a *LexicalRealisationDescription* instance that is linked to the syntactic frame instance, and which specifies the argument that is realised, along with the lexical item that realises the respective argument. This is achieved by means of the relations *argument* and *lexicalItem*, which link the lexical realisation instance to the argument instance and the lexical item instance respectively. This is, again, in clear contrast to the LMF approach, where the lexical realisation of syntactic arguments within the MWE is encoded indirectly via the rank of a particular component.

5.2.4.7 Potential lexical realisations

Closely related to the previous description is the description of *potential* lexical fillers. For example, VDE specifies the following valence pattern and example for a sense of »*to learn*« (cf. Herbst *et al.*, 2005: p. 477f).

(5.3) + something/a lot/etc.$_P$ + about N/V-ing

(5.4) »*You'll learn lots of worthwhile things about the little known American war with Ecuador of 1802.*«

This pattern expresses that »*to learn*« subcategorises some kind of a quantifying argument, along with a prepositional phrase. On the one hand, one could model this at the level of syntactic categories. However, if one wants to express a preference for specific lexical items, as has been the case in VDE, we propose to deal with this similar to the lexical realisation of arguments in the valence description of MWEs. In particular, the respective frame is linked to a *LexicalRealisationDescription* instance which specifies – in addition to the realised argument and the realising lexical item – a value for the *hasQuantification* property.

5.2.4.8 Quantitative description

The final aspect of the valence description deals with the quantitative description of valence frames, e. g. in terms of corpus frequency. One straightforward approach would be to define a *hasFrequency* property for valence frames, and to specify the frequency for each particular valence frame instance. However, a certain valence frame that is e. g. used by more than one of the senses of a lexeme needs to specify its frequency value *in relation to* this particular sense. Therefore, our strategy is to have a class for frequency descriptions whose instances specify the frequency of a valence frame with respect to a sense or lexeme. Technically, an instance of *FrequencyDescription* is linked to the lexeme or a specific sense via the *hasQuantitativeDescription* relation, and this instance, which specifies the frequency value, is then linked to the respective frame via *describes*. This way, it is also possible to specify more than one frequency value for a particular valence frame instance, and to state e. g. with respect to which corpus the respective frequency value is to be interpreted.

5.2.4.9 Example valence representation

To summarise and illustrate the different aspects discussed above, we discuss in more detail the valence description of the collocation »*Kritik üben*« (Figure 5.16). The general definition of the valence description is provided in the appendix in the form of a UML diagram.

As can be seen in Figure 5.16, the top part defines a syntactic frame of the type *SubjectObjectFrame* for a support reading of »*üben*«, which is linked to both the sense instance and the lexeme instance. In addition to specifying the predicate of the frame to be »*üben*«, the frame instance is linked to two *ValenceArgument* instances with syntactic category *NP*, which realise the grammatical functions *subject* and *directObject* respectively. Finally, the subject argument is specified to have the semantic type *human*. As was mentioned on page 97f above, the semantically weak support reading does not specify a semantic valence frame. In contrast to this, the instance representing a sense of »*Kritik*« does specify a semantic valence frame of the type *Judgment_communication*, in addition to a syntactic *PObjectFrame* that subcategorises a prepositional phrase with »*an*«. The corresponding valence argument realises the *prepObject* function of the syntactic frame, as well as the *Evaluee* role of the semantic frame.

As was explained above, a collocation can be linked to its components either at the level of lexemes or at the level of senses – depending on which kind of information is available. Here, we assume that semantic information is available, and thus the sense of »*Kritik üben*« is linked to its components via the corresponding *hasBase* and *hasCollocate* relations. In order to capture the fact that the collocation uses the syntactic frames of its components, we link the syntactic frame instance of »*Kritik üben*«, which is of type *SubjectObjectPObjectFrame*, to the syntactic frames of the components by means of the *usesFrame* relation. For the semantic frames the situation is different, since the collocate is not linked to a semantic frame. In the case at hand, the collocation as a whole takes over the meaning of the base »*Kritik*«, and thus the semantic frame of the collocation is of type *Judgment_communication* as well. In addition to this, the semantic frame of the collocation not only uses the semantic frame of the base – thus obtaining the corresponding syntax-semantics mapping of the *prepObject/Evaluee* – but further assigns to the *subject* the semantic role *Communicator*. As this role is not part of the original semantic frame of »*Kritik*«, it is assigned directly by the frame instance of the collocation. In addition to this, it should be noted that »*Kritik*« itself is not assigned a semantic role within the collocation. This is due to the fact that, although it is not the syntactic head of the collocation, it is sort of the »semantic head« of the collocation, as it is the source of the semantic content (*frame evoking element* in FrameNet terminology; Baker *et al.*, 1998). Since »*üben*« itself is semantically weak and does not assign semantic roles itself, there is no semantic role that could be assigned to »*Kritik*«[21]. Finally, the syntactic frame instance of »*Kritik üben*« is linked to a *LexicalRealisationDescription* instance, which specifies that »*Kritik*« fills the *directObject* slot of »*üben*«. The result of all this is that »*Kritik üben*« has the valence frame *'üben<subject|NP|Communicator, directObject|NP[= 'Kritik<prepObject|an-PP|Evaluee>']>'*.

[21] Recall that one could assign to »*Kritik*« the *Supported* role, assuming that »*üben*« evokes a *Support* frame (cf. Burchardt *et al.*, 2006). However, we consider this information not necessary here.

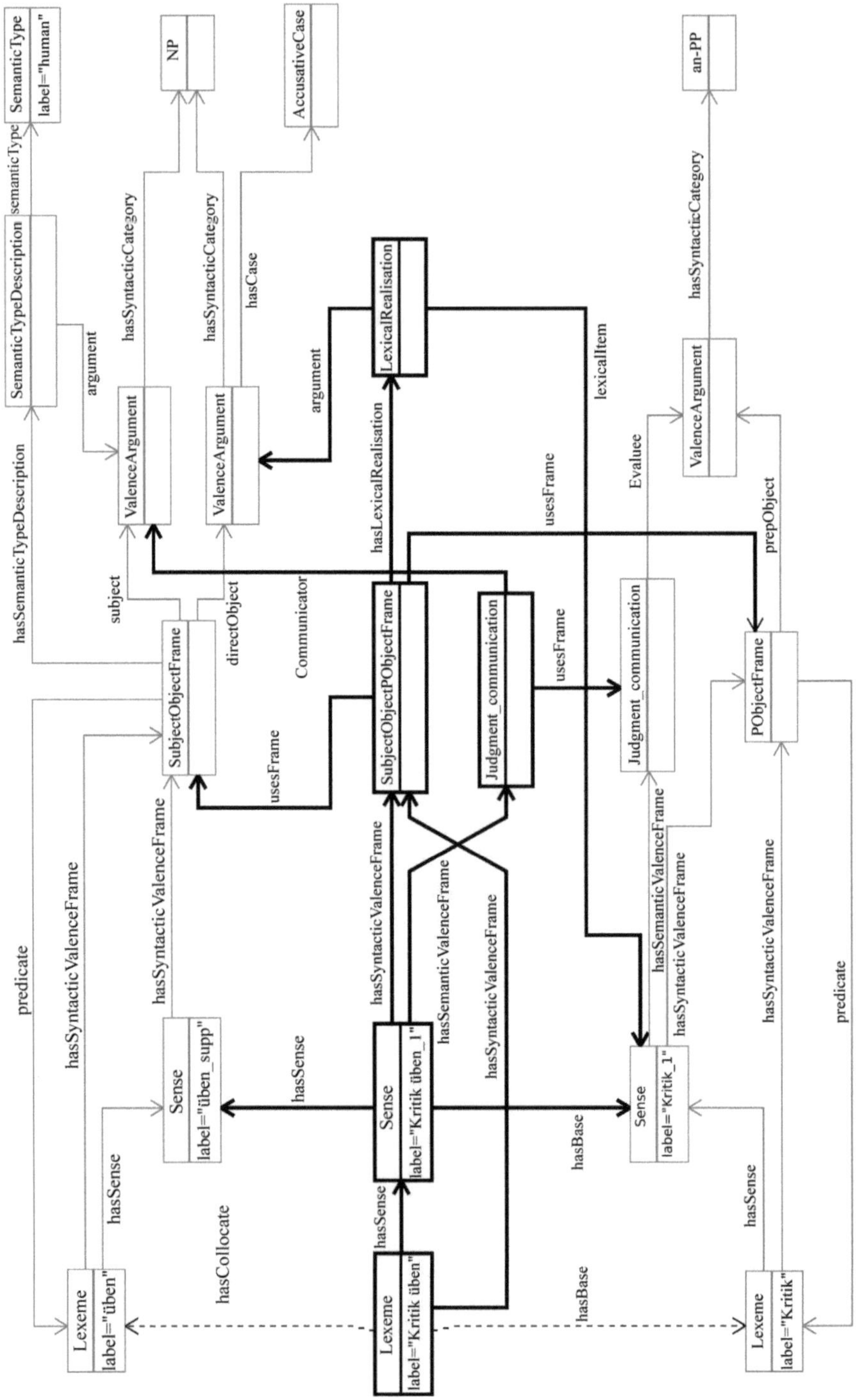

Figure 5.16: Valence representation of »*Kritik üben*«

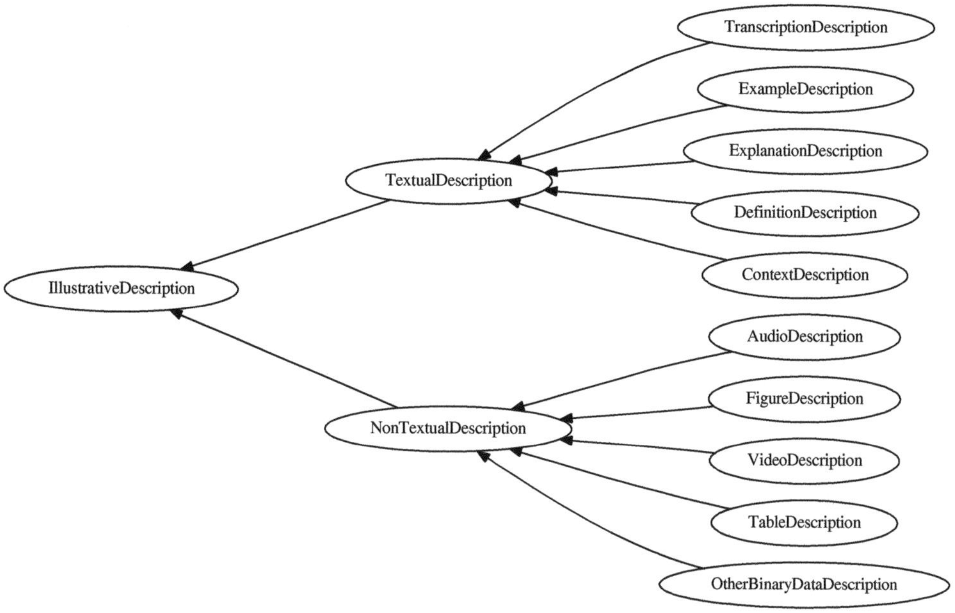

Figure 5.17: Subclasses of *IllustrativeDescription*

5.2.5 Illustrative Description

Similar to the modelling of orthographic information (see Section 5.2.3), *illustrative descriptions* like example sentences, definitions, figures etc. can be modelled in a rather straightforward way. Technically, they are instances of classes *ExampleDescription*, *DefinitionDescription* or *FigureDescription*. Figure 5.17 displays the hierarchy of illustrative descriptions, which is based on (ISO/FDIS 12620, 2009) and ISOcat[22].

Instances of *TextualDescription* and its subclasses specify their content in terms of the property *hasContent*. As was discussed in (Spohr, 2005: p. 23), the content of example sentences can itself contain XML markup. Instances of *NonTextualDescription* typically refer to some URL that indicates the location where the respective non-textual entity, e. g. a picture or a sound file, can be found. This is done by means of the property *hasExternalResource*. Moreover, both types of illustrative descriptions may specify the source of their content, if applicable, by means of the *hasSource* property. Similar to LMF, illustrative descriptions are linked to instances of particular senses. Figure A.8 on page 205 shows illustrative descriptions for the two senses of »*Dekor*«.

[22] http://www.isocat.org

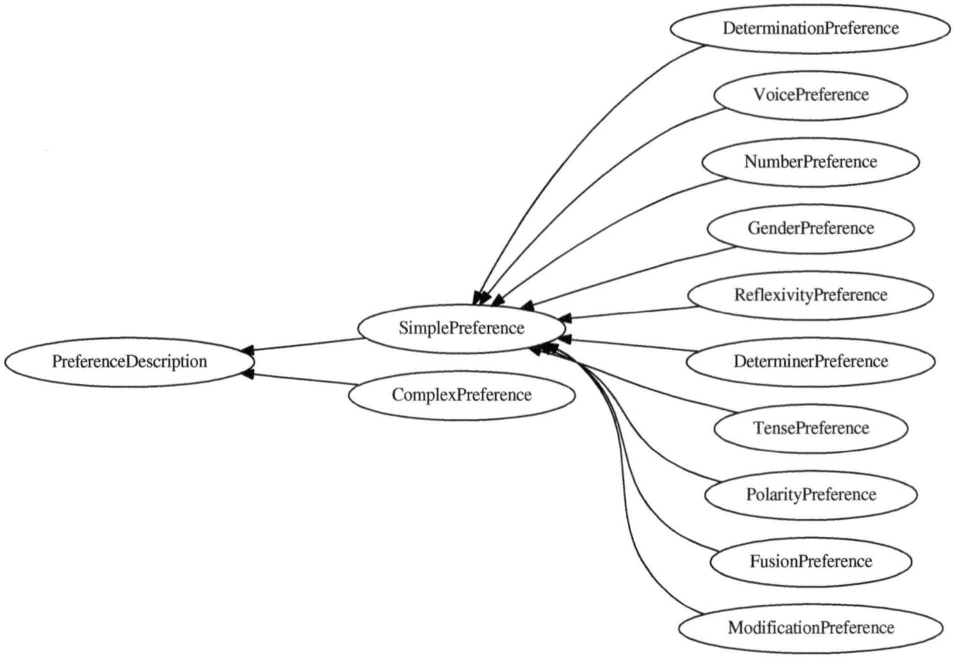

Figure 5.18: Subclasses of *PreferenceDescription*

5.2.6 Preference Description

The last type of description that is to be discussed in detail concerns the expression of preferences and restrictions. Here, we need to express e. g. that the base »*Abschied*« of the $V + N_{obj}$ collocation »*Abschied nehmen*« (»*to say goodbye*«) always occurs in the singular and in 77.6% of the occurrences observed in a given corpus without a determiner, or that one sense of »*Dekor*« always selects neuter gender and the singular form. In order to express these in a uniform way, we propose to model both preferences and absolute restrictions as instances of a class *PreferenceDescription*. Figure 5.18 shows the hierarchy of different types of preferences defined in the model, which can be extended to cover further types if necessary.

As can be seen in the figure, there are two main types of preference descriptions, simple and complex ones. While instances of *SimplePreference* typically express a single preference like the ones just mentioned, a *ComplexPreference* can be used to model preferences which have a common quantification (see also Spohr, 2005: pp. 24-26). Each instance of a preference description is linked to a lexical item via the *hasPreference* property, e. g. *Dekor_2 hasPreference GenderPreference_1* or *Dekor_2 hasPreference NumberPreference_1*. These instances then specify the value of their preference, e. g. *NumberPreference_1 hasNumber*

SingularNumber, as well as the quantification, e. g. *NumberPreference_1 hasQuantification "100.0"*. In order to express preferences for collocations such as the one mentioned above, we make use of a property called *describes*. In order to represent the preferences for »*Abschied nehmen*«, we thus make the following statements.

(5.5)	*Abschied_nehmen*	*hasBase*	*Abschied*
	Abschied_nehmen	*hasPreference*	*NumberPreference_x*
	NumberPreference_x	*hasNumber*	*SingularNumber*
	NumberPreference_x	*hasQuantification*	*"100.0"*
	NumberPreference_x	*describes*	*Abschied*
	Abschied_nehmen	*hasPreference*	*DeterminationPreference_y*
	DeterminationPreference_y	*hasDetermination*	*false*
	DeterminationPreference_y	*hasQuantification*	*"77.6"*
	DeterminationPreference_y	*describes*	*Abschied*

The interpretation of these statements is as follows. The collocation *Abschied_nehmen* has an absolute preference for singular number with respect to its base *Abschied*, and a *77.6%* preference for not having a determiner in front of its base.[23] A different way of modelling this circumstance would be to have a property like *hasBasePreference* which specifies the preference without reference to the lexical item by means of *describes*. Without a direct reference to the actual base, however, the fact that the values of the *hasBasePreference* property refer to the lexical item that is the value of *hasBase* would then have to be reconstructed. In other words, it would be bound to the internal names of the properties (cf. comments in Section 5.2.4.3). On the other hand, a representation like *Abschied hasPreference NumberPreference_x* would be problematic, since *Abschied* may show this preference behaviour only in this particular word combination. For these reasons, we consider such preferences rather a property of the collocation with respect to its components rather than of the components themselves, and therefore, we model them as such.

5.3 Formalisation in Description Logics

In this section, we will provide details on the formalisations of the MLR model. In general, the immediate interpretation of the description logic axioms that will be discussed in the following is that of *well-formedness constraints*. For example, if *a* is an instance of a class *X*, then it is *necessary* that *a* adheres to the formal definition of *X* in order to be a valid instance. Therefore, such axioms are primarily used for consistency control (see Section 6.1.2). However, the formalisations can also be formulated as *necessary and sufficient* conditions (cf. Section 4.2.4.2 above), meaning that if any instance *b* in the MLR conforms to the set of axioms that has been defined for a particular class *Y*, then *b* is *inferred* to be an instance of *Y*

[23] Note that in addition to the *DeterminationPreference* class, the MLR model provides a class for *DeterminerPreference*. This latter class is used to express preferences for a particular kind of determiner, e. g. definite vs. indefinite article.

as well. On the one hand, this is a further aspect of consistency control that ensures that the formal definitions of the classes in the MLR model are correct and complete. On the other hand, as was mentioned in Section 4.3.3 in the context of *value partitions*, it can be used for inferences in the MLR in general.

In order to avoid redundancy, a large portion of these formalisations will not be discussed at length here. Instead, we will limit the discussion to a number of classes that we consider appropriate for illustrating the general characteristics of the MLR model. Moreover, all of these classes belong to the lexical part of the MLR model, as their formal details are more interesting from a metalexicographical perspective than the formalisations of the descriptive entities. Readers who are not interested in any of the formal aspects of the MLR model may skip this section and continue with Section 5.4 on page 108.

5.3.1 Lexical Entities in General

The *LexicalEntity* class is defined at the top level of the model, together with the *DescriptiveEntity* class. The subclasses of *LexicalEntity* are *Lexeme*, *Form* and *Sense*, and we want to express that any instance of *LexicalEntity* has to be an instance of any of these. In other words, we do not want to have any instances which are direct instances of *LexicalEntity* without instantiating any of its subclasses. In order to express this, we define a so-called *covering axiom* (see e. g. Horridge *et al.*, 2004: p. 75f) that consists of the union of the subclasses of *LexicalEntity*. This axiom states that an instance of *LexicalEntity* is an instance of either *Lexeme*, *Form* or *Sense*.

(5.6) $$\begin{aligned} \mathit{LexicalEntity} \equiv\ & \mathit{owl{:}Thing} \sqcap \\ & (\neg\ \mathit{DescriptiveEntity}) \sqcap \\ & (\mathit{Lexeme} \sqcup \mathit{Form} \sqcup \mathit{Sense}) \end{aligned}$$

The definition in (5.6) expresses that *LexicalEntity* is equivalent to the intersection of *owl:Thing* with the complement of *DescriptiveEntity* and the union of *Lexeme*, *Form* and *Sense*. This means that an instance of *LexicalEntity* is an instance of either *Lexeme*, *Form* or *Sense* and not an instance of *DescriptiveEntity*.

5.3.1.1 Lexemes

The definition of the class *Lexeme* adds further restrictions to the ones defined for *LexicalEntity*. However, it is important to remember that the ones defined for *LexicalEntity* still hold for instances of *Lexeme*. Therefore, the *Lexeme* class is disjoint with *DescriptiveEntity* as well.

As was mentioned in the previous sections of this chapter, most lexical relations – although centered around senses – have been defined for lexemes as well. In order to ensure that lexemes have lexical relations only to other lexemes, not to senses, we specify that all values of the *hasLexicalRelationTo* property are instances of *Lexeme* (see (5.7)). Together with the next two axioms, which specify that *Lexeme* is disjoint with *Sense* and *Form*, we can ensure that lexemes do not have any lexical relations to senses. To see the necessity of the disjointness axioms, consider a case in which a *Lexeme* is linked to a *Sense* via *hasLexicalRelationTo*. If the reasoner is run to check the consistency of the data, then this *Sense* instance would, on the basis of the axiom $\forall hasLexicalRelationTo.Lexeme$, be inferred as an instance of *Lexeme*, since there is no restriction that would specify that a *Sense* cannot be a *Lexeme* at the same time. Therefore, this axiom is only reasonable in combination with the disjointness of *Lexeme* and *Sense*, which would cause an inconsistency in the aforementioned case.

In addition to these axioms, we state that a *Lexeme* is linked to a *Form* instance via *hasLemma*, that a lexeme needs to specify a syntactic category, and that – similar to the covering axiom defined for *LexicalEntity* – *Lexeme* instances instantiate either *BoundUnit*, *FreeUnit* or *Clitic*.

(5.7) $$\begin{aligned} Lexeme \equiv\ & LexicalEntity\ \sqcap \\ & (\forall hasLexicalRelationTo.Lexeme)\ \sqcap \\ & (\neg\ Sense)\ \sqcap \\ & (\neg\ Form)\ \sqcap \\ & (\exists hasLemma.Form)\ \sqcap \\ & (\exists hasPartOfSpeech.SyntacticCategory)\ \sqcap \\ & (BoundUnit \sqcup FreeUnit \sqcup Clitic) \end{aligned}$$

5.3.1.2 Forms

The definition of the second subclass of *LexicalEntity*, namely *Form*, is shown in (5.8). The first axiom states that a *Form* instance has to be either the lemma or one of the word forms of a *Lexeme*. Similar to the definition of *Lexeme*, the *Form* class is defined as disjoint with the other subclasses of *LexicalEntity*. Moreover, we specify that a *Form* instance instantiates either *InflectedForm* or *UninflectedForm*. Finally, a *Form* needs to have at least one *FormDescription*.

(5.8) $$\begin{aligned} Form \equiv\ & LexicalEntity\ \sqcap \\ & ((\exists isLemmaOf.Lexeme) \sqcup (\exists isWordFormOf.Lexeme))\ \sqcap \\ & (\neg\ Lexeme)\ \sqcap \\ & (\neg\ Sense)\ \sqcap \\ & (InflectedForm \sqcup UninflectedForm)\ \sqcap \\ & (\exists hasFormDescription.FormDescription) \end{aligned}$$

5.3.1.3 Senses

The formal definition of *Sense* is much more complex than that of *Lexeme* and *Form*. This is for three reasons: (i) all lexical relations have *Sense* in their domain, and thus, instances of *Sense* are much more interrelated with other lexical entities in the model than instances of *Form*; (ii) there are no further subclasses defined underneath *Sense*, which means that the *Sense* class carries a large amount of instances, whereas in the case of *Lexeme*, only the subclasses are instantiated; and (iii), instances of *Sense* can be senses of virtually any kind of *Lexeme*, which means that, in sum, the definition of *Sense* is almost as complex as the definitions of all the subclasses of *Lexeme* together.

In order to define *Sense* such that the consistency of the data in the MLR can be ensured, it is necessary to state that the instances of *Sense* make use of only those relations which are defined for the types of *Lexeme* that they are senses of. More precisely, if a sense makes use of the *hasBase* or *hasCollocate* relations, then it has to be a sense of some kind of *Collocation*. Conversely, if a sense makes use of the *isBaseOf* or *isCollocateOf* relations, then the values of these relations need to be instances that are senses of some kind of *Collocation*. Due to the fact that all lexical relations either have an inverse like *hasBase/isBaseOf* or have been defined as symmetric (like *hasMorphologicalRelationTo*), it suffices to state such definitions in only one direction, e. g. either from a collocation to its components or from the components to the collocation. Moreover, since lexical relations are organised hierarchically, restrictions do not have to be defined at the level of the actual relations (e. g. *hasBase* and *hasCollocate*), but of their superordinate relations (e. g. *isCollocationOf* in the case at hand). In sum, the restrictions have to involve only those lexical relations whose domain or range differs from that of its superordinate relation. For example, since the relation *hasCompound* restricts its range with respect to that of its superproperty *isMorphologicalComponentOf* to instances of *Compound*, the definition of *Sense* needs to include the axiom that if a sense makes use of the *hasCompound* relation, then the value of *hasCompound* needs to be a sense of an instance of *Compound*. (5.9) shows part of the axioms defined for *Sense*.

(5.9)
$$
\begin{aligned}
Sense \equiv\ & LexicalEntity \sqcap \\
& (\forall hasLexicalRelationTo.Sense) \sqcap \\
& (\exists isSenseOf.Lexeme) \sqcap \\
& (\neg\ Lexeme) \sqcap (\neg\ Form) \sqcap \\
& (\forall hasCollocation.(\exists isSenseOf.Collocation)) \sqcap \\
& (\forall isMorphologicalComponentOf. \\
& \qquad\qquad (\exists isSenseOf.ComplexFreeUnit)) \sqcap \\
& (\forall hasCompound.(\exists isSenseOf.Compound)) \sqcap \\
& \ldots
\end{aligned}
$$

The first lines state that a *Sense* is a *LexicalEntity* that has lexical relations only to other instances of *Sense*. This is to avoid that a *Sense* instance is linked to a *Lexeme* instance. Moreover, a *Sense* needs to be connected to a *Lexeme* via *isSenseOf*, in order to avoid that there are dangling senses that are not connected to any lexemes.[24] Finally, similar to the definitions for *Lexeme* and *Form*, instances of *Sense* cannot be instances of *Lexeme* or *Form*. The remaining axioms define the restrictions that stem from the domains and ranges of the different lexical relations in the sense that was just explained.

5.3.2 Specific Types of Lexemes

In the following, we will present the description logic formalisation of specific types of lexemes. Similar to the discussion in Section 5.1.2.2, we will focus on simple vs. complex collocations as well as specific subtypes thereof.

---

[24] Due to the fact that *isSenseOf* has been defined as a functional property, no further axiom is required to ensure that a *Sense* instance is connected to exactly one *Lexeme* instance.

5.3.2.1 Simple collocations

An instance of *SimpleCollocation* is defined as a *Collocation* whose values of *isCollocationOf* (i. e. the superproperty of *hasBase* and *hasCollocate*) can only refer to instances of *SyntacticallySimpleFreeUnit*. Moreover, *SimpleCollocation* is disjoint with *ComplexCollocation* and, like the classes discussed above, cannot be instantiated itself, but only through one of its subclasses.

(5.10) $\mathit{SimpleCollocation} \equiv \mathit{Collocation} \sqcap$
$(\forall \mathit{isCollocationOf.SyntacticallySimpleFreeUnit}) \sqcap$
$(\neg\ \mathit{ComplexCollocation}) \sqcap$
$(\mathit{Adj\text{-}Adv} \sqcup \mathit{N\text{-}Adj} \sqcup \mathit{N\text{-}N\_gen\text{-}obj} \sqcup \mathit{N\_quant\text{-}N} \sqcup$
$\mathit{Prep\text{-}N} \sqcup \mathit{V\text{-}Adj\_pred} \sqcup \mathit{V\text{-}Adv\_adv} \sqcup \mathit{V\text{-}N\_acc\text{-}obj} \sqcup$
$\mathit{V\text{-}N\_dat\text{-}obj} \sqcup \mathit{V\text{-}N\_subj} \sqcup \mathit{V\text{-}NP\_adv} \sqcup \mathit{V\text{-}PP\_pobj})$

$V + N\ (Object_{acc})$ collocations form one subtype of simple collocations. As was mentioned in Section 5.1.2.2, they refer to collocations where the base fills the direct (accusative) object slot of the collocate. Therefore, we define the class *V-N_obj-acc* as a type of *SimpleCollocation* whose base has as part of speech some instance of *NOUN* (e. g. *CommonNoun*) and whose collocate is some kind of *VERB* that subcategorises an accusative object. Moreover, a *V-N_obj-acc* collocation has only one collocate, so we restrict the cardinality of *hasCollocate* to one. Finally, collocations of type *V-N_obj-acc* have the part of speech *VerbPhrase* and are disjoint with all the other types of *SimpleCollocation*.

(5.11) $\mathit{V\text{-}N\_obj\text{-}acc} \equiv \mathit{SimpleCollocation} \sqcap$
$(\exists \mathit{hasBase}.(\exists \mathit{hasPartOfSpeech.NOUN})) \sqcap$
$(\exists \mathit{hasCollocate}.((\exists \mathit{hasPartOfSpeech.VERB}) \sqcap$
$(\exists \mathit{hasSyntacticValenceFrame}.(\exists \mathit{accObject.ValenceArgument})))) \sqcap$
$(= 1\ \mathit{hasCollocate\ owl{:}Thing}) \sqcap$
$(\exists \mathit{hasPartOfSpeech}.\{\mathit{VerbPhrase}\}) \sqcap$
$(\neg\ (\mathit{Adj\text{-}Adv} \sqcup \mathit{N\text{-}Adj} \sqcup \ldots \sqcup \mathit{V\text{-}PP\_pobj}))$

5.3.2.2 Complex collocations

For complex collocations, we will show the formalisation of collocational chains, i. e. collocations that merge two collocations such that the base of one collocation is the collocate of the other. The definition states that a *CollocationalChain* is a *MergedCollocation* that merges a collocation which has a base that is the collocate of something that is merged in a collocational chain. The same applies to the collocate. Note, however, that this definition is only approximative and does not suffice for consistency checking purposes. For example, it could be the case that a collocational chain C_1 is defined which merges a collocation whose base is the collocate of a collocation that is merged in a different collocational chain C_2.

In other words, there is no way to ensure that C_1 and C_2 have to refer to the same instance of *CollocationalChain*. Although such a configuration would involve a considerable amount of ill intent during the editing of the lexical resource, it is nonetheless possible and would require a query-based consistency check if desired.

(5.12) $CollocationalChain \equiv MergedCollocation \sqcap$
$(\exists mergesCollocation.(\exists hasBase.(\exists isCollocateOf.(\exists isMergedIn.CollocationalChain)))) \sqcap$
$(\exists mergesCollocation.(\exists hasCollocate.(\exists isBaseOf.(\exists isMergedIn.CollocationalChain))))$

The last type of lexical entity to be discussed here is a specific kind of *RecursiveCollocation*, namely *V + (Prep + N)*. The definition states that a *V.Prep-N* collocation is a *RecursiveCollocation* whose base is a *Prep-N* collocation and whose collocate is something that has a verbal part of speech. Finally, collocations of type *V.Prep-N* are verb phrases.

(5.13) $V.Prep\text{-}N \equiv RecursiveCollocation \sqcap$
$(\exists hasBase.Prep\text{-}N) \sqcap$
$(\exists hasCollocate.(\exists hasPartOfSpeech.VERB)) \sqcap$
$(\exists hasPartOfSpeech.\{VerbPhrase\})$

5.4 Modelling Lexicographical Functions and NLP Requirements

As was mentioned in Section 2.3 above, the core aspect of a *multifunctional* lexical resource is its ability to serve multiple lexicographical functions as well as NLP applications. According to Tarp (2008), each of these functions is defined on the basis of types of potential users, user situations as well as user needs (cf. Section 2.2). Therefore, what is needed in order to be able to accommodate multiple functions in one lexical resource, as well as the possibility to serve the needs of NLP applications, is a formal tool that specifies which elements of the lexical description are needed in a particular situation and how they are presented to the user. In this section, we will present our interpretation of Tarp's account, and our approach to representing the relevant notions in our lexicon model.

5.4.1 Preliminary Remarks

Irrespective of whether one agrees with Tarp's classification, the following should be noted[25]. It seems intuitively correct that there are indications in a lexical entry that are more relevant to certain types of users in certain types of situations than to other users in different situations. The classification proposed in Tarp (2008) simply represents one way to account for this. Moreover, access to these indications needs to be different for different types of users in different user situations, as does the presentation of these indications. Therefore, there needs to be a way to ensure a uniform treatment of those "more relevant" and "less relevant" pieces of information across different user and situation types. Commercial dictionary writing systems such as iLEX (Erlandsen, 2004) or TLex (Joffe, 2009) offer ways to specify e. g. what a dictionary article should look like. However, the formal means of dealing with user

[25] This is in part intended as a response to justified criticism expressed by the audience of the eLEX 2009 conference in Louvain-la-Neuve, Belgium.

needs as outlined in this section do not only move away from detailed layout specifications for individual information pieces. They introduce a layer of abstraction that enables a parameterisation of the components which perform the actual presentation (e. g. microstructural specifications such as *»move indications that match primary needs up in the article«*), as well as a customisation of the lexical content that a user has access to (e. g. macrostructural filters like *»ignore this lexical item«*) – all this without touching the actual data. For these reasons, the suggestions in this section should be seen as orthogonal to mere layout specifications of lexical entries e. g. by means of XSLT, and it is in this context that the present approach needs to be positioned and evaluated.

5.4.2 Types of Users and User Situations

According to Tarp (2008), potential users are characterised by factors such as their mother tongue, their proficiency of the mother tongue (or the second language in question), as well as their general cultural and linguistic background. This not only means that e. g. sophisticated linguistic vocabulary like *"diaintegrative marking"* will not be understood by most of the users of a dictionary, but also that more basic vocabulary like *"grammatical gender"* or *"collocation"* should be presented to users in a form that makes it easy for them to understand the kinds of information that are presented to them. In addition to this, the language proficiency of the user can also have an effect on the kind of lexical data that should be presented. For example, specialised English vocabulary from the economic domain may not be among the suitable lexical candidates that a language learner who has just started learning the language should be exposed to. Therefore, a model of lexicographical functions needs to be powerful enough to enable such filters.

As for different types of user situations, Tarp (2008) distinguishes between *cognitive* and *communicative situations* (cf. Section 2.1). While the former term refers to situations in which a user wishes to acquire more knowledge e. g. about a given subject or a specific lexical item, the latter covers situations in which the user wishes to satisfy a specific communicative need, such as the desire to understand a text (receptive situation) or to write a text (productive situation). In addition, each of these situations may possibly involve the mother tongue, a second language, or both. According to Tarp, the specific situation a user is in has an immediate effect on his or her needs. For example, while a potential dictionary user in a text-productive situation may need to get information about collocational behaviour (e. g. *»which verb does 'Mord' usually combine with?«*; ⇒ *»Mord + begehen«* (*»to murder«*)), users in a text-receptive situation will typically only need information on those collocations whose meaning is non-compositional, such as idiomatic collocations (e. g. *»auf den Plan treten«* (*»to appear on the scene«*; literally: *»to step onto the plan«*)), since the meaning of other collocations can be inferred from their lexical components.

In sum, the type of potential users as well as the situation they are in determine their needs, i. e. the kinds of information that should be presented to them, as well as how they should be presented. Generalising over the types of users mentioned in Tarp (2008), this view can be extended to any other type of user or application for which there is a need to extract subsets of the data or their description, e. g. for a valence dictionary or a domain-specific dictionary.

5.4.3 Access and Presentation Status

As was discussed in Section 2.1 above, Tarp (2008) classifies different types of user needs as *function-related* (information-seeking) or *usage-related* (information- or instruction-seeking), depending on whether they occur in extra-lexicographical situations or whether they only occur when the lexicographical situation, i. e. the consultation of a dictionary, takes place. Tarp labels these different types of needs as *primary* and *secondary* needs respectively (cf. Tarp, 2008: p. 56f), where primary needs are those that cause potential dictionary users to become actual dictionary users, while secondary needs are those that arise in the actual dictionary users in order to satisfy their primary needs. From the point of view of the designer of a lexicon model, both types of needs have to be accounted for, either (i) by the way the user of the lexical resource has access to lexicographical data, or (ii) by the way these are presented to the user.

As for (i), for example, the user interfaces to the *Base lexicale du français*[26] (BLF; Verlinde *et al.* (2007); *lexical database for French*) and the *Ordbogen over faste vendinger*[27] (OFV; *the dictionaries of fixed expressions*) confront users with simple questions that should help them find the information they need. In the case of BLF, such a question is e. g. *»is it 'le' or 'la'?«*, which is directed towards users in a text-productive situation who are uncertain of the gender of a particular French lexical item. In OFV, users are confronted with the phrase *»I am looking for information in the dictionary because I want to have support in understanding an expression.«*[28]. In Tarp's terminology, both are direct ways of determining the communicative situation that a user is in, as well as his or her primary need[29], by means of offering predefined queries that take over from the user the task of posing a query him- or herself. Moreover, they predetermine the kinds of information that are presented, since users are only presented with the information that they have asked for. This prevents overloading the user with information.

Access-related issues also include needs which have been labelled *»... as lemmata«* in Tarp (2008). As was already discussed in Section 2.2, a need like *»orthographical variants/mistakes as lemmata«* (see e. g. table 4.3 in Tarp, 2008: p. 69) simply means that users should be able to have access to a lexical entry not only through the standard orthography of the respective lexical item, but also through variants or even misspellings. As such, point (i) rather affects the design of interfaces than the actual lexicographical data (cf. Section 6.2.2.1), and may not be solved by a model of lexicographical functions alone. However, a model may at least provide support in determining the way in which access to certain kinds of information is enabled. Primary needs could be regarded as those pieces of information that should be made accessible to the user, and as such, a model that specifies the *access status* of a kind of indication will certainly help to achieve this.

Point (ii) above is more closely linked to questions of modelling, and can be solved more easily by representational means. In general, it refers to the structure of a lexical entry, or more precisely, the structure of what is presented to a user as a result to a query. While this

---

26 http://ilt.kuleuven.be/blf/

27 http://www.ordbogen.com/opslag.php?dict=fvdd

28 The Danish original is *»Jeg søger information i ordbogen, fordi jeg vil have hjælp til at forstå en vending«*.

29 In fact, both *gender* and *meaning of idioms* are listed as primary needs in text production and text reception respectively (cf. tables 4.2 and 4.4 in Tarp, 2008: p. 69f).

can be accomplished by means of specific instructions in layout tools such as XSLT in a straightforward way, it seems more reasonable to have a formal means that generalises over particular types of indications and thus enables a uniform treatment of needs across different lexicographical functions.

These considerations suggest a model that defines the *presentation status* of indications with respect to specific types of user situations. As was mentioned before, Tarp's classification of primary and secondary needs provides a solid and extensible working basis for the definition of such a model. Moreover, this model can be used to capture types of users that differ with respect to their mother tongues or the proficiency level thereof, as well as with respect to their linguistic background.

For example, while it may be relevant for an expert lexicographer to know that *»Rede«* (*»speech«*) is the *base* of the collocation *»Rede halten«* (*»give a speech«*), this degree of detail may be confusing rather than helpful to users who are lexicographically less trained. For them, it suffices to learn that *»Rede«* combines with *»halten«*. As was shown in Section 5.1.3, the hierarchical organisation of classes and properties in OWL, along with the built-in subsumption inference, allow for a nice solution to this: while the lexical data specify that *»Rede«* and *»Rede halten«* are linked via the specific property *isBaseOf*, they are automatically inferred to be linked via the more general property *hasCollocationalRelationTo* property as well. In the context of user needs, one could state that for a user in a text-productive situation, *hasCollocationalRelationTo* has the presentation status of a relevant indication (*primary* in Tarp, 2008: p. 70), whereas *hasBase* is a property that should be ignored. Similarly, one could state e. g. that in terms of access, the distinction between quasi-synonymy and synonymy is not relevant for non-expert users, as they may be looking for a word *Y* that means (roughly) the same as a word *X*, without the need for *X* and *Y* to be strict synonyms. Therefore, the corresponding relations would be ignored in the search interface when accessing the lexical resource, whereas their superordinate relation *hasSynonymicRelationTo* is offered to non-expert users. At the level of presentation, however, it is important to indicate to a non-expert user that *Y* is only a *near* synonym of *X*. Therefore both *hasSynonym* and *hasQuasiSynonym* would be displayed in a lexical entry. This shows that indications which are relevant for presentation in a lexical entry, such as example sentences, are not necessarily relevant in the query form. Rather, access status specifications could e. g. be used to avoid overloading the user with search options.

In addition to determining *what* is relevant in which situation, this mechanism provides a rather elegant solution for hiding implementational details of the model, such as the class and relation hierarchies, from the user. For example, classes like *SyntacticallyComplexFreeUnit*, which have a formal justification as they are used for structuring the information in the model, need not be displayed to users and can thus be ignored in access to and presentation of the information. However, this mechanism does not express *how* e. g. *hasCollocationalRelationTo* needs to be presented to different types of users who differ, for example, with respect to their mother tongue or linguistic background knowledge. In order to achieve this, a model should not only specify the access and presentation status of an indication, but also the *labels* with which it is presented to different types of users in different languages. This will be explained in more detail in the following subsection.

5.4.4 Labels and Interface Languages

As was mentioned above, this part of the model refers to the characteristics of different types of users, such as their language proficiency or general linguistic knowledge. This means that individual pieces of lexicographical information need to be presented to different types of users in a different way. Coming back to the example discussed in the previous section, the *hasCollocationalRelationTo* edges between *»Rede«* and its collocations like *»Rede halten«* or *»flammende Rede«* may be presented to lexicographically proficient German users as *»Kollokationen«*, whereas it might be more appropriate to present them as *»Typische Wortverbindungen«* to a non-expert language learner. Moreover, respective English users might prefer the corresponding information in the form of *»Collocations«* and *»Typical word combinations«* respectively. In other words, each item of the metalanguage (i. e. classes like *SupportVerbConstruction*, properties like *hasSynonym* and instances like *AccusativeCase*) needs to have a label for different types of users and in various languages, so that users get the information they want in their preferred language, and in a form that they can understand. As these *interface languages* should be treated completely independently from both the metalanguage and the object language, it is advisable to introduce a separate layer on top of the linguistic model and the lexical content that deals with this user-specific content.

5.4.5 Putting Things Together: User Profiles

In order to accommodate all the findings discussed in the previous subsections, we propose to model a *user profile layer* on top of the lexical data and the linguistic model. In this layer, each individual user profile targets the needs of a particular group of users in a particular user situation. For example, while one profile could be designed for a linguistically untrained user in a text-receptive situation in the mother tongue, another profile would serve linguistically trained users in an L2 production situation. Each of these profiles is stored in a separate file and specifies – for all kinds of entities in the linguistic model – the access and presentation status and the labels in different interface languages. Moreover, this mechanism can be used to specify labels and status for the lexical data themselves. For example, one could specify that a word like the German *»gabelig«* (*»forked«*), which has an orthographic variant *»gablig«*, has the label *»gab(e)lig«*. Clearly, this is not a form that should as such be stored as value for the *hasOrthographicForm* property (cf. Section 5.1 above), since it does not match any of the individual variants and a search for "gab(e)lig" itself is rather unlikely. However, it may nonetheless be a valid form to present to a user, and thus, such forms can be specified as labels if desired. In addition to this, as was mentioned in Section 5.4.2, it may be necessary to define macrostrutural filters in case certain vocabulary is considered inappropriate for certain groups of users. Here, a special status could be assigned to those lexical items that should be filtered out. Figure 5.19 summarises the situation just described.

As can be seen in the figure, the user profile layer is situated on top of the linguistic model and the lexical data. This way, a clear separation of metalanguage (i. e. the linguistic model; cf. Sections 5.1 and 5.2), object languages (i. e. the dictionary content) and interface languages (i. e. the labels and languages; cf. Section 5.4.4) is achieved, which enables a straightforward adding of further profiles and thus an extension of the user profile layer. As can further be seen, each individual user profile file imports individual dictionary content files

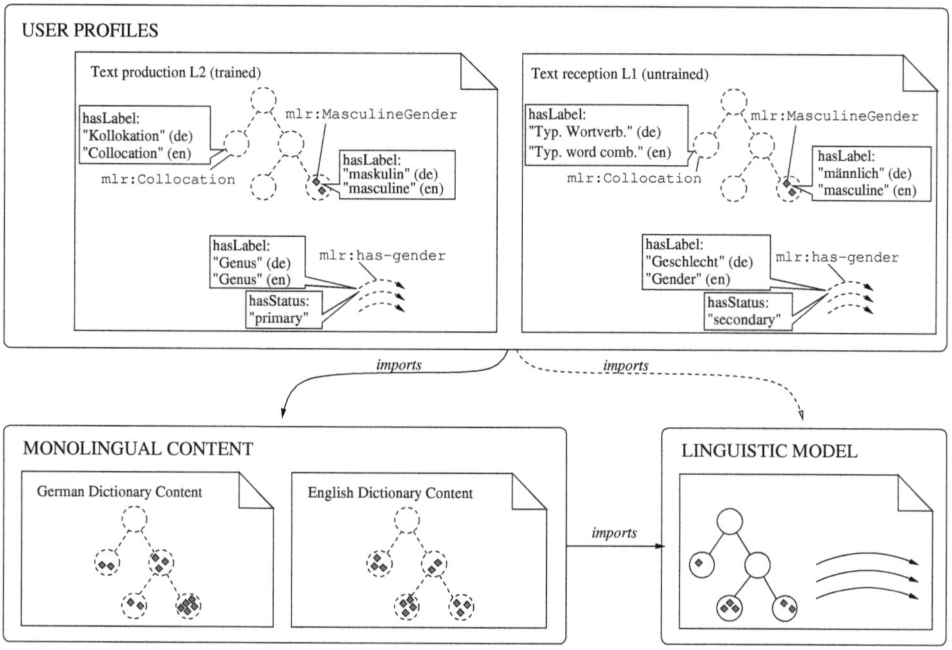

Figure 5.19: User profiles in relation to the lexicon model and data

– like e. g. a monolingual German dictionary or a monolingual English dictionary – so that the specification of labels for lexical items that was just mentioned can be done. Moreover, as the monolingual dictionaries import the linguistic model, and since imports are transitive in OWL, each user profile also imports the linguistic model and can thus assign access and presentation status as well as labels to linguistic data categories and indications defined there.

In more technical terms, as most data categories and indications are modelled as classes or properties, we need to be able to make statements not only about instances of classes, but also about classes and properties themselves. Since such *metaproperties* go beyond the expressivity of OWL DL, this means that we need to leave its computationally safe realms and use features that require OWL Full. However, it is important to note that this does not necessarily conflict with our intention to define our model with the means provided by OWL DL. Due to the independence of metalanguage, object language and interface language in our model, the computational properties of the model itself are not affected, and thus, the favourable features of OWL DL, such as consistency checking or inference, can still be performed by means of a description logic reasoner.[30]

In particular, we define metaproperties *hasLabel* and *hasStatus* (with subproperties *hasAccessStatus* and *hasPresentationStatus*), which have in their domain the metaclasses *owl:Thing*,

[30] See Section 5.5.1 for details on how this independence is achieved technically.

as well as *owl:Class* and *rdf:Property*. Since (i) each instance in the model is an instance of *owl:Thing*, (ii) each class is an instance of *owl:Class* and (iii) each property an instance of *rdf:Property*, all kinds of entities are covered. As for the ranges of our metaproperties, both *hasLabel* and *hasStatus* have the XML Schema datatype *xsd:string*. For *hasStatus*, however, the range is further restricted. Instead of allowing for all kinds of string values, the range is limited to the values *primary*, *secondary*, *ignore*, and *include* by means of the *owl:oneOf* construct (see Bechhofer *et al.*, 2004: Section 6.2). While *primary* and *secondary* refer to the status of user needs as defined by Tarp (2008)[31], *ignore* is a status that can be used for the definition of both macrostructural filters and as a means to spare users from hierarchical overhead and indications that are unnecessary for them (cf. Sections 5.4.2 and 5.4.3). The *include* status is primarily intended for kinds of indications that are more complex and whose descriptions are not immediately connected to the lexical item. One prominent example of this is the description of valence information, where e. g. the path from a lexical item (or a sense) to the syntactic category of its argument is *hasSyntacticValenceFrame* ∘ *hasSyntacticArgument* ∘ *hasSyntacticCategory*. For a primary need *syntactic properties*, which Tarp lists e. g. for text-productive situations, it would not make sense to assign primary status to *hasSyntacticCategory*, since it is not as such a syntactic property of the lexical item. Instead, the property *hasSyntacticValenceFrame*, which is basically the *entry point* to syntactic valence information, is assigned primary status, and the properties that follow in the chain are assigned the *include* status, such as the properties of *hasSyntacticArgument* and *hasSyntacticCategory*. However, even more basic indications like *hasExample* make use of this status, since the actual content of the example is stored in the property *hasContent*. For the module that performs the processing of this informations, this is like an instruction to follow this path and include the information in the processing.

5.4.5.1 Metamodel of user profiles

Since all user profiles have in common that they are defined by means of the *hasLabel* and *hasStatus* properties, it makes sense to define a sort of *metamodel* that imports the linguistic model and provides the necessary properties for making statements about the resources therein. Such a metamodel could then serve as a kind of template for the creation of specific user profiles. However, we still need a way to identify which profile a certain label or status description belongs to. For example, if we have a statement like *MasculineGender hasLabel "männlich"@de* in one profile and *MasculineGender hasLabel "maskulin"@de* in another, but both properties have been defined in the same metamodel, we need to make sure that the source of each statement can be identified easily. As was mentioned in Section 4.2.1 above, XML namespaces provide a nice solution to this issue.

Since each profile is defined in its own file, it can receive its own namespace. This means that we are able to define several *hasLabel* and *hasStatus* properties which can be addressed and differentiated by means of their namespaces (or the prefixes defined for these), e. g. *prefix1:hasLabel* vs. *prefix2:hasLabel*. In addition to this, though, we also need a way to capture

[31] At this point, it seems again necessary to refer to the fact that Tarp's classification is only taken as a basis, and that other status values could be used that seem more plausible to other lexicographers. As was mentioned above, the main point is that certain types of needs are treated uniformly across different user and situation types.

the fact that all of these *hasLabel* properties still describe essentially the same, e. g. if one wants to extract all *hasLabel* statements. One way of doing this would be to make use of the equivalence of their *local names*. However, we would not like to rely on methods that require string comparison or even parsing of entity names. Even if the naming scheme in a model should be as transparent as possible, internal names should not be used to convey information as such (cf. the comments on LMF in Section 5.2.4.3). In addition to this, from an application perspective, queries that involve string comparison or string-based filtering of results are typically less efficient than ones that make use of a more restricted pattern in the first place. This is because in a SPARQL pattern like the one in (5.14), all statements matching `?entity ?property ?label` – which would, in fact, be true of *all* statements in the resource – are extracted before the result is filtered for those matching `"hasLabel"`.

(5.14)
```
SELECT ?label
WHERE {?entity ?property ?label
       FILTER regex(str(?property), "hasLabel")}
```

This problem is aggravated if we not only want to extract the values for *hasLabel*, but also for *hasStatus*. If, on the other hand, we are able to restrict the possible values for the variable `?property` beforehand, only the relevant ones would be extracted. In order to achieve this restriction, we propose to organise the relevant metaproperties in a hierarchy that allows for the extraction using underspecified graph patterns in queries. In particular, we create a separate *user profile model*, which defines a general property *hasUserProfileRelationTo* that has the metaproperties *hasLabel* and *hasStatus* as subproperties. By keeping this user profile model separate from the linguistic model, we can ensure that the latter remains within the scope of description logics – which would not have been the case if it had contained metaproperties. A specific profile (e. g. text reception in the mother-tongue) then imports this user profile model and assigns to the entities defined therein a namespace prefix (e. g. *up:*). The effect is that *hasLabel* and *hasStatus* can then be addressed in the specific user profile by *up:hasLabel* and *up:hasStatus* respectively. However, in order to be able to differentiate between statements that originate from different profiles, each individual profile needs to have its own set of properties, so that e. g. the user status statements originating from a profile describing L1 text reception could be identified by means of *x recl1:hasStatus y*, whereas statements from an L2 production profile would be identified e. g. by *x prodl2:hasStatus y*. Therefore, an individual user profile defines its own *hasLabel* and *hasStatus* properties as subproperties of *up:hasLabel* and *up:hasStatus* respectively. In the end, the hierarchy of profile-relevant metaproperties looks like the one in Figure 5.20, with the profile-specific properties being subsumed by the general ones. The main advantage of this approach with respect to querying is that all labels can be extracted using the underspecified property *up:hasLabel*, all status information by means of *up:hasStatus*, and all profile-relevant statements in general by means of *up:hasUserProfileRelationTo*. In particular, the query that was shown in (5.14) can now be rephrased as follows.

(5.15)
```
SELECT ?label
WHERE {?entity up:hasLabel ?label}
```

Since *up:hasLabel* subsumes all more specific properties, such as *recl1:hasLabel*, *prodl2:hasLabel* and so on, the respective statements are extracted as well. Moreover, the predicate that

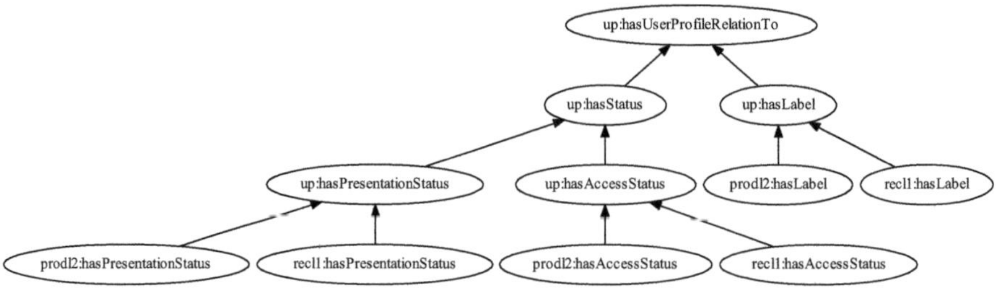

Figure 5.20: Hierarchy of user profile relations

stands between `?entity` and `?label` in the query is now restricted in the graph pattern already, and thus no filtering of the results needs to be performed.

5.4.5.2 Specific user profiles

In this subsection, we will present two specific user profiles that have been defined on the basis of the account in Tarp (2008). In particular, we will focus on parts of the definition of a user profile for text-receptive situations in the mother tongue (e. g. a native speaker of German reading a German text), and of a user profile for text-productive situations in a foreign language (e. g. a native speaker of German writing an English text). Moreover, we assume that the information that needs to be displayed in a lexical entry, i. e. the *presentation status* of the lexicographic indications, is primarily determined by Tarp's analysis. These specifications are complemented by label and status specifications for linguistically trained vs. untrained users, which we will discuss after having gone into the details of the types of situations.

As will become clear in the course of this discussion, for some types of information it is more straightforward to find an immediate counterpart in the lexicon model, while others may involve combinations of properties or non-trivial paths through the model graph. For example, due to the complexity of the description of lemmas and word forms and the thus necessary complexity of the model (cf. Section 5.2.3 above), the need for information about orthography involves a chain of at least two properties, starting from the *Form* instance via *hasFormDescription* and *hasOrthographicForm* to the actual string value (see Tables 5.6 and 5.7 on pages 120 and 122 respectively). However, although Tarp (2008) does not explicitly state this, the need for orthography commonly involves information on syllabification in productive situations as well. Therefore, *orthography* needs to be mapped to several properties.

Further needs may even refer to features that lie outside the scope of what a model of user needs can provide. For example, the primary need to obtain information about the meaning of a lemma can be met in several distinct ways: (i) users could be offered the choice to pick the relevant output indications in the consultation interface, e. g. »*Definitionen*«, »*Beispielsätze*«; (ii) users do not select their output indications, but are instead presented with the lexical entry in a way that makes meaning indications more salient or displays them further up in the entry; or (iii) a user could be asked a question like »What does x mean?« (cf. Tarp, 2008: p. 122; see also BLF).

Case (i) represents a *need-specific* consultation, and a model that provides access and presentation status of indications can support the organisation of the user interface, without actually selecting a complete user profile. In case (ii), the presentation of the user interface as well as the lexical entry is (more or less) completely determined on the basis of the model. Thus, we consider case (ii) a *profile-specific* consultation. Case (iii) is closely related to (i) except for the fact that a model of user needs can only be of very limited support. A question like »What does x mean?« needs to be hard-coded somewhere, as does the internal query into which it is to be translated. As this can be done in the actual user interface, it does not require a formalisation of user needs in the form of a model – at the cost of modularity and maintainability. In the following, we will mainly focus on solutions involving (i) and (ii), as these appear to be more interesting from a modelling perspective.

Text reception in a mother tongue

Meaning of lemmata. Although Tarp's conception and use of the term *lemma* seems rather suboptimal in this context, we interpret it in the way suggested by Piotrowski (2009: p. 485), namely as »any element that allows one access to an entry«. Thus, this first need has been searched for, including e. g. inflected word forms. Therefore, we map this kind of need to any kind of indication that we believe conveys the meaning of a lexical item. Among these are e. g. the properties *hasDefinition* or *hasExample*. As the actual string content is stored in the property *hasContent*, it receives the *include* presentation status. In contrast to Tarp, who lists lexical semantic relations like *hasSynonym* and *hasAntonym* only for productive situations for reasons of variety in expression, we include them also for the text-receptive situation, as we consider them useful in determining the correct meaning of a lexical item. Therefore, these properties get primary presentation status as well. Moreover, we can set the presentation status of *hasLexicalSemanticRelationTo* to *ignore*, as it does not contribute to the meaning as such.

Idioms and meaning of idioms. The need for idioms and their meaning is more straightforward. Here, we assign primary presentation status to the property *hasIdiom*. However, its superproperty *hasIdiomaticRelationTo* as well as its sibling *isIdiomOf* are not assigned primary presentation status. While *isIdiomOf* links an idiom to the components it consists of and may thus still be a relvant indication when viewing the lexical entry of the idiom, *hasIdiomaticRelationTo* can be ignored. Since meaning-related properties already have primary presentation status, no further steps are necessary here.

Proverbs and meaning of proverbs. Like the previous need, but with the properties *hasProverbialRelationTo*, *hasProverb* and *isProverbOf*.

Pragmatic and cultural restrictions. This need refers to pragmatic style or register indications. In our model, these are treated by means of diasystematic markings. Therefore, the subproperties of *hasMarking* receive primary presentation status.

Irregular inflection forms as lemmata. In straightforward terms, this need means that a user should be able to have access to a the lexical entry of »*gehen*« (»*to go*«) by searching for the irregular inflection form »*ging*« (»*went*«). In order to achieve this, any search for a lexical item should not only involve base forms, but also inflected forms. This can be achieved by generally mapping the search to *hasOrthographicForm*, since the form descriptions of base forms as well as inflected forms make use of this property. As *hasOrthographicForm* is only accesible via *hasFormDescription*, the latter receives *include* presentation status. As was mentioned in Section 5.1.1 above, a further way of dealing with this would be to have a morphological analyser that processes the search term and returns the matching lemma. This would be very much in line with Tarp's concept of a *leximat* (Tarp, 2008: p. 120ff). However, if word forms are not stored in the lexicon as full forms, then we are not able to make statements about them. For example, we might want to be able to say that the plural form »*Dekors*« of »*Dekor*« is far more common than the other plural form »*Dekore*«. This is only possible if both »*Dekors*« and »*Dekore*« are stored in the lexicon. Therefore, we say that this need is treated by means of the *hasOrthographicForm* property.

Lemmata. This need refers to lexical items in general. More explicitly, it means that users need to be able to search for lexical entries by means of lemmata, which is achieved by simply giving them a text field where they can specify the lemma. Therefore, no specific steps have to be done in the user profile model.

Orthography. Orthography is generally mapped to the property chain *hasFormDescription* ∘ *hasOrthographicForm*. Again, since *hasFormDescription* is only used to make *hasOrthographicForm* accessible, it receives *include* presentation status. In text-productive or proof-reading situations, the need for orthography also includes the property *hasSyllabification*. However, we do not consider it necessary in a receptive situation.

Orthographical variants as lemmata. As with irregular inflection forms, orthographic variants specify their written form by means of the *hasOrthographicForm* property. Thus, by mapping the search to this property, orthographical variants are captured as well.

Orthographical mistakes as lemmata. In contrast to the needs discussed so far, orthographic mistakes are not stored in any property value in the lexicon. On the one hand, this is due to the fact that listing all potential mistakes – frequent and »accidental« ones – would inflate the lexicon unnecessarily. On the other hand, much more elegant ways for dealing with this problem exist. For example, in case the search for a certain form results in an empty result set, one could start a search based on measures like edit distance (Levenshtein, 1966). Such a search would propose entries whose orthographic forms are closest to the term that has been searched for. This way, a search for »*persöhnlich*«, which is a common incorrect spelling of »*persönlich*« (»*personal*«), would point the user to the entry of »*persönlich*«, without actually storing »*persöhnlich*« as a potential misspelling of »*persönlich*«.

Word combinations as lemmata. This need refers to the need to be able to search for word comincations. Since MWEs have the presentation status of treatment units in our model, no further step is required.

Word class. This need can be mapped directly to the property *hasPartOfSpeech*, which is assigned primary presentation status.

Gender. As with the word class, the need for gender information can be mapped directly to a single property, namely *hasGender*.

Summary. Table 5.6 provides a quick summary of this user profile. In the table, every property or chain of properties is expressed relative to *Lexeme*, *Sense* or *Form*, as these represent the potential starting points. Those needs listed above the horizontal line are assigned primary presentation status, while those below have secondary presentation status. An asterisk ('*') indicates that the subproperties of the mentioned property are assigned the respective presentation status.

Text production in a foreign language

In this profile, we will only focus on those needs that have not been discussed in the previous profile, or which have to be treated in a fundamentally different way. These are *word formation*, *inflection*, *syntactic properties*, *L2 collocations*, and *L2 derivatives*.

Word formation. The need to have information on word formation can be mapped to the subproperties of *hasMorphologicalRelationTo*, namely *hasCompound/isCompoundOf* and *hasDerivation/isDerivationOf*.

Inflection. On the one hand, this need can be addressed by displaying the inflectional class with an appropriate label, e. g. the statement *Frau hasDmorInflectionalClass NFem_0_en* as *"Flexion: -, -en"*. In the mother tongue, a trained user can be expected to be able to match *"-, -en"* to the genitive singular and nominative plural respectively, and to be able to infer all the remaining forms in the paradigm. However, this is not necessarily the case of language learners – irrespective of whether they are linguistically trained or not. Similar to the need »irregular inflection forms as lemmata« discussed in the text-receptive situation on page 118, we have the possibility to store all inflection forms as full forms in the lexicon and to display them according to their *hasOrthographicForm* and morpho-syntactic properties like *hasNumber*, *hasCase* or *hasTense*. Admittedly, this would mean an incredibly large number of forms to be stored. Therefore, another way of dealing with this is to make use of a morphological NLP tool that generates on demand all the forms in the paradigm on the basis of the inflectional class that a lexical item belongs to. In this case, the actual treatment of this need lies outside of the scope of the user need model. Therefore, a solution that involves the user need model would assign a presentation status to the properties mentioned above. We emphasise, however, that a solution involving a morphological generator would be the preferred one.

Type of information in (Tarp, 2008)	Presentation status of properties: Primary	Include
Meaning of lemmata	*hasDefinition*, *hasExample*, *hasExplanation*, *hasSynonymicRelationTo**, *hasAntonymicRelationTo**	*hasContent*
Idioms	*hasIdiom*	
Meaning of idioms	meaning indications	*hasIdiom*
Proverbs	*hasProverb*	
Meaning of proverbs	meaning indications	*hasProverb*
Pragmatic and cultural restrictions	*hasMarking**	
Irregular inflection forms as lemmata	search covers all values of *hasOrthographicForm*	*hasFormDescription*
	Secondary	Include
Lemmata	treated in interface	
Orthography	*hasOrthographicForm*	*hasFormDescription*
Orthographical variants as lemmata	search covers all values of *hasOrthographicForm*	*hasFormDescription*
(Orthographical mistakes as lemmata)	tolerant search	
Irregular inflection forms as lemmata	search covers all values of *hasOrthographicForm*	*hasFormDescription*
Word combinations as lemmata	word combinations are treatment units	
Word class	*hasPartOfSpeech*	
Genus	*hasGender*	

Table 5.6: Primary and secondary needs of linguistically untrained users in a text-receptive situation in the mother tongue

Syntactic properties. The need for syntactic properties refers to general syntactic usage of the lexical item. This includes syntactic valence descriptions as well as morpho-syntactic preferences. Due to the complexity of the valence description, a lot of properties receive *include* presentation status, such as the subproperties of *hasSyntacticArgument*, *hasLexicalRealisation* or *usesFrame*. However, the main property that is assigned *primary* presentation status is the one that actually introduces the syntactic valence description, namely *hasSyntacticValenceFrame*. On the side of morpho-syntactic preferences, the properties that are assigned primary presentation status are the subproperties of *hasMorphoSyntacticPreference*, such as *hasNumberPreference* or *hasDeterminationPreference*.

L2 collocations. For addressing this need, we assign primary presentation status to the direct subproperties of *hasCollocationalRelationTo*, namely *hasCollocation* and *isCollocationOf*.

L2 derivatives. This need is very generally mapped to the property *hasDerivation* and *isDerivationOf*.

Summary. Table 5.7 summarises the mappings between Tarp's user needs and the entities in our model.

Linguistically trained vs. untrained users

In the following, we complement the analyses shown on the previous pages with specifications based on the linguistic background of the user. This includes defining "understandable" labels for users with varying linguistic background – such as *"Stil"/"Style"* for *hasDiaphasicMarking* or *"Typische Wortverbindung"/"Typical word combination"* for *Collocation* –, as well as different presentation and access status specifications indicating what should be offered in the query form and lexical entry presentation respectively. To illustrate the general approach, we limit the discussion to a selection of subproperties of *hasLexicalSemanticRelationTo*.

As can be seen in Table 5.8, the status specifications of lexical-semantic relations are rather different depending on the linguistic background knowledge of a user. We assume that untrained users need not be aware of the difference between synonyms and quasi-synonyms for the purpose of querying the lexicon. In other words, if linguistically untrained users wish to query for (near) synonyms of a word, they are offered e. g. "Means (roughly) the same as" in the interface. This is the label of *hasSynonymicRelationTo*, the superproperty of both *hasSynonym* and *hasQuasiSynonym*, and therefore subsumes the more specific properties as well. As was mentioned on page 111 above, however, the distinction between strict and near synonyms is relevant to untrained users when displaying a lexical entry. Therefore, the specific properties have the corresponding presentation status and are displayed as "Means the same as" and "Means roughly the same as" respectively. As for linguistically trained users, the distinction between synonyms and quasi-synonyms is relevant both with respect to access and presentation, and can thus be displayed with accurate labels in linguistic terminology.

When combining these specifications with the ones for text-receptive and text-productive situations discussed on the previous pages, indications which are irrelevant for specific user

Type of information in (Tarp, 2008)	Presentation status of properties: Primary	Include
L2 words		
• orthography	*hasOrthographicForm*, *hasHyphenation*	*hasFormDescription*
• word class	*hasPartOfSpeech*	
• genus	*hasGender*	
• pragmatic and cultural restrictions	*hasMarking**	
• inflection	*hasWordForm*	*hasFormDescription*, *hasOrthographicForm*, *hasNumber*, *hasCase*, *hasTense*
• word formation	*hasMorphologicalRelationTo**	
• (morpho-)syntactic properties	*hasSyntacticValenceFrame*, *hasMorphoSyntacticPreference**	*usesFrame*, *hasSyntacticArgument**, *hasSyntacticCategory*, *hasCase*, *hasLexicalRealisation*, *argument*, *lexicalItem*
L2 collocations	*hasCollocation*, *isCollocationOf*	
L2 idioms	*hasIdiom*	
L2 proverbs	*hasProverb*	
L2 derivatives	*hasDerivation*	
L2 synonyms, antonyms, hyponyms, etc.	*hasLexicalSemanticRelationTo**	
	Secondary	Include
L2 lemmata	treated in interface	
• orthography	*hasOrthographicForm*, *hasHyphenation*	*hasFormDescription*
• word class	*hasPartOfSpeech*	
• genus	*hasGender*	
Orthographical variants as lemmata	search covers all values of *hasOrthographicForm*	*hasFormDescription*
(Orthographical mistakes as lemmata)	tolerant search	
Meaning of L2 lemmata	*hasDefinition*, *hasExample*, *hasExplanation*	*hasContent*
Meaning of L2 idioms	meaning indications	*hasIdiom*
Meaning of L2 proverbs	meaning indications	*hasProverb*

Table 5.7: Primary and secondary needs of linguistically trained users in a text-productive situation in a foreign language – production directly in the foreign language

MLR entity	Trained			Untrained		
	A	P	Label	A	P	Labels
hasLexicalSemanticRelationTo						
hasSynonymicRelationTo				×		"Means (roughly) the same as"
hasSynonym	×	×	"Synonym"		×	"Means the same as"
hasQuasiSynonym	×	×	"Quasi-synonym"		×	"Means roughly the same as"
hasAntonymicRelationTo				×		"Means (roughly) the opposite of"
hasAntonym	×	×	"Antonym"		×	"Means the opposite of"
hasQuasiAntonym	×	×	"Quasi-antonym"		×	"Means roughly the opposite of"

Table 5.8: A(ccess) and P(resentation) status and labels for linguistically trained vs. untrained users (× marks a property as being displayed)

types are ignored even though they are relevant with respect to the situation type. To see that this is reasonable, consider a linguistically trained user in a text-receptive situation. According to Table 5.6, all subproperties of *hasLexicalSemanticRelationTo* are considered relevant. However, the user-specific profile for trained users specifies that *hasLexicalSemanticRelationTo* itself, as well as *hasSynonymicRelationTo* and *hasAntonymicRelationTo*, are irrelevant for both access and presentation. Therefore, these three relations are hidden from the linguistically trained user, and only the specific relations which are in fact relevant are displayed.

5.4.6 NLP Profiles

In contrast to the user needs discussed in the previous subsection, the situation for NLP applications is fundamentally different. On the one hand, it seems difficult to transfer the classification of primary and secondary needs, which is based on the notion of *potential dictionary users* in *communicative situations*, to the field of NLP. For example, while it is conceivable that an NLP tool like a syntactic parser has specific needs, such as the one to obtain information on the syntactic behaviour of a lexical item or on its word class, it seems critical to assume that any of these needs has a different status than any other one: both of them have to be made available, and have to be extractable from the resource when needed. Besides, NLP tools very often serve more than one purpose, and thus the creation of a clear-cut typology with well-defined needs is not always possible. In addition to this, the typical interaction of an NLP tool with the lexical resource would not be based on what the lexicographer thinks is necessary for a certain type of NLP tool, but rather on what the tool needs for a specific task. This indicates that the interaction should rather be approached by an application programming interface (API) that provides methods that allow for the extraction of word class information as well as all valence-related information from the lexicon. As all this is done with respect to the same underlying data source, the lexical resource is truely multifunctional. On the other hand, it is conceivable to specify certain labels for specific pieces of information. For example, it may be beneficial for the extraction of valence information to make use of labels for the entities that represent the syntactic features, e. g. *"Object"* or *"NP"*. Such specifications could also be hard-coded in the API, but a modularisation of this part of the description makes it more adaptable at a later stage. Therefore, it is conceivable to create an API that makes use of an external file that specifies labels for the internal names in the model. The API will be explained in detail in Section 6.3.1.

5.5 Architecture of the MLR Model

The previous sections have introduced the different components of the MLR model and shown how they are used to capture different aspects of a lexical resource. In this section, we will illustrate how these components are organised into different layers, as well as how these layers are interrelated. In addition to this, Section 5.5.3 will summarise the quantitative aspects of the model, such as the number of classes and properties that have been defined.

5.5.1 Interrelationships between Components of the MLR Model

The basic component of the MLR model is the *Linguistic Model.* As was mentioned in Sections 5.1 and 5.2, it consists of a lexical part and a descriptive part which are indicated by means of the *LexicalEntity* and *DescriptiveEntity* classes. However, it is also possible to organise the linguistic model with a higher degree of modularity than the one presented above. In addition to distinguishing between these two classes, one could also physically separate them by storing them in two different OWL files. This way, lexical entities and descriptive entities would be part of different models and would receive different namespaces. In the MLR model, it has not been done since it was considered more practicable to be able to address all entities in the linguistic model by means of the same namespace prefix, e. g. in the context of designing a graphical user interface to the lexicon (see Section 6.2.2.1). However, the two classes could still be separated physically at a later stage if desired.

On top of the linguistic model is defined the *Monolingual Content Model.* Technically, this model consists of a file that imports the linguistic model and serves as a template for creating specific monolingual content files. In other words, a content file for monolingual German dictionary data is a copy of the monolingual content model which instantiates the lexical classes therein and has its own unique namespace. In addition to the linguistic model and the monolingual content model, the MLR model contains a *User Profile Model* which provides properties for specifying the access to as well as the presentation of the dictionary data, and labels with which the information will be shown to the user (see Section 5.4). The user profile

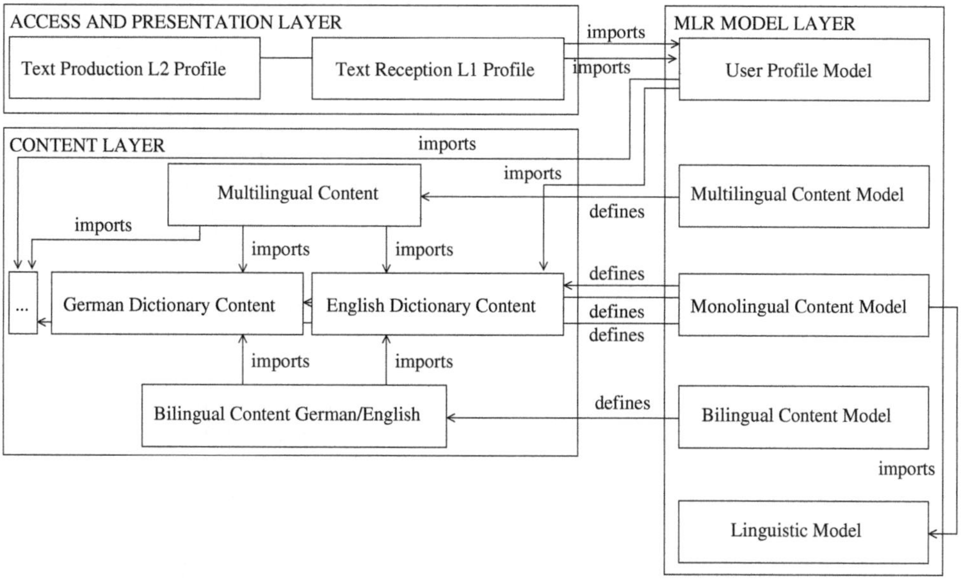

Figure 5.21: The different components of the MLR model and their interrelationships

model is imported by the specific user profiles, each of which adds its own subproperties to the ones defined in the user profile model and formalises the needs of a particular type of user in a particular situation.

In total, the various components which make up the MLR model (i. e. the linguistic model, the content model and the user profile model) constitute the *MLR Model Layer*, whereas the individual content files as well as the individual user profiles constitute the *Content Layer* and the *Access and Presentation Layer*. As was mentioned at the beginning of this chapter, this separation of layers reflects the distinction between *metalanguage* – represented by the MLR model layer –, *object language* (content layer) and *interface language* (access and presentation layer). This is summarised in Figure 5.21.

5.5.2 Bilingual and Multilingual Perspectives

In addition to the monolingual content model, the MLR model layer contains models for bilingual and multilingual content as well. As can be seen in Figure 5.21, we propose to model bilingual and multilingual dictionary content by creating views on several monolingual dictionaries (see also Spohr and Heid (2006) and Polguère (2009)). In the case of bilingual dictionary content, this is achieved by means of the *Bilingual Content Model*, which provides a symmetric relation for directly linking lexical items (*hasTranslationEquivalent*), as well as the *hasParaphrase* property for specifying paraphrases in cases where there is no direct correspondence of a particular lexical entity in the other language. As pointed out by Spohr and Heid (2006), such paraphrases do not affect the monolingual dictionaries in any way, as they are part of the bilingual dictionary only. This is ensured by the unique namespace that is assigned to a particular bilingual content file, and thus to the *hasTranslationEquivalent* and *hasParaphrase* properties. Technically, a bilingual content file is a copy of the bilingual content model which imports two monolingual dictionary content files and links their lexical entities by means of these relations. This way of dealing with bilingual dictionaries without affecting the monolingual dictionaries they are made up of indicates that the model proposed here offers an elegant solution to a problem that seems to be an unresolved issue in the otherwise rather flexible and unrestricted lexical systems approach (see Polguère (2009): p. 54).

For modelling multilingual dictionary content, we propose to devise an *interlingua* – similar e. g. to the *interlingual index* in EuroWordNet (Vossen, 1998) – to which the lexical entities in the individual monolingual content files are linked (see also Sérasset and Mangeot-Lerebours (2001)). This interlingua is defined as part of the *Multilingual Content Model*, along with a *denotes* relation that is used for linking the lexical entities to the concepts of the interlingua. Similar to the bilingual content, the multilingual content file imports several monolingual content files and links their lexical entities to the interlingua defined in the multilingual content model, by means of the *denotes* relation.

As pointed out by Tarp, »traditional learner's dictionaries that are *either* monolingual or bilingual only have a limited useful value« (Tarp, 2008: p. 151). By modelling bilingual dictionaries as combinations of monolingual dictionaries on the basis of a single underlying database, the architecture proposed in the MLR model offers an elegant way of representing a dictionary that can be both monolingual *and* bilingual, and which provides the relevant data depending on the specific communicative situation.

In order to ensure a monolingual consultation, the search can always be restricted to those entities which are defined in a specific monolingual dictionary. This can be done e. g. by means of filtering for the respective XML namespace (cf. Spohr and Heid, 2006), to ensure that all the entities and relations that are displayed to a user are part of the particular monolingual content file that is relevant in the respective situation.

As was discussed in the context of a user profile for an L2 text-productive situation in Section 5.4.5, Tarp's account of user needs distinguishes between those needs which refer to the L1, and those which refer to the L2. For example, in the aforementioned situation, a user needs to be given information on L2 orthography and the meaning of L2 lemmata, while this information is not relevant for the lexical items of the L1. However, for some users German is the L1 and e. g. English is the L2, whereas for other users English is the L1 and German the L2. So how can a single monolingual dictionary function as an L1 dictionary for some users, while it represents an L2 dictionary for other users? Here, the XML namespace technology can be used in combination with SPARQL. In particular, it is possible assign prefixes like *l1:* or *l2:* to particular namespaces within a SPARQL query. While the namespace of an entity is fixed, the prefix can be assigned to it dynamically at the point the consultation takes place, i. e. the moment the query is stated. This way, as is shown in (5.16) and (5.17), a prefix like *l2:* can in one SPARQL query identify instances of the German monolingual dictionary and in a later consultation refer to instances of the English monolingual dictionary, while the SPARQL query itself remains the same. For the generation of lexical entries, one can then e. g. define processing instructions for instances within the namespace indicated by the *l1:*

prefix and the *l2:* prefix respectively, without having the need to use the actual namespace.

(5.16)
```
PREFIX l1:  <http://www.example.org/english.owl#>
PREFIX l2:  <http://www.example.org/german.owl#>
SELECT ...
```

(5.17)
```
PREFIX l1:  <http://www.example.org/german.owl#>
PREFIX l2:  <http://www.example.org/english.owl#>
SELECT ...
```

5.5.3 Metrics of the MLR Model

In the final section of this chapter, we provide some quantitative details on the model, in terms of the number of entities that have been defined. As was mentioned at the beginning of this chapter, the core component of the MLR model is the *linguistic model*, and the other models basically represent views onto the data in the lexical resource. The linguistic model itself has been defined within the scope of OWL DL, which has been achieved by storing the metaproperties which are required for the definition of user profiles separate from the linguistic model. More precisely, the expressivity of the linguistic model is equivalent to the $\mathcal{SHOIN}$(D) description logic, as it makes use of all the constructs available in OWL DL. Table 5.9 shows the numbers for the different kinds of entities in the model. Note, however, that these numbers do not include any instances of lexical entities, as they are part of the lexical data and thus not included in the MLR model.

Type of entity	Lexical part	Descriptive part
Class	71	1,229
Property/relation	55	6,557
Individual	0	522

Table 5.9: Number of entities in the MLR model

6 Towards a Multifunctional Lexical Resource

While the previous chapter has focused on the model for a multifunctional lexical resource (MLR) and discussed in detail its components, this chapter is devoted to the discussion of how it can be integrated into an architecture for an MLR that contains modules for storing, accessing and presenting the content of the lexical resource to different kinds of users. This discussion will first deal with the acquisition of lexical data from different existing resources (Section 6.1.1) and then focus on the definition of mechanisms which ensure the consistency and integrity of both model and data by means of description logic axioms, as well as through SeRQL queries (see Section 6.1.2). The workflow of these processes, from the initial data extraction and unification to the storage of consistent lexical content, is summarised in Section 6.1.3.

In addition to this, we will demonstrate how the structure of the MLR model and the representations therein can support the definition of a graphical user interface (GUI; see Section 6.2) that enables user-oriented access to as well as function-based presentation of the data in the lexicon. Similarly, we will provide details on the application programming interfaces that can be used by NLP applications in order to access the MLR data directly or to export them in a standard exchange format (Section 6.3). Finally, Section 6.4 sketches a potential architecture for a multifunctional lexical resource that combines all of these aspects.

6.1 Lexicon Compilation

6.1.1 Extraction and Unification of Data from Existing Resources

Before we turn to the discussion of the modules just mentioned, we will provide details on the extraction and unification of data that we have taken from two different resources for German, namely the SALSA corpus release 1.0[1] and a database of collocations that has been acquired at the Institute for Natural Language Processing of the University of Stuttgart (see Weller and Heid, 2010). This has been done in order to have a solid background against which to evaluate the processability of the representations in the MLR model, as well as their scalability when dealing with considerable amounts of data. The data as well as the extraction and unification process will be described in the following subsection. The result of this process in terms of the number of entities contained in the MLR is summarised on page 133.

6.1.1.1 Data sources and relevant lexicographic information

SALSA corpus release 1.0. The *Saarbrücken Lexical Semantics Acquisition* (SALSA) corpus (Burchardt *et al.*, 2006) is a manually created German corpus resource containing annotation on multiple layers of linguistic description. In particular, it adds a layer of lexical-

[1] Downloadable from http://www.coli.uni-saarland.de/projects/salsa/corpus/.

semantic annotation to the morphologically and syntactically annotated TIGER treebank (Brants *et al.*, 2002). For this annotation, SALSA uses the FrameNet paradigm (Baker *et al.*, 1998), where a *frame* represents a prototypical situation (e. g. a *commercial transaction*) and comes with its set of *frame elements* (or semantic roles) which represent the participant or props that are involved in this situation (e. g. *buyer*, *seller* and *goods*). A frame is said to be *evoked* by a *frame-evoking element*, which is called the *target* of the frame annotation. In the case of SALSA, the focus of the annotation has been on verbs, which means that a vast majority of the frame targets are verbs. In general, however, a frame can also be evoked by lexical units of other word classes, such as nouns or adjectives. According to Burchardt *et al.* (2008a), the SALSA corpus release 1.0 features more than 16,500 frame annotations for about 500 lemmas in over 13,000 sentences. These annotations are either available in one very large XML file, or as several individual XML files, with each file containing the annotations of a particular lemma. Since the latter option can be processed much more efficiently, we have opted for this one (see also Section 6.1.2.2). In particular, this means that we create one output OWL file for each input XML file.

As was mentioned in Section 5.2.4.6, collocations have been annotated in the SALSA corpus by means of a SUPPORT frame, which is evoked by the main predicate of the collocation and assigns to its argument the SUPPORTED role. For example, a collocation like »*in Schwung bringen*« (»*to leverage*«) is annotated as *[in Schwung*$_{\text{SUPPORT.SUPPORTED}}$*] bringen*. On the one hand, this strategy makes them fairly easy to extract. On the other hand, however, further arguments that the collocation might have are ignored. Therefore, although in a sentence like »*Die Maßnahmen brachten die Wirtschaft in Schwung.*« (»*The measures have leveraged the economy.*«) we would say that »*die Wirtschaft*« is an argument of the collocation, it is not annotated as such, and can therefore not be extracted. Nonetheless, the SALSA corpus contains very detailed syntactic and semantic valence information for verbal targets and thus represents an ideal resource for filling the MLR model with data. In particular, we have identified the following kinds of information that can be extracted from the SALSA corpus and fed into the MLR model.

Instances of *Lexeme*, *Form* and *Sense*. For each frame annotation, one can check if the frame-evoking element has already been created as a *Lexeme*. If this is not the case, then the *Lexeme* instance can be created, along with the *Form* instance, which is linked to the lexeme by means of *hasLemma/isLemmaOf*. In the case of annotations of the SUPPORT frame, the lexeme and the lemma need to be constructed on the basis of the frame-evoking element as well as the contents of the SUPPORTED role.

For each combination of a lexeme with a particular frame, a *Sense* instance is created. For example, we create a single instance for all frame annotations of »*bringen*« with the PLACING frame, and one instance for all its annotations with BRINGING. In fact, this represents a very nice way of distinguishing between senses internally – as opposed to having only e. g. »*bringen*$_1$« and »*bringen*$_2$«. This way, it is possible to check whether a certain sense has already been created[2]. In addition to this, the sentence that contains the respective frame annotation can be extracted and linked to the sense.

[2] This refers only to the *internal representation* of the sense. It may be perfectly appropriate to *present* the different senses as »*bringen*$_1$«, »*bringen*$_2$« etc. to the user. However, if the senses have to be identified like this internally, then it is very difficult to determine whether a specific sense has already been created, especially in a setting where the data are not derived manually.

Lexical-semantic relations. One of the assumptions underlying FrameNet is that synonyms and antonyms are usually defined within the same frame. However, the exact nature of this relation is left unspecified. For example, while the lexical units »*new*«, »*old*« and »*fresh*« all evoke the AGE frame, the lexical-semantic relations between them are different. The relation between »*new*« and »*fresh*« could be considered a case of *quasi synonymy*, whereas »*new*« and »*old*« stand in an antonym relation to each other (see e. g. Burchardt *et al.*, 2005). Therefore, in order to still make use of the information that items which evoke the same frame are semantically related, we can link them by means of the general *hasLexicalSemanticRelationTo* property. For the purpose of evaluating the representations in the MLR model, this degree of detail suffices and, in fact, this shows how underspecified information can be accommodated in the MLR model as well.

Syntactic and semantic valence information. For the extraction of semantic valence information, the strategy is to represent frame annotations in the MLR model as semantic valence frames. In other words, for an annotation of »*bringen*« with the PLACING frame, an instance of the *SemanticFrame* subclass *Placing* is created. For each annotated frame element in this frame annotation, a *ValenceArgument* instance is created and linked to the instance representing the respective syntactic category. Moreover, the *Placing* instance is linked to these *ValenceArgument* instances using the properties that represent the respective semantic roles.

In order to extract information on the syntactic functions realised by the arguments of the frame annotation, the path through the functional edges in the syntactic annotation tree is followed (cf. Burchardt *et al.*, 2008a: p. 22f). Depending on the governable syntactic functions that are identified this way, an instance of the corresponding *SyntacticFrame* subclass (e. g. *SubjectObjectFrame*) is created and linked via the syntactic function properties to the *ValenceArgument* instances that have been created before. The resulting statements for an annotation of »*bringen*« with the PLACING frame are as follows.

(6.1)	*Lexeme_bringen*	*hasSyntacticValenceFrame*	$SynFrame_1$
	$Sense\_bringen_1$	*hasSyntacticValenceFrame*	$SynFrame_1$
	$Sense\_bringen_1$	*hasSemanticValenceFrame*	$SemFrame_1$
	$SemFrame_1$	*rdf:type*	*Placing*
	$SynFrame_1$	*rdf:type*	*SubjectObjectFrame*
	$Arg_{1/2/3}$	*rdf:type*	*ValenceArgument*
	$SemFrame_1$	*Placing.Cause*	Arg_1
	$SemFrame_1$	*Placing.Theme*	Arg_2
	$SemFrame_1$	*Placing.Goal*	Arg_3
	$SynFrame_1$	*subject*	Arg_1
	$SynFrame_1$	*accObject*	Arg_2
	$SynFrame_1$	*adjunct*	Arg_3
	Arg_1	*hasSyntacticCategory*	*NounPhrase*
	Arg_2	*hasSyntacticCategory*	*NounPhrase*
	Arg_3	*hasSyntacticCategory*	*PrepositionPhrase*

As is shown in the statements above, a syntactic frame is linked to both the lexeme and the sense, whereas instances representing semantic valence frames are attached to the respective *Sense* instance (cf. Section 5.2.4 above).

Frequency counts. For each annotation of a particular frame with a lexeme, the frequency count of the corresponding *Sense* instance can be increased, as well as the frequency of recurring identical frames. As was mentioned in Section 5.2.4, this means that the sense is linked to a *FrequencyDescription* instance by means of *hasFrequencyDescription*, which is in turn linked to the respective valence frames via *describes*. This way, we can extract frequency information for lexemes, for the senses of a lexeme, for a syntactic frame with respect to a lexeme and with respect to a sense, as well as for a semantic frame with respect to a sense. For example, $SynFrame_1$ in (6.1) has a frequency of 20 with respect to the PLACING reading of *»bringen«* and a frequency of 18 with respect to its BRINGING reading, with the total frequency of the PLACING reading of *»bringen«* being 33. In order to be able to interpret these frequencies correctly, the respective frequency descriptions specify the source of the frequency as "SALSA".

Collocations DB of Weller and Heid (2010). The second data source is a DB of automatically extracted syntactic patterns (e. g. *noun + verb* or *adjective + noun + verb*) along with frequency counts of several morpho-syntactic features. For example, the entry of *»in Schwung bringen«* states that it has occurred 87 times, that in 84 of these occurrences the base has been in the singular and in 86 without a determiner, and that in 73 cases it has subcategorised a direct object. In addition to this, an entry specifies the head noun of the base of the collocation, which is trivial in the case of *»in Schwung bringen«*. In a collocation like *»auf Talfahrt befinden«* (*»to tumble«*), however, the entry specifies that *»Fahrt«* is the head noun of the compound *»Talfahrt«*. Such information can be used to check e. g. if a collocation that replaces the compound base with the head noun (i. e. *»auf Fahrt befinden«*) exists as well.

The database contains millions of entries for the syntactic patterns that have been used in the automatic extraction, not all of which can be considered valid MWEs in the sense that they should be stored in a lexicon. According to Weller and Heid (2010), manual investigation of the 500 most frequent entries of each pattern reveals that the *preposition + noun + verb* pattern and the *noun + verb* pattern provide the best results. Therefore, the strategy that will be followed here is to look up in the DB the *Noun + Verb* and *Noun + PP* collocations that have been extracted from the SALSA corpus, and to unify their representations with the information from the DB. In order to get a better impression as to the scalability of the MLR, we further add the 2,500 most frequent entries of each of these two types. For this, we process an XML file[3] that contains both these most frequent collocations and the ones contained in the SALSA corpus (which are not necessarily among the top 2,500 ones from the collocations DB), order the entries by their verb lemma, and check whether an OWL file exists for the respective verb lemma. If this is the case, we unify the representations of the collocations which have been annotated in SALSA with the information from the DB. Collocations which are not part of the respective SALSA OWL file are simply added. In case there is no existing OWL file for a particular verb lemma – i. e. it has not been annotated in SALSA – we create a new OWL file for that lemma and create the respective instances according to the data in the XML file. In particular, the following types of information can be extracted from the DB.

Morpho-syntactic preferences. Each collocation that has been extracted from the SALSA corpus on the basis of the SUPPORT frame can be looked up in the DB in order to retrieve

[3] I should like to thank Marion Weller for making these data available.

its frequency count as well as that of its morpho-syntactic properties. On the basis of these figures, it is possible to calculate morpho-syntactic preferences. For this calculation, we need to apply different strategies. For example, while it might be considered a preference if in 60% of the occurrences the base noun had an indefinite article (as opposed to definite, demonstrative or possessive determiners), it is not necessarily a preference if the base occurred with any kind of determiner in 60% of the cases. In the following, we provide details on the heuristics used in order to determine whether a particular collocation has a morpho-syntactic preference. These represent values which have been considered reasonable values for the identification of preferences, but which can also be altered at any time if more reasonable values are determined.

Number, polarity, reflexivity and determiner preferences:
: In order to have any of these preferences, we define that the relative frequency of one of the possible values (e. g. plural vs. singular number, negative vs. positive polarity or definite vs. indefinite vs. demonstrative determiner) is at least 60%. It should be noted that due to the fact that the data have been extracted automatically, the number value cannot always be determined unambiguously. Therefore, for number preferences, the frequency is calculated relative to the unambiguous cases only. Similarly, in the case of determiner preferences, the frequency is relative to cases which have any determination only.

Determination and modification preferences:
: A *DeterminationPreference* or *ModificationPreference* instance is created if the relative frequency of having any determiner or modification is at least 75% – then we have a positive preference – or if it is below 25%, in which case there is a negative preference. We do not consider the range between 75% and 25% to express any preference with respect to determination or modification, although the appropriateness of this threshold would need empirical investigation.

Fusion preferences:
: This kind of preference only applies to collocations which contain at least a preposition and a noun, e. g. $V + PP_prep - object$, and indicates whether the preposition and the determiner of the base noun are fused. For example, in the collocation »*ans Licht kommen*« (»*to appear; to come to light*«) the preposition »*an*« and the determiner »*das*« of the base noun are always fused to »*ans*«. As fusion applies to definite articles only, the calculation of this kind of preference is relative to cases with definite articles only. In general, we say that a fusion preference exists if at least 20% of the occurrences have a definite article (since there are five types of determiners which are distinguished in the DB), and if at least 75% of them are fused. The threshold of 20% is used in order to exclude cases where in e. g. one of the 100 occurrences the base had a definite article that was fused with the preposition, whereas the remaining 99 occurrences have been with an indefinite article.

Syntactic valence information:
: The final kind of information is not so much a preference as an indication of the syntactic valence of the collocation. For collocations which have a direct object in at least 25% of the cases, we create a *SubjectObjectFrame* instance and a *hasSyntacticValenceFrame* link from the collocation.

Morphological relations. As was mentioned above, the DB specifies the head noun of each collocation. This information is used in two respects. First, we can create the *Lexeme*, *Form* and *Sense* instances for the head noun in the MLR and link the *Sense* instance to the sense of the base noun by means of *isHeadOfCompound*. Second, we check if a collocation exists in the DB where the base noun is replaced with the head noun. If this is the case, we add it to the MLR and create a *hasMorphologicalRelationTo* link between the two collocations. The effect of this is that the collocations can be displayed in each other's entries.

More example sentences and frequency counts. Since each collocation entry specifies the corpus sentences that contain the respective collocation, they can be extracted and added as further example sentences of the collocation. Moreover, the frequency values of the collocation can be extracted and stored as well, with an indication of the source upon which the frequency count is based.

6.1.1.2 Storing the MLR data

After applying the extraction steps described above to the data in the SALSA corpus and the database of collocations, we store the thus acquired OWL files in a form that makes it possible to query them. As was mentioned in Section 4.2.7.3, several so-called RDF triplestores exist which combine scalable storage technology with efficient query engines, offering access to RDFS data by means of standard query languages like SPARQL. However, since the MLR model makes use of vocabulary that has been defined in OWL, we are in need of a storage component that is capable of offering support not only for RDFS, but also for at least the most fundamental OWL constructs. For example, if we state a query that is to extract the synonyms of a particular lexical entity, the triplestore should also enable the extraction of those synonyms that have been inferred on the basis of the symmetry and transitivity of the *hasSynonym* property.

As of 2011, one of the most scalable databases offering OWL inference is the OWLIM family of repositories developed by Ontotext[4]. OWLIM offers reasoning based on forward chaining of entailment rules for a subset of OWL and has been implemented as a storage and inference layer for the Sesame framework (Broekstra *et al.*, 2002). After presenting the main features of the Sesame framework and the OWLIM repository, we summarise the size of the MLR in terms of the number of entities it contains (see Table 6.1 on page 135).

The Sesame framework. The Sesame framework[5] is an open-source RDF triplestore written in Java. It offers a variety of backends for storing data in repositories – such as in-memory, relational databases and native RDF – which can be queried by means of the W3C standard query language SPARQL as well as Sesame's own query language SeRQL (cf. Section 4.2.6 above). In order to keep Sesame independent of a particular storage backend, and thus extensible, its architecture provides a layer for implementing the communication with the various storage backends, the so-called *storage and inference layer* (SAIL; Broekstra *et al.*, 2002). This layer represents a low-level application programming interface which provides

[4] See http://www.ontotext.com/owlim. See also Kiryakov *et al.* (2005).
[5] See http://www.openrdf.org/.

interfaces that can be implemented according to a specific backend, while the methods for accessing the data are uniform across all storage backends.

The core component of Sesame is an HTTP server consisting of Java Servlets that enable access to Sesame repositories over HTTP[6]. In addition to this, Sesame provides the *Sesame Workbench*, which serves as a graphical user interface to the Sesame HTTP server. Since the Sesame workbench is also implemented as a Java web application, it can be accessed through a web browser. The Sesame workbench enables the creation of new repositories on the server and the deletion of existing ones, as well as exploration (e. g. by stating queries or exporting the repository) and modification (e. g. by adding or removing statements). For programmatic access to the repositories, Sesame offers a repository application programming interface so that exploration and modification can be performed from within other applications. Among others, this application programming interface provides mechanisms for retrieving individual statements (i. e. RDF triples) and for evaluating SPARQL and SeRQL queries. By connection with a repository stored on the Sesame HTTP server, this can also be done remotely (see Sections 6.3.1 and 6.4 for more details). Finally, statements and query results can be exported in several formats, such as the SPARQL Query Results XML Format (Beckett and Broekstra, 2008), RDF/XML, Turtle and N-Triples (cf. Section 4.2.8 above).

The OWLIM SAIL. As was mentioned above, OWLIM has been implemented as a SAIL, which means that it is available as a repository type in Sesame. OWLIM performs reasoning based on forward-chaining of entailment rules with the *Triple Reasoning and Rule Entailment Engine* (TRREE[7]), which starts »from the known facts and [performs] inference in an inductive fashion« (Kiryakov *et al.*, 2005: p. 183). In other words, the possible inferences that can be drawn are calculated when the statements are added to the repository, and thus no further reasoning is required at the moment a query is stated. As a result, queries can be evaluated more efficiently, while data addition and deletion are more time-consuming. As such, OWLIM supports the dialect OWL Horst (ter Horst, 2005), which extends RDFS with reasoning with typed literals and supports several OWL constructs, such as *owl:FunctionalProperty*, *owl:SymmetricProperty*, *owl:sameAs*. However, it may also be extended by adding custom rules to the predefined rule sets in the TRREE.

OWLIM is available in two versions, namely SwiftOWLIM and BigOWLIM. While SwiftOWLIM performs reasoning and query evaluation in-memory and is thus very fast, BigOWLIM operates with file-based indices and is thus more scalable. According to the product website, it is capable of performing reasoning against 12 billion RDF triples, making it »the most scalable inference engine«[8] and the ideal candidate for storing and querying the MLR data. Moreover, due to the architecture of Sesame, the storage component can be nicely integrated into a client-server architecture (see Section 6.4).

Size of the MLR. After extracting data from the SALSA corpus and enriching them with information from the collocations DB, we store them in a Sesame BigOWLIM repository, along with the MLR model itself and the OWL files containing the user profiles that have been described in Section 5.4.5 above. The size of the resulting resource comprises almost

6 See http://www.openrdf.org/doc/sesame2/users/ch03.html.

7 See http://owlim.ontotext.com/display/OWLIMv42/Primer+Introduction+to+OWLIM#PrimerIntroductiontoOWLIM-TheTRREEEngine.

8 See http://www.ontotext.com/owlim/benchmark-results.

TYPE OF ENTITY	NUMBER OF INSTANCES
Lexical entities	42,300
Lexemes	13,819
Forms	13,819
Senses	14,662
Collocations	10,167
Verbs	1,365
Nouns	2,286
Lexical-semantic relations between senses	1,328
Morphological relations between senses	1,658
Syntactic valence frames	3,631
Types	12
Semantic valence frames	3,695
Types	677
Morpho-syntactic preferences	32,811
Number preferences	9,201
Determination preferences	8,017
Modification preferences	6,493
Determiner preferences	6,229
Fusion preferences	2,411
Reflexivity preferences	358
Polarity preferences	102
Example descriptions	44,099
Total number of instances	168,383
Total number of RDF statements	10,272,349

Table 6.1: Number of entities in the MLR

14,000 lexemes with roughly 14,500 senses, 3,000 lexical relations, 7,200 valence frame instances and more than 44,000 example sentences. In total, these make up over 10,000,000 RDF statements. Table 6.1 displays the exact counts for different types of entities in the MLR repository.[9]

6.1.2 Consistency Control

In this section, we will focus on rather formal aspects of the MLR, before turning to the multifunctional aspects of the MLR in terms of its usability for human users and NLP applications in Sections 6.2 and 6.3. In particular, we will discuss how an OWL DL model

[9] BigOWLIM is available under an RDBMS-like commercial licence. A free research and evaluation copy of version 3.2.6 has been kindly made available by Ontotext (Sirma Group). It has been installed on a Sesame 2.3.0 HTTP server.

can support mechanisms for ensuring the consistency and integrity of the lexicon. As was explained in Section 3.1.2 above, this refers to both the data in the MLR as well as the model itself, which is in contrast to the related approaches discussed in Section 3.2, where consistency and integrity – given their sparse mention in the relevant literature – seem to be of minor importance.

In version 3.2.6, which is the version used here, OWLIM provides only limited support for consistency checking based on description logic axioms, although inclusion of this functionality seems to be planned[10]. This is partly to do with the fact that OWLIM does not fully support the OWL DL language constructs. However, there are other reasoners which fully support OWL DL, although as was pointed out in Section 4.2.7.2 above, these typically do not scale very well. Nonetheless, since the MLR data are distributed over several OWL files, these reasoners can still be used to check the consistency of the files *offline*, i. e. before they are stored in the BigOWLIM repository. This strategy has been successfully applied in the development of the SALSA lexicon (cf. Spohr *et al.*, 2007). Moreover, Burchardt *et al.* (2008a) report a powerful combination of such logic-based consistency checking techniques with query-based consistency checks. In the following, we briefly introduce the main features of the approach presented in Burchardt *et al.* (2008a), before discussing how it can be applied in the context of the MLR.

6.1.2.1 Consistency control in the SALSA lexicon

As was mentioned above, Burchardt *et al.* (2008a) have presented a way to combine axiom-based with query-based consistency checking. More precisely, they have used a description logic reasoner to detect instances of corpus annotations which are inconsistent with respect to the underlying framework. In order to be able to do this, their lexicon model contains a formalisation of FrameNet as well as of the SALSA annotation scheme, including axioms that specify e. g. which frame elements (FEs) can be annotated for a particular frame, as well as which FEs exclude each other and can therefore not be part of the same frame annotation. Annotations which do not satisfy these conditions are thus identified as inconsistent. In addition to checking the consistency of the annotations, however, this formalisation can also be used to check the logical consistency of the underlying framework itself.

Earlier versions of the SALSA lexicon model contained axioms which restricted the core and non-core FEs for particular frames. For example, the definition of the class representing the PLACING frame contained, among others, the following axiom, which states that annotations of the PLACING frame can only have the mentioned core FEs.

(6.2) $Placing \sqsubseteq \forall hasCoreRole.(Placing.Agent \sqcup Placing.Goal \sqcup Placing.Theme \sqcup \ldots)$

According to FrameNet, the PLACING frame is inherited by the DISPERSAL frame. This was represented in the lexicon model by means of the subclass relationship between the two frames. The class definition of DISPERSAL thus contained the axioms in (6.3), which specify the subclass relationship between DISPERSAL and PLACING as well as the core and non-core FEs which can be annotated for instances of the DISPERSAL frame.

---

10 http://www.mail-archive.com/topbraid-composer-users@googlegroups.com/msg00554.html.

(6.3) $Dispersal \sqsubseteq Placing \sqcap$
$\forall hasCoreRole.(Dispersal.Agent \sqcup Dispersal.Individuals \sqcup \ldots) \sqcap$
$\forall hasNonCoreRole.(Dispersal.Goal\_area \sqcup Dispersal.Source \sqcup \ldots)$

These axioms were based on the assumption that for frames which inherit from each other, the corresponding FEs should also stand in inheritance relations to each other, since – due to the monotonicity of OWL – the axioms defined for the PLACING class have to hold for its subclass DISPERSAL as well. More precisely, in order to be consistent, the core FEs of DISPERSAL have to be subclasses of the core FEs of PLACING, since otherwise the DISPERSAL class cannot satisfy the conditions in (6.2) and (6.3) at the same time. While this would appear to be a reasonable interrelation between FEs, it turned out to be incorrect, as the inheritance relations between the FEs are like the ones shown in (6.4).

(6.4) $Dispersal.Agent \sqsubseteq Placing.Agent$
$Dispersal.Individuals \sqsubseteq Placing.Theme$
$Dispersal.Goal\_area \sqsubseteq Placing.Goal$
$\ldots$

While the core FEs DISPERSAL.AGENT and DISPERSAL.INDIVIDUALS do in fact inherit from the corresponding core FEs of the PLACING frame, (6.4) shows that DISPERSAL.GOAL_AREA, which is a non-core FE, inherits from the core FE PLACING.GOAL. Therefore, the DISPERSAL class does not satisfy the conditions in the definition of PLACING, although it has been asserted as its subclass, and thus, the reasoner classifies the model as inconsistent. The two possible interpretations of this circumstance are that either the definition of FrameNet is too informal in that it allows non-core FEs to inherit from core FEs and vice versa, or that the assumption that this should not be the case is too strict. However, as one of the aims of the SALSA lexicon model had been to provide a consistent formalisation of FrameNet, the answer to this question was not in the focus. Instead, this case provided important evidence that the reasoner delivered crucial input for the refinement of the model, as without a reformulation of these conditions it would have been logically inconsistent.

In addition to this axiom-based consistency checking, the SALSA lexicon contains a mechanism for query-based consistency and integrity checks operating directly on a Sesame MySQL RDFS repository. Although this moves away from the axiomatisation in description logics, it still benefits from the built-in subsumption inference of OWL. According to Burchardt *et al.* (2008a), it was possible to detect complex cases of annotation inconsistencies involving the FrameNet hierarchy this way. For example, they have formulated a SeRQL query that checks for cases in which two frame annotations have the same target in a sentence, such as one verb evoking two different frames. While this is in general possible, the query further checked whether these frames and their FEs inherit from each other. If this was the case, then the assumption was that those FEs which inherit from each other should also be assigned to the same syntactic constituents in the sentence. However, this was not always the case, and the inconsistent annotations were returned by the query.

Most of these consistency queries follow the general structure that is shown in (6.5). As can be seen, this makes use of the SeRQL `MINUS` operator, which is equivalent to the set complement in that it returns the results of the first query which are not in the results of the second query[11].

[11] See http://www.openrdf.org/doc/sesame2/users/ch09.html#section-minus.

```
(6.5) SELECT *
      FROM [any pattern X]

      MINUS

      SELECT *
      FROM [well-formed cases of X]
```

In particular, the queries subtract from any particular pattern the well-formed ones (see also Spohr, 2005). In order to extract frame annotations that do not have any annotated FEs, for example, the first part of the query would extract all frame annotations and subtract from them the ones that have annotated FEs. The result set thus consists of those which do not have any FEs.

6.1.2.2 Consistency control in the MLR

The consistency checking mechanism developed in the SALSA project can be transferred to the MLR in the following way. First, the MLR model file as well as the OWL files containing the descriptions of the individual lemmas are checked with a description logic reasoner[12] on the basis of the formalisation of the MLR model presented in Section 5.3. If they are found to be consistent, they are loaded into a temporary BigOWLIM repository. Once all data have been checked and added in this way, a series of predefined consistency queries is evaluated against this repository, returning the entities which do not conform to the specifications. These are then corrected and fed into this repository again, where they are re-checked for their consistency. Once all inconsistencies have been removed, the data are loaded into the MLR BigOWLIM repository, from where they can then be accessed by human users and NLP applications. In the following, we will briefly present some example cases of inconsistencies that may arise, and discuss the problems that have been encountered.

Axiom-based checking. An example case of a potential model inconsistency has been discussed in Section 4.3.4 above. Below, we will focus on examples of data inconsistencies involving the formalisation of the *Sense* class, with the relevant axioms repeated in (6.6). These express that a *Sense* instance can have lexical relations only to other *Sense* instances, and not e. g. to instances of the *Lexeme* class. Moreover, it can only be linked via *hasCollocation* to instances which are senses of a collocation, and finally, *Sense* instances cannot be instances of the *Lexeme* class.

(6.6) $$\begin{aligned} Sense \equiv\ & (\forall has\text{-}lexical\text{-}relation\text{-}to.Sense) \sqcap \\ & (\forall has\text{-}collocation.(\exists is\text{-}sense\text{-}of.Collocation)) \sqcap \\ & (\neg Lexeme) \sqcap \\ & \ldots \end{aligned}$$

In order to test these constraints, we have created an instance *Sense_1* and linked it to an instance of the *Lexeme* class via the *hasLexicalRelationTo* property. Example 6.7 shows part of the output obtained after running the Pellet reasoner on these data.

[12] We have used Pellet 2.0.1, which is an open-source OWL DL reasoner based on tableaux algorithms (cf. Sirin *et al.*, 2007).

(6.7) `Clash: Individual namespace#Sense_1 is forced to belong to class namespace#Lexeme and its complement`

Due to the *hasLexicalRelationTo* link between a sense and a lexeme, in combination with the first restriction in (6.6), the reasoner infers that either the sense is and instance of the *Lexeme* class, or the lexeme of the *Sense* class.

In a slightly more complex configuration, we link *Sense_1* to an instance *Sense_2* via *isBaseOf*. *Sense_2* itself is the sense of an instance of *SyntacticallySimpleFreeUnit*, which is one of the complements of the *Collocation* class. After running the Pellet reasoner on these data, the following answer is obtained.

(6.8)
```
Clash: Individual namespace#SyntacticallySimpleFreeUnit_3 is forced to
belong to class namespace#SyntacticallyComplexFreeUnit and its
complement

Explanation:
  subClassOf(Collocation, SyntacticallyComplexFreeUnit)
  prop(hasSense, SyntacticallySimpleFreeUnit_3, Sense_2)
  subProperty(isBaseOf, hasCollocation)
  type(SyntacticallySimpleFreeUnit_3, SyntacticallySimpleFreeUnit)
  type(Sense_1, Sense)
  subClassOf(Sense, all(hasCollocation, some(isSenseOf, Collocation)))
  functional(isSenseOf)
  inverseProperty(isSenseOf, hasSense)
  disjointWith(SyntacticallyComplexFreeUnit, SyntacticallySimpleFreeUnit)
  prop(isBaseOf, Sense_1, Sense_2)
```

As can be seen in (6.8), Pellet returns not only the inconsistent entity itself, but also an explanation as to why it has been classified as inconsistent. In particular, (6.8) shows that due to the *hasSense* link between *SyntacticallySimpleFreeUnit_3* and *Sense_2* as well as the *isBaseOf* link between *Sense_1* and *Sense_2*, *SyntacticallySimpleFreeUnit_3* is inferred as a *Collocation*. This is a subclass of *SyntacticallyComplexFreeUnit*, which is the complement of *SyntacticallySimpleFreeUnit*. Therefore, *SyntacticallySimpleFreeUnit_3* is inferred as an instance of both a class and its complement, which is a logical contradiction.

The explanation nicely illustrates the interplay between the formal definitions of both classes and properties, which is reflected e. g. in the subsumption inference from a more specific class like *Collocation* to the more general *SyntacticallyComplexFreeUnit*, as well as inferences based on the fact that *isSenseOf* is a functional property. In addition to this, it demonstrates that recent years have seen considerable improvement as far as feedback from the reasoner is concerned, as this was reported as one of the disadvantages at the time the SALSA lexicon was compiled (see Burchardt *et al.*, 2008a).

However, there are also some issues connected with axiom-based consistency checking. In addition to the afore-mentioned scalability issues of reasoners which fully support OWL DL, a tableau-based reasoner like Pellet will stop as soon as it has found a contradiction. In essence, this means that inconsistencies need to be dealt with iteratively, as each inconsistency requires another run of the reasoner in order to be detected and corrected. In addition to this, some of the formal assumptions made by OWL may lead to confusion when interpreting the output of the reasoner. As was mentioned in Section 4.2.4, OWL makes the open world assumption, whereas it does not make the unique name assumption. The effect of this is that what has not been explicitly stated as false is not assumed to be false. In the context of the data in a lexical resource, this means that unless there is some fact that states e. g. that a specific lexeme does not have a value for the *hasPartOfSpeech* property, the simple omission of such value does not render the respective lexeme inconsistent. Rather, the reasoner infers from the axiom $\exists has\text{-}part\text{-}of\text{-}speech.SyntacticCategory$ (cf. (5.7) on page 105) that there is some value for *hasPartOfSpeech* – whether it has been specified or not. Similar holds for example (6.7) mentioned above, where there would not have been a clash unless *Lexeme* and *Sense* had been defined as disjoint.

This behaviour has been identified as unsuitable for many applications which lie outside the scope of the Semantic Web, such as lexical resources, as these typically require a closed world. For these reasons, there have been recent proposals for mechanisms that enable the interpretation of description logic existential restrictions as integrity constraints in OWL (see Motik *et al.* (2007a,b); see also Sirin and Tao, 2009). While these seem very promising, they have not yet been implemented in scalable systems, and for the time being, integrity constraints thus need to be formalised in the form of queries rather than axioms. Nonetheless, these queries still benefit considerably from the semantics of OWL.

Query-based checking. As was mentioned above, axiom-based consistency checking can be complemented by formulating integrity constraints in the form of queries which extract specific configurations from the MLR. Here, we have found that Sesame's own query language SeRQL is more suitable for this task than SPARQL, as it provides the appropriate set operators that are needed. In the following, we will first present one query which checks for the completeness of the description of *Lexeme* instances, in that the presence of a value for the *hasPartOfSpeech* property is queried. The second case that will be discussed below represents a more complex case of a data inconsistency. In particular, this query extracts instances of $V + N_{obj}$ collocations whose collocate does not subcategorise a nominal direct object.

In order to extract instances which are inconsistent with respect to the first case just mentioned, we fill the query template shown in (6.5) above such that the first part of the query matches all instances of *Lexeme*, while the second part subtracts those instances which specify a value for the *hasPartOfSpeech* property.

(6.9)
```
SELECT LEXEME
FROM {LEXEME} rdf:type {mlr:Lexeme}

MINUS

SELECT LEXEME
FROM {LEXEME} rdf:type {mlr:Lexeme};
                mlr:hasPartOfSpeech {}
```

The query in (6.9) illustrates the general pattern that can be applied to other descriptions as well in order to ensure data integrity. For example, a similar query is stated in order to check whether all *Sense* instances are linked to a *Lexeme* instance. In addition to this, the queries make heavy use of underspecified information, in the sense that they are typically formulated by means of very general classes and properties. In the repository, these general statements have been inferred from the more specific ones by means of the forward-chaining algorithm of BigOWLIM and thus match with the patterns used in the queries.

The second case to be discussed here is more complex in that it involves several properties that are checked. As was just mentioned, the query in (6.10) is to extract instances of $V + N_{obj}$ collocations whose collocate does not subcategorise a nominal direct object. However, the query also extracts those instances which deviate from the well-formed configuration in a different respect. For example, it also extracts cases of $V + N_{obj}$ collocations which have no collocate at all as well as those whose collocate either (i) has no value for *hasPartOfSpeech*, (ii) is not a verb, (iii) has no valence frame, (iv) has only valence frames without direct accusative objects, or (v) has only valence frames with direct accusative objects that are not noun phrases.

(6.10)
```
SELECT COLLOCATION
FROM {COLLOCATION} rdf:type {mlr:V-N_obj}

MINUS

SELECT COLLOCATION
FROM {COLLOCATION} rdf:type {mlr:V-N_obj};
                   mlr:hasCollocate {COLLOCATE},
     {COLLOCATE} mlr:hasPartOfSpeech {} rdf:type {mlr:VERB},
     {COLLOCATE} mlr:hasSyntacticValenceFrame {}
                 mlr:accObject {}
                  mlr:hasSyntacticCategory {mlr:NounPhrase}
```

The constraints needed in order to identify instances which are inconsistent with respect to (6.10) have also been expressed in terms of necessary conditions in description logics. In particular, the axiom ($\exists$*has-collocate*.(($\exists$*has-part-of-speech.VERB*) $\sqcap$ ($\exists$*has-syntactic-valence-frame*. ($\exists$*acc-object.ValenceArgument*)))) in the definition of the *V-N_acc-obj* class (cf. (5.11) on page 107) also renders all $V + N_{obj}$ collocations inconsistent whose collocate does not subcategorise a nominal direct accusative object. However, this requires an additional assertion which expresses that the collocate has no further syntactic valence frames beyond the ones that have been asserted, i. e. a maximum cardinality restriction = *n has-syntactic-valence-frame owl:Thing*, where *n* is the number of syntactic frames that the collocate is linked to. If this fact is missing, the reasoner infers that there is some additional valence frame that satisfies the condition. In order to avoid these additional statements, we have decided to formulate this constraint as well in terms of a SeRQL query, although the respective axioms are still part of the MLR model – in view of future developments in the area of OWL integrity constraints.

6.1.3 Workflow of the Lexicon Compilation Process

The workflow of the processes described in the previous two sections is illustrated in Figure 6.1. As can be seen there, we start from the SALSA XML data, which are distributed over several XML files, and convert each of them separately into OWL (cf. Section 6.1.1.1). While this has advantages with respect to the performance of the conversion process, it requires an extra mechanism in order to make sure that the descriptions of lexical entities which occur in different XML files are not created more than once. For example, the XML file containing the frame annotations of *»kommen«* contains the collocation *»in Schwierigkeiten kommen«* (*»to* *get into trouble«*). In order to create the entry of this collocation, one would now create the entity representing the collocation, as well as the ones representing the base and the collocate, and link the entities by means of the *hasBase* and *hasCollocate* relations. However, while these entities might not have been created yet in the file that is currently being processed, they might have been created in one of the files that had been converted earlier. For example, the entry of the base *»Schwierigkeit«* has already been created during the conversion of the XML file which contains the annotations of *»bringen«* – in the context of the collocation *»in Schwierigkeiten bringen«* – and should therefore not be created again. For this reason, the converted SALSA data are stored in a temporary BigOWLIM repository. During the conversion of an XML file, this repository is queried for existing entities that match the lemma and part-of-speech of the lexeme that is to be created. If this is the case, then the direct *rdf:type* and the internal name of the entity are extracted. In addition to this, an entity with the same name and type is created in the currently converted file, as otherwise there would be no instance to link to. However, since this instance has the same namespace and ID as the one existing in the repository, the two instances are automatically unified by BigOWLIM when the current file is added to the SALSA repository, and they are thus not duplicates.[13]

Once all SALSA data have been converted that way, the XML file containing the data from the collocations DB is processed. As was mentioned above, this is done by means of ordering the entries in this file and checking for each verb lemma whether a corresponding OWL file has been created. If this is the case, then the SALSA representations are unified with the ones from the collocations DB. In case no file exists for a particular verb lemma, a new OWL file is created which contains the information extracted from the collocations DB. As the DB may provide entries of collocations whose components are contained in SALSA, although the collocations themselves are not, this unification process again involves interaction with the SALSA repository, in order to avoid the creation of duplicate instances.

For each OWL file that is created this way, the Pellet OWL DL reasoner is run to determine the logical consistency of the data with respect to the definitions in the MLR model. If the reasoner detects an inconsistency, the respective file is revised, which may result in a manual correction of the respective inconsistency or a potential correction of the extraction routines. This process is repeated until the file has passed the logical consistency check. Once this is the case, all data are stored in a temporary BigOWLIM repository, and the query-based consistency checks are evaluated. Similar to the axiom-based procedure, this may involve iterative manual correction in both the OWL file and the extraction routines. If all data have passed the tests on this intermediate repository, the OWL files are stored in the final MLR BigOWLIM repository, from where they can be accessed by human users and NLP applications.

---

[13] Another way of querying for such instances would be to create lexemes with an internal name like `Lexeme_lemma`, where `lemma` is the lemma of the respective entity. However, as this would assign meaning to the internal names of entities, it has not been done.

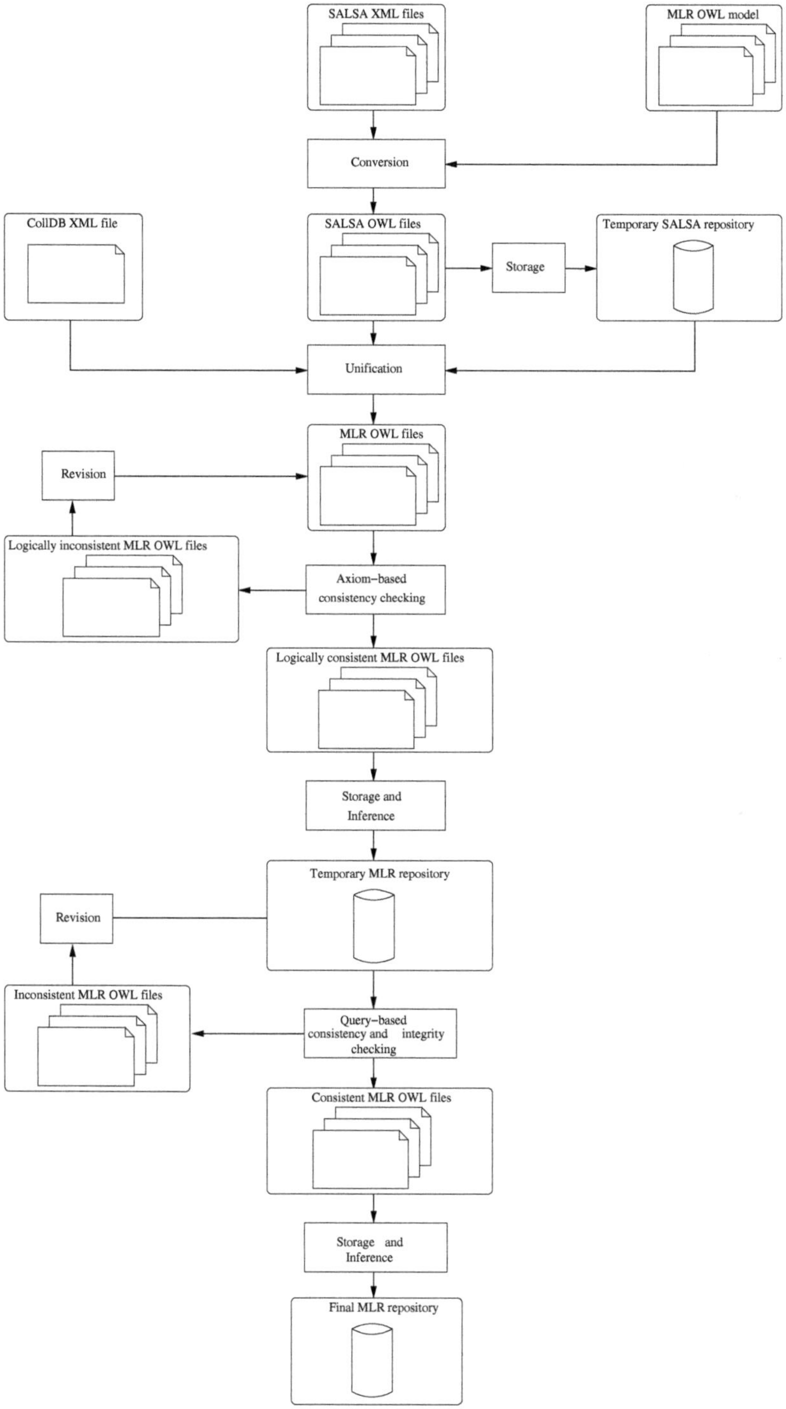

Figure 6.1: Workflow of the lexicon compilation process

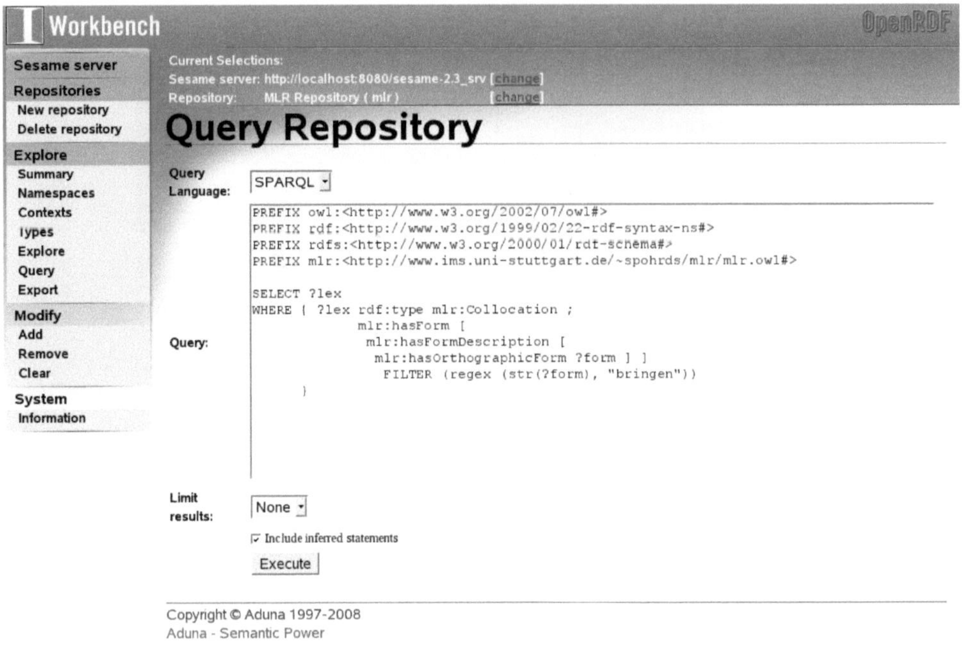

Figure 6.2: Screenshot of a SPARQL query in the Sesame workbench

6.2 User-oriented Lexicon Access and Presentation

With the MLR data stored in a scalable and consistent form, we now turn to the ways in which they can be accessed by human users (Section 6.2.2.1) as well as presented to them (Section 6.2.3). In the following, we will start by showing how the MLR can be accessed through the Sesame workbench, and assess its suitability for serving as a graphical user interface for the MLR. Afterwards, we discuss how the model structure can support the definition of a custom graphical user interface (GUI). Regarding presentation, we will discuss how lexical entries can be generated from the RDF statements by means of SPARQL and the user profiles discussed in Section 5.4.5.

6.2.1 Access and Presentation in the Sesame Workbench

As was mentioned above, the MLR can be accessed through the Sesame workbench, which offers query support for SPARQL and SeRQL. Figure 6.2 displays a screenshot of the query form containing a SPARQL query that extracts from the MLR all instances of the class *Collocation* which have a lemma or a word-form that matches with »*bringen*«.

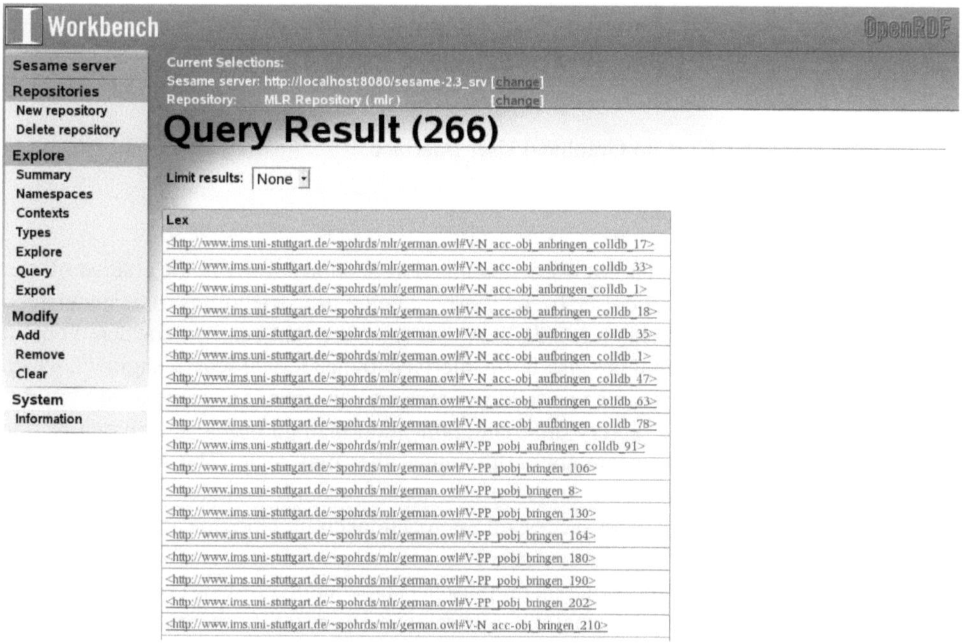

Figure 6.3: Screenshot of the results of a SPARQL query in the Sesame workbench

The figure illustrates a number of issues with the Sesame workbench[14]. The most obvious of these is the fact that the user requires command of SPARQL in order to be able to formulate a query. While this knowledge can be found in experts who are familiar with Semantic Web technology, it can certainly not be expected from the average dictionary user. Moreover, even if the knowledge is there, the formulation of a felicitous query still requires highly detailed knowledge of the internal structures of the MLR model, such as the correct paths in the model graph, the exact names of predicates as well as the namespaces. This kind of expertise can only be expected of people who have been directly involved in the development of the MLR model, or who have invested a considerable amount of effort in getting familiar with it. In any case, it cannot be expected of a user. Finally, from a presentation point of view, the user is confronted with far too much metadata, such as details on the namespaces and XML Schema Datatypes. Similar issues apply to the presentation of query results, as shown in Figure 6.3.

In sum, it can be stated that it is not possible to integrate support from the model – e. g. for the formulation of queries or for the presentation of the results –, and we thus consider the Sesame workbench to be unsuitable of serving as a GUI to the MLR. For this reason, the MLR is in need of a custom GUI. Here, the fact that the model has been defined in a typed

[14] The following points are not to be understood as criticism of the Sesame workbench in general, but rather of its suitability to serve as a GUI for the MLR. Needless to say that it has not been developed for such purposes.

formalism offers a number of ways for supporting the definition of such a GUI. Below, we will focus on the access functionality, as well as the presentation of lexical entries.

6.2.2 Access through a Custom Graphical User Interface

6.2.2.1 General considerations[15]

A fundamental requirement that has been mentioned in Section 3.1.3.1 in the context of user interfaces is that they have to be user-friendly, where being user-friendly is to be understood as easy-to-use (see e. g. de Schryver, 2003). A user interface that can be considered one of the most user-friendly ones in this sense is the interface to the Google search engine[16], which offers at first not much more than a text field where users can specify a search term.

While an ED is, of course, a very different application than an online search engine, the fundamental needs of their users are not as different as they may seem. The users want information, which is – in the context of an electronic lexical resource – centered around lexical items. Therefore, the intuitive and successful approach taken by Google can in principle be transferred to the MLR graphical user interface as well, by providing users first with a simple text field for specifying a string value that represents some lemma or word-form. While this may seem too simple in terms of what the user can specify, recall from Section 3.2.3.3 that although a user interface like the one of BLF is very rich in terms of specifying what the result of a particular query should look like[17], the user's involvement in formulating the actual query essentially consists in entering a string value in one or two text fields. Depending on which text field this value is specified in, the user is presented with different kinds of results.

In contrast to this, in an approach like the one followed in the present study, which deals with user needs in terms of a metamodel that regulates the presentation of the indications in lexical entries (cf. Section 5.4.5 above), the complexity of the user interface can be reduced to offering just one central text field initially, since the kind of information that is presented to the user is determined on the basis of the properties of the selected profile (see Section 6.2.3).

Internally, the value that is specified in the text field can be inserted into the skeleton of a SPARQL query like the one in (6.11), which is passed on to the Sesame server. This query extracts all *Lexeme* instances which have a lemma or a word-form that matches the specified string. Formally, the query follows the path from the *Lexeme* instance to the value of *hasOrthographicForm*, via *hasLemma*/*hasWordForm* and *hasFormDescription*. Here, we can make use of the underspecified *hasSenseOrFormRelationTo* property, i. e. the superproperty of *hasLemma* and *hasWordForm*. In addition to avoiding a (less efficient) disjunction in the query, its symmetry and transitivity further allows us to follow the inferred direct connection from a sense to the forms of its lexeme (cf. Section 5.1.3). Therefore, if we omitted the `rdf:type mlr:Lexeme` pattern, `?lex` would match with instances of both *Lexeme* and *Sense*. The benefit of this will become evident in later query examples.

---

15 A custom graphical user interface has been developed as part of an undergraduate thesis, under the supervision of the author (see Müller, 2010). As further implementational aspects can be found there, this section will focus on more abstract aspects of the graphical user interface, such as the general ideas and design considerations.

16 See http://www.google.com/.

17 For example, after an »*Is it le or la?*« query, the user is shown information on grammatical gender, whereas after an »*Is it a frequent word combination*« query the result consists in frequency counts.

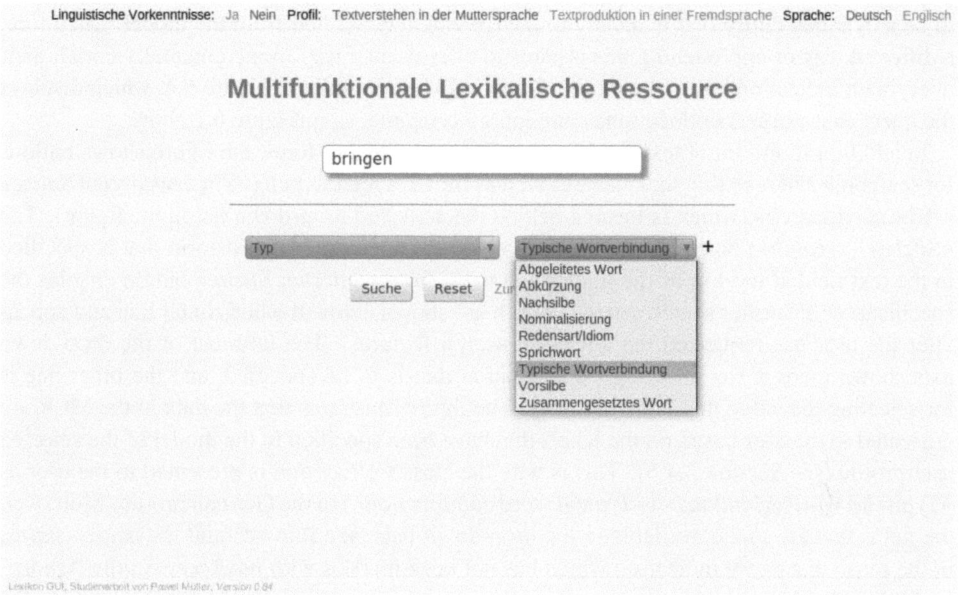

Figure 6.4: Layout of the graphical user interface, with basic search and more advanced search features

(6.11)
```
SELECT ?lex
WHERE { ?lex rdf:type mlr:Lexeme;
             mlr:hasSenseOrFormRelationTo [
              mlr:hasFormDescription [
               mlr:hasOrthographicForm ?form ] ]
                FILTER (regex(str(?form), ''user input'')) }
```

At the same time as offering users a straightforward way of accessing the MLR, the fact that SPARQL is only needed internally further solves one of the crucial problems identified above in the context of the Sesame workbench, namely that knowledge of SPARQL is required to formulate even the simplest query. However, especially more advanced users like expert lexicographers do not only search by lemma, and in fact, non-lemma-based access has been highlighted as one of the crucial requirements on the MLR (cf. Section 3.1.2.1). Therefore, it is necessary to offer advanced search options, which can be made available on demand and should also require as little knowledge of the internal structure of the model as possible. One way of achieving this is to offer a search form that contains various fields, such as *»Word class«* or *»Gender«*, each of which is hard-coded in the graphical user interface and has next to it a text field for specifying the value (see e. g. the DiCouèbe GUI). The problem with this approach is that the GUI is a static entity that is only consistent with a particular version of the model, and in case the model is modified, e. g. by adding further properties, the GUI needs to be modified as well. In contrast to this, however, we would like the graphical user interface to be a dynamic entity that is ideally to a large extent generated from the model. Therefore, a different way of approaching this issue is to offer users a way to incrementally enrich their query with indications from the model. This could be done like in Figure 6.4, which displays the query that extracts collocations containing *»bringen«*, as in Figure 6.2 above.

In addition to the inital text field for specifying the search term, the figure shows buttons for searching and resetting the query, as well as for advanced search (*»Zur erweiterten Suche«* *»Advanced search«*, which is located behind the activated drop-down list in the figure). The *»Suche«* (*»search«*) button is used for searching for a lemma or word-form that is specified in the text field at the top of the figure, and the *»Zur erweiterten Suche«* button enables the specification of further search criteria, which are shown below the horizontal line and appear after the user has requested the advanced search features. The leftmost of the drop-down lists shown there is for selecting the indication that is to be specified, and the other one is for selecting the value that it should have. The figure illustrates that the data in the MLR are presented to the user based on the labels that have been specified in the model of the selected user profile (see Section 5.4.5). This is why the class *Collocation* is presented to the user as *»Typische Wortverbindung«* (*»Typical word combination«*) in the German profile. Moreover, the items that are made available in the drop-down lists take into account the *access status*, in the sense that every indication which has not been marked with *hasAccessStatus "ignore"* is displayed. As can be seen, the user has selected *»Linguistische Vorkenntnisse: Nein«* (*»Linguistic background: No«*), and is therefore presented with a rather short list of types of lexical entities. In addition to selecting the linguistic background knowledge, the profile and the language can be selected in the way shown in Figure 6.4, by means of a list of available profiles and supported interface languages in the top right-hand corner.[18]

The specifications that have been interactively selected by the user are then added to the template shown in (6.11) above, which yields a SPARQL query like the one in (6.12), where the parts written in italics represent those that have been specified by the user.

(6.12)
```
SELECT ?lex
WHERE { ?lex rdf:type mlr:Lexeme;
                 mlr:hasSenseOrFormRelationTo [
                  mlr:hasFormDescription [
                   mlr:hasOrthographicForm ?form ] ]
                    FILTER (regex(str(?form), ''bringen'')) .
        ?lex rdf:type mlr:Collocation }
```

As can further be seen in Figure 6.4, the graphical user interface provides a way to add further search specifications to the query. By clicking on the »+« sign, the user can specify additional search criteria that need to be matched by the searched term. We will call this way of adding further search criteria *vertical search*. While these search criteria can be specified in the form of drop-down lists as well, the specification of their values does not necessarily correspond to selecting a value from a list. For example, if one wants to search for a collocation that is synonymous with a particular word, users should ideally be offered a text field in which they can provide a lemma. This is exemplified in Figure 6.5, which contains a query that extracts collocations which are synonymous with *»bringen«*.[19]

---

[18] As the GUI developed by Müller (2010) is still in a prototype stage, not all functionalities shown in the screenshots have been fully implemented (see Müller (2010) for details).

[19] *»Bedeutet (ungefähr) das Gleiche wie«* means *»Means roughly the same as«*.

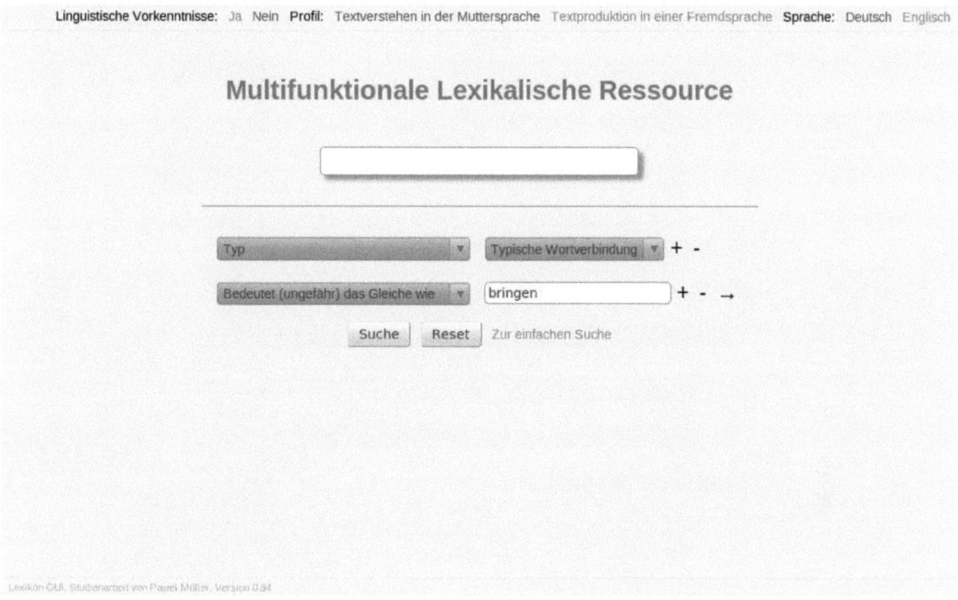

Figure 6.5: Example of a query with advanced search features

In addition to the queries presented so far, more complex queries can also be formulated in this graphical user interface. The query in Figure 6.6 extracts all collocations that consist of an adjective and a noun which is a synonym of »*Problem*«. A query like this could be stated e. g. in a text-productive situation by a non-native (but fairly advanced) speaker of German who wants to express that something is e. g. a big problem, and who would like to have some lexical choice with respect to the noun and the adjective. Possible results are for example the entries for »*großes/schwerwiegendes/erhebliches/ernstes/... Problem*« or »*große/erhebliche/enorme/ernsthafte/... Schwierigkeit(en)*«. The figure illustrates the specification of what we call *horizontal search*, which does not only involve properties of the initial search term, but also of the entities that are connected to it. As can be seen in the figure, horizontal search can be further refined through vertical search, by adding criteria like »*Word class*« or »*Synonymous with*«. The generated SPARQL query is shown in (6.13).[20]

(6.13)
```
SELECT ?lex
WHERE { ?lex rdf:type mlr:Lexeme .
```

[20] The heavy use of *hasSenseOrFormRelationTo* in the query is due to the fact that most lexical relations have been defined for both lexemes and senses, although they should ideally be defined between senses only (cf. Section 5.1.1). However, since knowledge in this detail is typically not available, we have to make sure that the query matches with both lexemes and senses. In the ideal case where this knowledge is available, *hasSenseOrFormRelationTo* would not need to be used this often. It is thus a problem originating from the quality of semi-automatically acquired data rather than of the model itself.

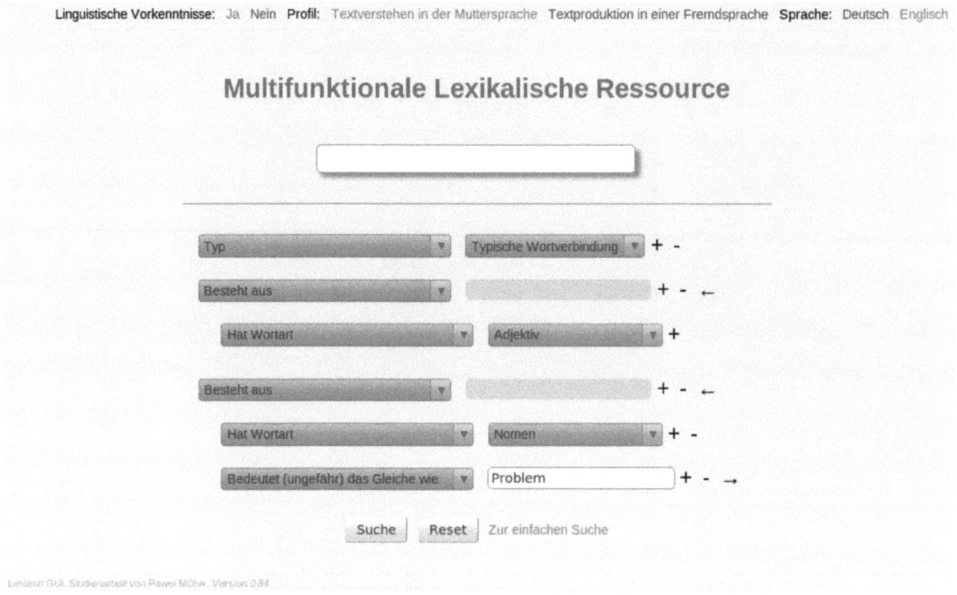

Figure 6.6: Example of a complex query in the graphical user interface

```
?lex mlr:hasSenseOrFormRelationTo [
      rdf:type mlr:Collocation ] .
?lex mlr:hasSenseOrFormRelationTo [
      mlr:hasCollocationalRelationTo ?a ] .
?a mlr:hasSenseOrFormRelationTo [
      mlr:hasPartOfSpeech mlr:PlainAdjective ] .
?lex mlr:hasSenseOrFormRelationTo [
      mlr:hasCollocationalRelationTo ?b ] .
?b mlr:hasSenseOrFormRelationTo [
      mlr:hasPartOfSpeech mlr:CommonNoun ] .
?b mlr:hasSenseOrFormRelationTo [
      mlr:hasSynonym ?c ] .
?c mlr:hasSenseOrFormRelationTo [
      mlr:hasFormDescription [
      mlr:hasOrthographicForm ?form ] ]
       FILTER (regex(str(?form), ''Problem'')) }
```

As was mentioned on the previous pages, the graphical user interface makes use of the labels defined in the user profile model for displaying the indications and values in the search form in an appropriate way. In addition to this, however, users are in need of more substantial support for the formulation of advanced queries. In particular, they should be offered only those properties which are relevant at a specific position in the query. For example, it would not be reasonable to offer a syntactic function like *subject* in the first drop-down list, since a lexical item does not have this property. Likewise, once a property has been selected, the list of offered values should consist of only those which can actually appear as values. If *hasPartOfSpeech* has been selected, for example, the drop-down list containing the values should not offer *AccusativeCase*.[21] Finally, for more complex query expressions, the selection should be reduced according to the continuations that are still possible. Therefore, if e. g. *hasValenceFrame* has been selected, a property like *hasMorphologicalRelationTo* should not appear in the list of possible continuations.

The MLR model can support this in various ways. First of all, the fact that it has been defined in a typed formalism is a prerequisite for being able to query for distinct indications in the first place. In addition to this, most indications have been modelled as properties, and therefore, their domains and ranges can provide vital support for the formulation of complex queries in the respects just mentioned (see also Section 5.2.1). In particular, we can specify that the properties which appear in the first (i. e. leftmost) drop-down lists are those which have *LexicalEntity* or any of its subclasses in their domain. This is because we assume that – even though the access is not necessarily lemma-based – the initial search criteria refer to a lexical entity. For example, even though we might search by properties such as part-of-speech and valence information (such as *»all verbs which subcategorise a sentential complement«*), the criteria specify the lexical entity.

Once a property has been selected, we need to process its range in order to determine the way in which the value specification is offered to the user. Here, we have identified four different cases that need to be covered in order to support the formulation of complex queries. In terms of the MLR model, these can be defined as follows.

Subproperties of *hasDescriptiveRelationTo* with *LinguisticFeature* in their range. These represent simple cases like *hasPartOfSpeech* or *hasGender*. Here, we propose to provide the user with a drop-down list for selecting the value. Since no further horizontal search seems necessary at this point (i. e. there are no properties which have e. g. *GrammaticalGender* in their domain), we call such properties horizontal end points.

Subproperties of *hasLexicalRelationTo*. As was mentioned above, specifying a value is not suitable for all kinds of properties. For lexical relations, there seems to be the need to offer users a choice as to how to continue. On the one hand, they might want to directly specify a lemma, as e. g. in a search for synonyms of *»bringen«*. Here, it would not be reasonable to have users select the *hasSynonym* property and then offer them a property like *hasForm*. Even though the model would support the reduction of the offered properties, this would involve too much formal detail of the underlying model, and too much overhead needed for stating the query. Rather, it seems more appropriate to offer a text field in which users can specify the lemma directly, and to transform this internally into a template similar to the one shown in (6.11) above – without the `rdf:type mlr:Lexeme` pattern. On the other hand, a user might not want to specify a lemma, but instead further restrict the synonym according to its properties. This kind of horizontal search was shown in Figure 6.6 above in the context of a collocation whose components should match certain criteria, such as a particular part-of-speech. Here, we can again make use of domain and range information. In case the user does

[21] Recall that those entities would be presented to the user not by their internal names, but by their labels depending on the selected user profile and interface language.

not want to specify a lemma but instead restrict the item in a different way, the properties that are available for specifying the restrictions are those that have in their domain the type that is in the range of the previously selected property. More formally, the set P_i of properties that are available to the user at a position i in the query after a property p_{i-1} has been selected consists of the properties q for which the following holds.

(6.14) $P_i = \{q | c \in Ran(p_{i-1}) \wedge d \in Dom(q) \wedge (c \subseteq d \vee d \subseteq c)\}$

where P_i is the set of properties available at i, p_{i-1} is the property selected at $i - 1$, and c and d are subclasses of *owl:Class*

As a result, we propose to give the user a choice between entering a string or specifying further criteria. As soon as a string is entered, no further horizontal search is possible at this point (i. e. it is a horizontal end point as well). Likewise, as soon as horizontal search criteria are entered, no string can be specified.

Other subproperties of *hasDescriptiveRelationTo*. A different strategy needs to be applied to descriptions which are more complex than e. g. *hasPartOfSpeech* or *hasGender*, such as example sentences or valence descriptions (cf. Section 5.2). In contrast to lexical relations, it seems unnecessary to offer users a way to provide a string value. Moreover, offering a drop-down list for selecting a value does not seem appropriate either, since it could be that the user wants to specify further criteria, such as a certain syntactic category for a particular syntactic function. Therefore, it seems reasonable to directly offer the user further horizontal search criteria once a property like this has been selected. More precisely, upon selecting a property like *hasValenceFrame*, further drop-down lists appear which contain the properties as determined by (6.14).

The *rdf:type* property. The strategies mentioned so far do not work for all properties. In particular, the *rdf:type* property needs to be assigned special treatment, as it has no domain or range information that could be used here. Therefore, (6.14) above needs to be modified as follows.

(6.14') $P_i = \{q | c \in Ran(p_{i-1}) \wedge d \in Dom(q) \wedge (c \subseteq d \vee d \subseteq c)\} \cup \{rdf{:}type\}$

where P_i is the set of properties available at i, p_{i-1} is the property selected at $i - 1$, and c and d are subclasses of *owl:Class*

Nonetheless, the values of *rdf:type* should certainly be restricted as well, since otherwise all classes in the MLR appear in the drop-down list. Therefore, if the user searches for collocations which are synonymous with entities of type *Compound*, it would be supportive to offer only those classes which are relevant, i. e. the classes which are – in the present case – in the range of the *hasSynonym* property. Formally, we can state that the set V_i of values that are available to the user if *rdf:type* has been selected at a position i in the query consists of the values v for which (6.15) holds. The *rdf:type* property is a horizontal end point as well.

(6.15) $V_i = \{v | u \in Ran(p_{i-1}) \wedge v \subseteq u\}$

where V_i is the set of values available at i, p_{i-1} is the property selected at $i - 1$, and u and v are subclasses of *owl:Class*

6.2.3 Function-based Presentation of Lexical Entries

As the previous section has shown, the MLR model supports the definition of the access functionality of a graphical user interface in a number of respects. In addition to this, it also supports the development of mechanisms which perform the presentation of the content of the lexical resource in a way that satisfies the needs of the user. In particular, these mechanisms make use of the user profiles presented in Section 5.4.5, which formalise the needs of different types of users in different communicative situations, based on the analysis in Tarp (2008). As was mentioned above, this differs from approaches like the one of the BLF interface, where users are required to select the appropriate result type themselves.

Given the access functionality just presented, we assume that the result is a list of lexemes which are displayed by means of their labels (see Figure 6.7 for the result of the query for collocations matching »*bringen*«). These labels do not necessarily correspond to the orthographic form – although for most syntactically simple lexical entities they probably do –, but may instead consist e. g. in a compact representation of spelling alternatives (cf. the example of »*gab(e)lig*« on page 112 above)[22]. In the case of collocations with very strong morphosyntactic preferences, the label could consist of the most common form, e. g. »*in Schwierigkeiten bringen*« (where the base is in the plural and without determination) and »*in die Bredouille bringen*« (where the base is in the singular and with definite article; both collocations mean »*to bring somebody into trouble*«).

By clicking on one of the items displayed in Figure 6.7, the respective lexeme is looked up in the MLR repository, and the statements that are relevant for the lexical entry are extracted. Technically, these statements make up a graph consisting of all the entities that the respective lexeme is linked to. Spohr (2008) has presented one way of extracting such statements from the repository by means of a SPARQL `DESCRIBE` query. However, we have identified three problems with respect to `DESCRIBE` queries. As was mentioned in Section 4.2.7.3, `DESCRIBE` does not have normative status in the SPARQL W3C recommendation (Prud'hommeaux and Seaborne, 2008), and the kind of statements that are returned depends on the SPARQL query processor rather than the query itself. Moreover, the evaluation of `DESCRIBE` queries tends to be rather inefficient compared to other SPARQL queries, such as `SELECT` and `CONSTRUCT`. Finally, `DESCRIBE` proves workable only for simple descriptions which are directly connected to the lexeme. However, as the details for more complex descriptions are also relevant for the lexical entry of the lexeme, the statements involving them need to be extracted as well, and the `DESCRIBE` query thus needs to be extended accordingly. This, in turn, aggravates the efficiency issues, and therefore, we consider `DESCRIBE` queries to be suboptimal for the extraction of the entry-relevant statements.

For these reasons, we have opted for a SPARQL `CONSTRUCT` query, as the form of the graph that is returned can be specified in the `CONSTRUCT` clause of the query, and since the evaluation of the query seems to scale even for large data sets. The `CONSTRUCT` query that is used for the extraction of the entry-relevant statements is shown in (6.16), where the *`selected item`* slot is filled with the internal name of the lexeme that the user has clicked on.

---

[22] Recall from Section 3.1.1 that de Schryver (2003) lists »text decompression« as one requirement on the presentation of lexical content. However, this refers to abbreviations which complicate the interpretation of particular indications, rather than representations which illustrate a certain circumstance in a more compact way – such as the fact that there are orthographic variants for a particular lexeme.

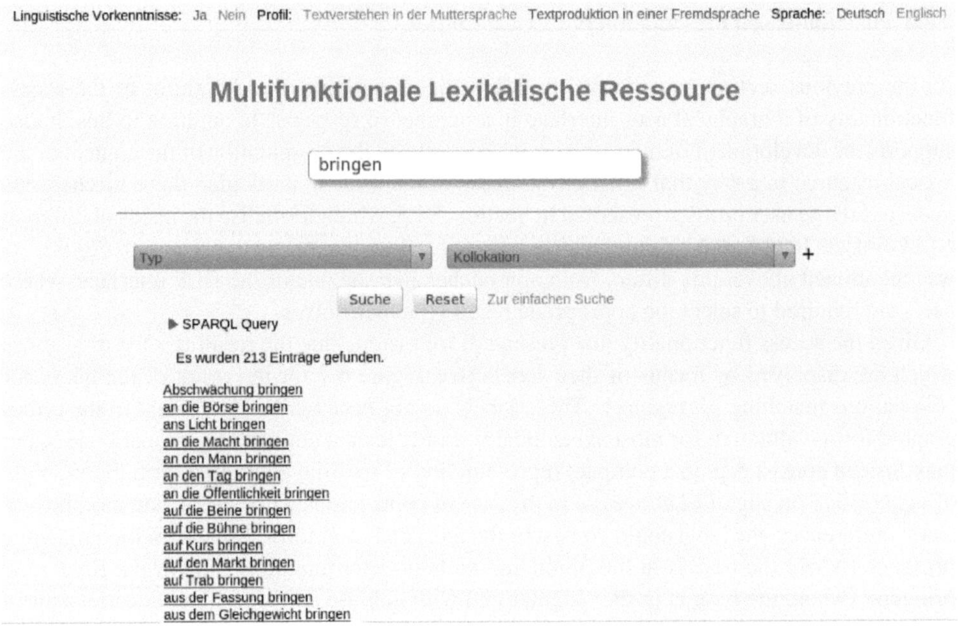

Figure 6.7: Result of a query for collocations matching *»bringen«*

```
(6.16) CONSTRUCT { ?s ?p ?o }
       WHERE {
              { <selected item> mlr:hasSenseOrFormRelationTo ?s }
        UNION { <selected item> mlr:hasSenseOrFormRelationTo ?x .
                       { ?x mlr:hasDescriptiveRelationTo ?s }
                 UNION { ?x mlr:hasLexicalRelationTo ?s }
                 UNION { ?x mlr:hasValenceFrame [
                             mlr:hasDescriptiveRelationTo ?s ] }
                 UNION { ?x mlr:hasValenceFrame [
                             mlr:usesFrame [
                              mlr:hasDescriptiveRelationTo ?s ] ] }
              } . ?s ?p ?o }
```

As can be seen in (6.16), the query makes use of underspecified properties almost exclusively. This is due to the fact that we want to keep it as general as possible, so that it does not need to be modified in case e. g. further more specific descriptive or lexical relations are added to the model. The query returns a graph consisting of statements `?s ?p ?o` which match the patterns specified in the `WHERE` clause. In particular, `?p` is any property that links `?s` to `?o`, where `?s` matches with the senses and forms of selected lexeme as well as – due to the symmetry, transitiv and (thus) reflexivity of `hasSenseOrFormRelationTo` – with the lexeme itself. In addition to this, `?s` matches with all entities that are linked to the lexeme, its senses or its forms via `hasDescriptiveRelationTo` or via `hasLexicalRelationTo`. Due to the complexity of the valence description, the subsequent lines are necessary, where `?s` matches with the arguments of a frame, the frames it uses, as well as the arguments of the frames it uses (cf. Section 5.2.4 above). The frame itself matches with `?x mlr:hasDescriptiveRelationTo ?s`, and its statements are thus part of the graph as well.

For processing the extracted statements, there are at least two options. Either, the result is serialised in RDF/XML and then processed e. g. by XSLT in order to produce the document that is displayed to the user, or the returned statements (i. e. the `GraphQueryResult` object that is returned[23]) are iterated directly in the program. Since the particular way in which this is done is not important in the context of the following discussion, we will present the query result as serialised in Turtle syntax, as it is more readable. The statements returned by the query in (6.16) after the user has clicked on *»in Schwierigkeiten bringen«* are shown in (6.17)[24].

(6.17)
```
@prefix xsd:  <http://www.w3.org/2001/XMLSchema#> .
@prefix de:  <http://www.ims.uni-stuttgart.de/~spohrds/mlr/german.owl#> .
@prefix mlr:  <http://www.ims.uni-stuttgart.de/~spohrds/mlr/mlr.owl#> .

de:V-PP_pobj_bringen_107
 a mlr:Lexeme , mlr:LexicalEntity , mlr:SimpleCollocation , mlr:V-PP_pobj ,
   mlr:Collocation , mlr:SyntacticallyComplexFreeUnit , mlr:FreeUnit ;
 mlr:hasUserProfileRelationTo "in Schwierigkeiten bringen"^^xsd:string ;
 mlr:hasLabel "in Schwierigkeiten bringen"^^xsd:string ;
 mlr:hasPartOfSpeech mlr:VerbPhrase ;
 mlr:hasDescriptiveRelationTo mlr:VerbPhrase ;
 mlr:hasLinguisticFeature mlr:VerbPhrase ;
 mlr:hasSyntacticFeature mlr:VerbPhrase ;
 mlr:hasForm de:UninflectedForm_bringen_109 ;
 mlr:hasSenseOrFormRelationTo de:Sense_bringen_110 ;
 mlr:hasSenseOrFormRelationTo de:V-PP_pobj_bringen_107 ;
 mlr:hasSenseOrFormRelationTo de:UninflectedForm_bringen_109 ;
 mlr:hasLemma de:UninflectedForm_bringen_109 ;
 mlr:hasSense de:Sense_bringen_110 ;
  ...
de:Sense_bringen_110
 a mlr:Sense , mlr:LexicalEntity ;
 mlr:hasLabel "in Schwierigkeiten bringen 1"^^xsd:string ;
 mlr:hasUserProfileRelationTo "in Schwierigkeiten bringen 1"^^xsd:string ;
 mlr:hasLexicalRelationTo de:Sense_bringen_5 ;
 mlr:hasLexicalRelationTo de:Sense_bringen_619 ;
 mlr:hasCollocate de:Sense_bringen_5 ;
 mlr:hasBase de:Sense_bringen_619 ;
 mlr:isCollocationOf de:Sense_bringen_5 ;
 mlr:isCollocationOf de:Sense_bringen_619 ;
 mlr:hasCollocationalRelationTo de:Sense_bringen_5 ;
 mlr:hasCollocationalRelationTo de:Sense_bringen_619 ;
  ...
 mlr:hasDescriptiveRelationTo de:NumberPreference_bringen_colldb_601 ;
 mlr:hasDescriptiveRelationTo de:DeterminationPreference_bringen_colldb_602 ;
 mlr:hasDescriptiveRelationTo de:DeterminerPreference_bringen_colldb_603 ;
 mlr:hasDescription de:NumberPreference_bringen_colldb_601 ;
```

---

23 Cf. the documentation at http://www.openrdf.org/doc/sesame2/2.3.0/apidocs/org/openrdf/query/GraphQueryResult.html.

24 `X a Y` means that X is of `rdf:type` Y.

```
mlr:hasDescription de:DeterminationPreference_bringen_colldb_602 ;
mlr:hasDescription de:DeterminerPreference_bringen_colldb_603 ;
mlr:hasPreference de:NumberPreference_bringen_colldb_601 ;
mlr:hasPreference de:DeterminationPreference_bringen_colldb_602 ;
mlr:hasPreference de:DeterminerPreference_bringen_colldb_603 ;
 ...
```

As (6.17) shows, the result contains a number of inferred statements as well. This is due to the fact that we want to be able to output lexical entries for different user profiles simply on the basis of the result of the query in (6.16), irrespective of which particular profile has been selected at the moment the query is evaluated. In other words, the query that is executed is the same for all profiles, and no further query to the repository is required if the user wishes to change the profile or the interface language. Therefore, the query result contains statements that may not be directly relevant for the entry of the current profile. For example, as was mentioned in Section 5.4.3, the detail that »*Schwierigkeit* is the *base* of the collocation is not necessarily relevant to an untrained user, while it is for an expert lexicographer.

Which statements are relevant in which profile, as well as the lables with which they are presented, is determined on the basis of the respective user profile model (see Section 5.4.5). There are several ways in which this information can be made available at this point. Here, we will simply assume that the information is extracted from the repository once, at the moment the application is started, and the result statements are stored in a data structure with efficient look-up, such as a Java HashMap[25]. The query that extracts these statements is shown in (6.18). Similar to the one in (6.16), this query also makes use of an underspecified pattern in order to extract all statements, not only the ones of a particular profile. For descriptive purposes, (6.19) displays a small fragment the statements in the form of their Turtle serialisation.

(6.18)
```
CONSTRUCT { ?s ?p ?o }
WHERE { ?p rdfs:subPropertyOf up:hasUserProfileRelationTo .
        ?s ?p ?o
         FILTER (?p != up:hasUserProfileRelationTo) }
```

(6.19)
```
@prefix xsd:  <http://www.w3.org/2001/XMLSchema#> .
@prefix recl1:  <http://www.ims.uni-stuttgart.de/~spohrds/mlr/recl1.owl#> .
@prefix prodl2:  <http://www.ims.uni-stuttgart.de/~spohrds/mlr/prodl2.owl#> .
@prefix mlr:  <http://www.ims.uni-stuttgart.de/~spohrds/mlr/mlr.owl#> .

mlr:hasExample
 recl1:hasAccessStatus "ignore"^^xsd:string ;
 recl1:hasPresentationStatus "primary"^^xsd:string ;
 prodl2:hasAccessStatus "ignore"^^xsd:string ;
 prodl2:hasPresentationStatus "secondary"^^xsd:string ;
 prodl2:hasLabel "Has example"@en ;
 prodl2:hasLabel "Hat Beispielsatz"@de ;
  ...
```

Example (6.19) shows that while `hasExample` should be ignored in both the text-receptive and the text-productive profile[26] in terms of access, it has primary status in the text-receptive

[25] See http://download.oracle.com/javase/1.4.2/docs/api/java/util/HashMap.html.

[26] The prefixes `recl1` and `prodl2` have been assigned to the namespaces of the respective profile models in the MLR repository.

profile and secondary status in the text-productive one (cf. Section 5.4.5). Moreover, (6.19) shows the labels that `hasExample` has in the text-productive profile, both in English and German. This way, it is possible to select only those indications that are relevant in the respective profile, and to present them in the language that has been selected by the user.

As was mentioned before, the lexical entry can now be generated from these statements. There are numerous ways of how the information can be presented to the user. In the graphical user interface to the BLF, for example, users are directed to a page which displays exactly the information that they have asked for, such as gender or frequency information. On this page, they are further given the possibility to learn more about the given lexeme by clicking on the respective link. A slightly different way, which will be followed here, is to interpret the account of user needs in Tarp (2008) such that all primary needs are immediately displayed to the user, whereas secondary needs are shown further down in the entry. In fact, this approach is closely related to the one taken by the Danish *Ordbogen over faste vendinger* (cf. Section 3.2.3.2 above).

While the approach taken by BLF seems to give users more power as to what they are presented with, it could be that there are cases in which a user does not have a single need at the moment the consultation takes place and would thus prefer more than one piece of information. In addition to this, the usage situation in BLF differs according to what is searched for, as the user needs to provide the search term in a different location in the graphical user interface. In contrast to this, the usage situation in the approach taken here is always the same and differs just with respect to the information that is presented. Therefore, the time that is needed in order to get familiar with the graphical user interface is likely to be shorter. However, these differences should not be understood as an attempt to argue that one of the approaches is essentially better than the other, as this would require extensive empirical analysis of user behaviour.

Figure 6.8 shows what the resulting lexical entry for the German noun »*Schwierigkeit*« (»*difficulty*«) in a text-productive situation could look like, based on the approach followed here. In the figure, indications which are primary needs according to Tarp (2008) appear at the top of the lexical entry, such as orthographic information as well as part-of-speech and gender. In addition to this, the inflected word forms – if any have been stored in the MLR – are displayed, e. g. by clicking on a »*Show word forms*« button. As was mentioned in Section 5.1.1, these could be word forms for which there is the need to store additional information. Further word forms could be generated by means of passing on the orthographic form – and possibly morphosyntactic properties like gender – to a morphological generation tool. Finally, the entry lists collocations as well as meaning indications like synonyms, each of which is linked to the entry of the respective item. For example, by clicking on »*in Schwierigkeiten bringen*«, the query in (6.16) is executed with the internal name of the respective lexeme, and the user is forwarded to the page displaying the generated lexical entry of this item. Primary needs can be separated from secondary needs, such as example sentences, by means of a horizontal dashed line. These secondary needs appear only after the user has requested them by clicking on the »*More information*« button. In addition to this, similar to BLF, further information can then be made available at the user's request, such as links to external sources. Technically, this can be done very straightforwardly by storing as values of the respective buttons URLs like `http://www.google.de/#hl=en&q=`[`lemma`] for Google search or `http://dict.leo.org/ende?lang=de& search=`[`lemma`] for look-up in the LEO online dictionary, and by filling the `lemma` slot accordingly. Finally, the user

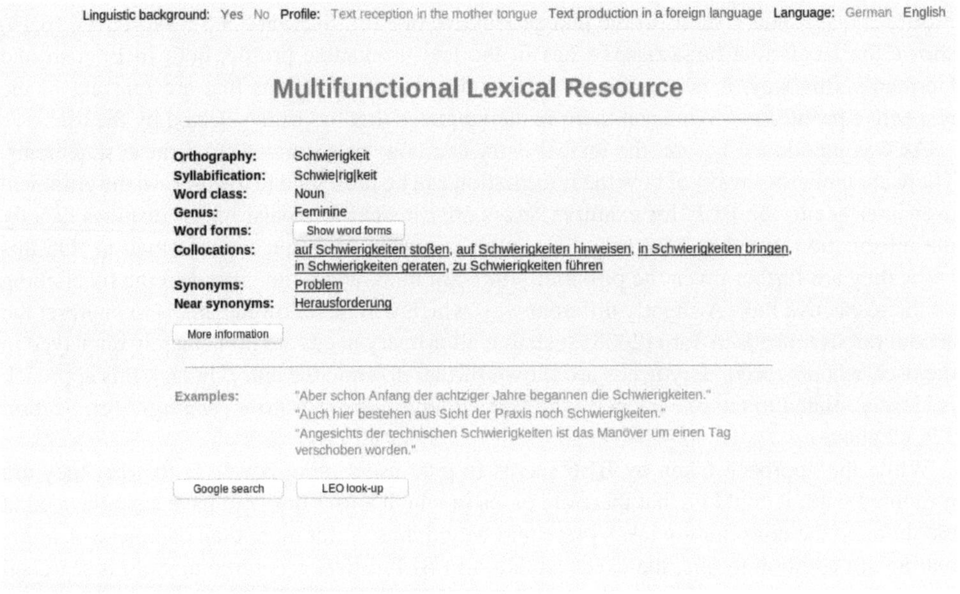

Figure 6.8: Schema of a lexical entry for a text-productive situation in a foreign language

can dynamically switch between different profiles and interface languages, e. g. by selecting a different profile in the drop-down list or by clicking on a different language in the top right-hand corner. By doing so, the statements that had been extracted by means of the query in (6.16) are processed according to the specifications in the currently selected user profile, and the lexical entry is generated again.

6.3 NLP-oriented Lexicon Access and Data Export

In addition to serving the needs of human users with respect to access and presentation, the MLR can serve NLP applications as well. As was mentioned in Section 3.1.3.2 above, there are two ways of approaching this, namely by means of an application programming interface (API) which allows for direct programmatic access to the MLR repository, and by offering conversion of the MLR data into standardised data exchange formats, such as LMF (ISO/FDIS 24613, 2008) or the TEI format for dictionary entries (The TEI Consortium, 2009: pp. 257-296). The two perspectives are discussed in the following sections.

6.3.1 Application Programming Interfaces

As was mentioned above, the Sesame framework provides an API for communicating with repositories by means of SPARQL and SeRQL, as well as at the level of RDF statements. According to the system documentation, this API has been developed in order to »give a developer-friendly access point to RDF repositories, offering various methods for querying and updating the data, while hiding a lot of the nitty gritty details of the underlying machinery«[27]. However, due to the fact that the Sesame repository API operates directly on the level of RDF triples, detailed knowledge of the model is needed in order to extract information from the MLR. The same is true if the query mechanism offered by the API is used, since in this case knowledge of both the model and the query language is needed. Therefore, we consider the Sesame repository API as such to be too closely linked to the underlying RDF structure as to serve as a direct API for communicating with the MLR repository. However, it can still be used as a good starting point for defining a custom API that abstracts away from the model structure and offers more straightforward extraction methods.

For these reasons, a custom Java API has been developed which builds on the Sesame repository API and hides Sesame-specific aspects of the connection, such as the URL of the Sesame server and the repository ID. In addition to this, it does not operate directly on the level of RDF triples and thus hides as much as possible of the internal structure of the model, like internal names and specific paths. Instead, it offers simple methods for the extraction of information about specific entities. Internally, most of these methods make use of SPARQL queries and the evaluation mechanism provided above in order to extract the relevant pieces of information from the repository. However, they do not require command of SPARQL from the developer of the NLP application. In the following, we will focus on the use of the API and illustrate it by means of an example.

The central access point for connecting with the MLR BigOWLIM repository is the `MLRConnection` class. Once the connection has been established, a `MLRConnection` object can be used to retrieve different kinds of information from the MLR, such as all the lexemes that are stored in the repository. Example (6.20) shows how valence information in the form of triples consisting of a grammatical function, a syntactic category and a semantic role can be extracted.

[27] See http://www.openrdf.org/doc/sesame2/users/ch08.html.

(6.20)

```
import de.uni_stuttgart.ims.spohrds.mlr.access.*;
import java.util.*;

public class ExampleApp {
  public static void main(String argv[]) {

    //establish a connection to the MLR repository
    MLRConnection mlr = new MLRConnection();

    //get all lexemes in the MLR
    List<Lexeme> lexemes = mlr.getLexemes();

    //get all lexemes whose orthographic form equals "bringen"
    //false means that it should be an exact match (i.e. no regex)
    lexemes = mlr.getLexemes("bringen", false);

    //get all lexemes whose orthographic form starts with "b"
    lexemes = mlr.getLexemes("^b", true);

    //iterate over lexemes whose orthographic form starts with "b"
    for (Iterator<Lexeme> lexIt = lexemes.iterator(); lexIt.hasNext(); ) {

      Lexeme lex = lexIt.next();

      //get the orthographic form of the current lexeme
      String orth = lex.getOrthographicForm();

      System.out.println("Valence frames of \""+orth+"\":");
      System.out.println("------------------------------");

     //get the semantic valence frames of the current lexeme and
     //iterate over them
     List<SemanticValenceFrame> frames = lex.getSemanticValenceFrames();
     Iterator<SemanticValenceFrame> frameIt = frames.iterator();

     while (frameIt.hasNext()) {

       //iterate over the arguments of the current frame
       SemanticValenceFrame frame = frameIt.next();
       Iterator<Argument> argIt = frame. getArguments().iterator();

        while (argIt.hasNext()) {

          Argument arg = argIt.next();

          //print the names of the function, the category and the role
          System.out.println(arg.getFunction().getName()
                       +", "+arg.getCategory().getName()
                       +", "+arg.getRole().getName());
        }
        System.out.println();
      }
      System.out.println("##############################");
    }
    mlr.close();
  }
}
```

As can be seen in line 8 of (6.20), a connection with the MLR repository is established by calling the `MLRConnection()` constructor. Since all repository-specific detail is implemented there, no further arguments are required. Lines 11, 15 and 18 illustrate different ways of retrieving lexemes from the MLR, namely by calling `MLRConnection.getLexemes()` either without arguments (for extracting all lexemes) or with a `String` and a `boolean` argument. Here, the string value is internally matched against the value of the *hasOrthographicForm* property, either exactly (in case the second argument is `false`) or as part of a regular expression (in case it is `true`). The iteration over the lexemes (lines 21 to 59) shows the extraction of the orthographic form of a lexeme by means of the `Lexeme.getOrthographicForm()` method (line 26). Note that this method has been defined for the `Lexeme` object, although in terms of the MLR model it would involve going via a *Form* and a *FormDescription* instance (cf. Section 5.2.3 above). This is due to the fact that, while we consider the distinction between *Lexeme* vs. *Form* instances crucial from a modelling perspective (see Section 5.1.1), we do not consider it significant in the context of an access application programming interface. Rather, it would introduce an unnecessary complication into the extraction process.

Line 33 shows the extraction of semantic valence information. Here, two important things need to be explained, namely that (i) similar to the case with the orthographic form above, the `getSemanticValenceFrames()` method is called directly on the `Lexeme` object, although – as was mentioned in Section 5.2.4 – semantic valence frames are linked only to senses; and (ii) the objects that are returned by `getSemanticValenceFrames()` are not equivalent to instances of the OWL class *SemanticFrame*. This is because we believe that the details of the internal representation of valence information, as well as the complexity of the syntax-semantics mapping, should be hidden from the application developer[28]. Therefore, we have implemented the `getSemanticValenceFrames()` method such that it returns a `List<SemanticValenceFrame>`, where each `SemanticValenceFrame` object consists of a `List<Argument>`, and each of these `Argument` objects, in turn, consists of a `Function`, a `Category` and a `Role` object. The arguments can be retrieved by means of `SemanticValenceFrame.getArguments()`, where each argument's function, category and role is accessible by means of the `Argument.getFunction()`, `getCategory()` and `getRole()` methods respectively (see lines 47 to 49). In addition to this, the `getSemanticValenceFrames()` method could also be called with a list of specific syntactic functions – more precisely, a `List<Function>` object – so that only those valence frames which have at least the mentioned syntactic functions are returned.

After running the example application just described, we get the following output.

(6.21)
```
Valence frames of "bauen":
------------------------------
subject, NounPhrase, Building.Agent
accObject, NounPhrase, Building.Created_entity

subject, NounPhrase, Building.Created_entity
```

[28] This does not mean that *Lexeme* and *Sense* are generally not distinguished in the application programming interface, since – in contrast to the *Lexeme* vs. *Form* distinction – we consider it very relevant in the context of an access application programming interface. Rather, by calling the `getSemanticValenceFrames()` method on the `Lexeme` object the frames of all senses of the lexeme are returned, whereas by calling it on a `Sense` object only the ones of that particular sense are returned.

```
subject, NounPhrase, Building.Agent

adjunct, PrepositionPhrase, Reliance.Intermediary
subject, NounPhrase, Reliance.Protagonist

adjunct, PrepositionPhrase, Reliance.Means
adjunct, PrepositionPhrase, Reliance.Instrument
subject, NounPhrase, Reliance.Protagonist

##############################
Valence frames of "beäugen":
------------------------------
accObject, NounPhrase, Perception_active.Phenomenon
subject, NounPhrase, Perception_active.Perceiver_agentive

##############################
Valence frames of "beanspruchen":
------------------------------
accObject, NounPhrase, Claim_ownership.Property
adjunct, PrepositionPhrase, Claim_ownership.Beneficiary
subject, NounPhrase, Claim_ownership.Claimant

accObject, NounPhrase, beanspruchen1-salsa.Abstract_property
adjunct, PrepositionPhrase, beanspruchen1-salsa.Beneficiary
subject, NounPhrase, beanspruchen1-salsa.Claimant

##############################
Valence frames of "beantragen":
------------------------------
accObject, NounPhrase, Request.Message
subject, NounPhrase, Request.Speaker

accObject, NounPhrase, Request.Message
subject, PrepositionPhrase, Request.Speaker

adjunct, PrepositionPhrase, Request.Addressee
comp, VerbPhrase, Request.Message
subject, NounPhrase, Request.Speaker

...
```

As the previous example shows, the access application programming interface has been defined such that only very little knowledge of the internal structure of the MLR is needed in order to extract information. In fact, one can say that no model expertise is needed at all, beyond knowing of the existence of entities like lexemes, senses and valence frames. This can, however, be acquired as well by looking at the Javadoc files.

6.3.2 Data Export

While the application programming interface presented in the previous section can be used to interactively extract individual pieces of information in the way described there, it can also be used to extract entire lexicon entries. Sesame has built-in support for exporting query results in several output formats, such as the SPARQL Query Results XML Format (see Section 4.2.6.1). However, these formats are only of limited use for exchanging data with NLP applications. Although general tools for processing them might exist for other applications, the internal structure of the model would still be reflected too much, and thus, model knowledge is required in order to interpret the data. Moreover, returning results to an application by means of the SPARQL Query Results XML Format makes sense only if the respective SPARQL query has been sent by the application as well. Thus, knowledge of SPARQL would again be required. For these reasons, the following subsection describes first experiments in exporting MLR data in the LMF format.[29]

6.3.2.1 Exporting the MLR data to LMF

The conversion of MLR data to specific output formats can be done by defining classes which implement the `ExportFormatWriter` Java interface. One of these classes is the `LMFWriter` class, which implements the methods defined in `ExportFormatWriter` such that the output file conforms to the LMF DTD version 16. For example, the XML root element of every file that is written by `LMFWriter` is a `LexicalResource` element which contains exactly one `GlobalInformation` and at least one `Lexicon` element.

The XML data shown in (6.22) have been obtained by invoking the `MLRConnection.exportEntries()` method with the `List<Lexeme>` object from example (6.20) above and with an `LMFWriter` object. Without going too much into the detail of the LMF representation, we will briefly explain a few aspects of the valence description. First, the value of the `subcategorizationFrames` attribute in `SyntacticBehaviour` is a string of IDREFs, each of which refers to the value of the `id` attribute of an `SubcategorizationFrame` element defined lower in the XML document. These IDs have been generated on the basis of the arguments that the corresponding frame contains. As can be seen, we have included adjuncts in the list of arguments. If desired, this can easily be restricted to the subproperties of *hasGovernableArgument* only, by adjusting the SPARQL query that extracts the syntactic valence frames in `Lexeme. getSyntacticValenceFrames()`. Finally, we have used the MLR-internal names (without their namespaces) as values for the syntactic arguments, since they have been chosen user-friendly enough in order to be processable. However, as was mentioned in Section 5.4.6, the naming could also be regulated by means of an NLP profile which specifies labels based on ISO/FDIS 12620.

(6.22)
```
<?xml version="1.0" encoding="UTF-8"?>
<!DOCTYPE LexicalResource SYSTEM
                         "http://www.tagmatica.fr/lmf/DTD_LMF_REV_16.dtd">
<LexicalResource dtdVersion="16">
  <GlobalInformation>
    <feat att="label" val="MLR output" />
    <feat att="languageCoding" val="UTF-8" />
  </GlobalInformation>
  <Lexicon>
    <LexicalEntry>
      <feat att="partOfSpeech" val="Verb" />
      <Lemma>
```

[29] We have implemented the conversion of syntactic valence information, as well as of basic lemma and part-of-speech information. A complete conversion of all indications in the MLR has not been developed at the time of writing this book. This is due to the fact that LMF has been subject to constant development in the course of carrying out this study.

```
    <feat att="writtenForm" val="bauen" />
  </Lemma>
  <SyntacticBehaviour
   subcategorizationFrames="subject.NounPhrase_accObject.NounPhrase
   adjunct.PrepositionPhrase_subject.NounPhrase
   adjunct.PrepositionPhrase_adjunct.PrepositionPhrase_subject.NounPhrase" />
</LexicalEntry>
<LexicalEntry>
  <feat att="partOfSpeech" val="Verb" />
  <Lemma>
    <feat att="writtenForm" val="beäugen" />
  </Lemma>
  <SyntacticBehaviour
   subcategorizationFrames="accObject.NounPhrase_subject.NounPhrase" />
</LexicalEntry>
<LexicalEntry>
  <feat att="partOfSpeech" val="Verb" />
  <Lemma>
    <feat att="writtenForm" val="beanspruchen" />
  </Lemma>
  <SyntacticBehaviour subcategorizationFrames="
   accObject.NounPhrase_adjunct.PrepositionPhrase_subject.NounPhrase" />
</LexicalEntry>
<LexicalEntry>
  <feat att="partOfSpeech" val="Verb" />
  <Lemma>
    <feat att="writtenForm" val="beantragen" />
  </Lemma>
  <SyntacticBehaviour
   subcategorizationFrames="accObject.NounPhrase_subject.NounPhrase
   accObject.NounPhrase_subject.PrepositionPhrase
   adjunct.PrepositionPhrase_comp.VerbPhrase_subject.NounPhrase ..." />
</LexicalEntry>
 ...
<SubcategorizationFrame id="subject.NounPhrase_accObject.NounPhrase">
  <SyntacticArgument>
    <feat att="syntacticFunction" val="subject" />
    <feat att="syntacticConstituent" val="NounPhrase" />
  </SyntacticArgument>
  <SyntacticArgument>
    <feat att="syntacticFunction" val="accObject" />
    <feat att="syntacticConstituent" val="NounPhrase" />
  </SyntacticArgument>
</SubcategorizationFrame>
<SubcategorizationFrame id="subject.NounPhrase">
  <SyntacticArgument>
    <feat att="syntacticFunction" val="subject" />
    <feat att="syntacticConstituent" val="NounPhrase" />
  </SyntacticArgument>
</SubcategorizationFrame>
<SubcategorizationFrame id="adjunct.PrepositionPhrase_subject.NounPhrase">
  <SyntacticArgument>
    <feat att="syntacticFunction" val="adjunct" />
    <feat att="syntacticConstituent" val="PrepositionPhrase" />
  </SyntacticArgument>
  <SyntacticArgument>
    <feat att="syntacticFunction" val="subject" />
    <feat att="syntacticConstituent" val="NounPhrase" />
```

```
      </SyntacticArgument>
    </SubcategorizationFrame>
      ...
  <Lexicon>
<LexicalResource>
```

6.4 Sketch of an MLR Architecture

In the previous sections of this chapter, we have presented different aspects of defining a multifunctional lexical resource on top of the graph-based OWL model that has been introduced in Chapter 5. Starting from the acquisition of lexical data from existing resources in Section 6.1.1, it has been shown that the semantics of OWL and RDFS in combination with a description logic reasoner and SeRQL queries yields a powerful mechanism capable of ensuring the consistency and integrity of the lexical data, as well as the consistency of the MLR model itself (Section 6.1.2). Finally, the multifunctionality of the lexical resource has been demonstrated in terms of its ability to serve human users and NLP applications (Sections 6.2 and 6.3). In the final section of this chapter, we will summarise the discussion by proposing a high-level architecture for a system that accommodates all of these aspects. After a brief introduction of the main components of this system in Section 6.4.1, we close the discussion by explaining the general processing steps involved in human usage scenarios of the MLR.

6.4.1 Basic Components

The basic component of the proposed MLR architecture is the *Sesame server* (shown at the bottom of Figure 6.9 on page 167). It contains the MLR BigOWLIM repository that was the output of the data acquisition and consistency checking processes described on page 143, and can be accessed by means of the Sesame repository and SAIL application programming interfaces.[30] The Sesame server interacts with the *MLR server*, which is the main component mediating between the MLR data and the human users. In particular, human users interact with the MLR through the graphical user interface discussed in Section 6.2.2. In addition to the query functionality and the presentation of lexical entries, the graphical user interface can provide further functionalities for exporting lexical entries e. g. to PDF format (by means of XSL-FO, as in Schunk, 2006) as well as links which forward the user to external resources, such as the Google search engine or the LEO online dictionary (cf. Section 6.2.2). On the NLP application side, the MLR application programming interface is used for interacting with the MLR. As was shown in Section 6.3, this application programming interface can be used to either extract data from the MLR interactively, or by means of a standard data exchange format like LMF. Moreover, as it has been implemented on top of the Sesame repository application programming interface, it can by-pass the MLR server and interact directly with the Sesame server.

[30] More detail on the internal architecture of Sesame can be found in the user documentation available at http://www.openrdf.org/doc/sesame/users/userguide.html#d0e129.

6.4.2 Processing Steps in a Human Usage Scenario

As can be seen in Figure 6.9, the MLR server contains several modules which can be classified as *access*, *presentation* and *processing* modules. The access module translates the queries that have been stated by means of the graphical user interface (cf. Section 6.2.2) into a SPARQL `SELECT` query. This is passed on to the Sesame server, which returns the query result to the MLR server. In case the query result is empty, this can have three reasons. Either (i) there is no subgraph which matches the specific pattern that the user has queried for, which can be the case especially if very complex patterns are expressed; (ii) the user has entered an inflected word form which is not stored as such in the MLR repository; or (iii) the user has entered a typographical error. In case (i), the empty result set needs to be returned to the graphical user interface. Although there are conceivable ways of dealing with this issue, we will not attempt at arguing for a specific one here. For example, the query could be incrementally underspecified by removing individual patterns from the query and checking whether these return results. However, to determine which of the patterns provided by the user are less relevant than others is a non-trivial task. In addition to this, there would need to be a way of unambiguously indicating to the user that the returned result is not exactly what had been asked for. Otherwise, this could lead to a misinterpretation of the presented data. Cases (ii) and (iii), however, can be resolved in a way that does not require further interaction with the user, for example by re-processing the string values provided by the user by means of a morphological analyser. If the morphological analyser is capable of finding a base form for a string value, this string is replaced with the base form in the SPARQL query, and the repository is queried again. In case the morphological analyser does not find a base form, then it is very likely that there has been a typographical error on the user's side. In order to deal with this, a distance measure algorithm like the one presented by Levenshtein (1966) is used in order to determine the closest distance between the string provided by the user and the lemmas that have been stored in the MLR repository. Here, a disjunction of e. g. the three closest matches returned by the algorithm could replace the user-provided string, and the SPARQL query is evaluated again. As all this happens without the user taking notice, it would resemble a *passive leximat* in the terminology of Tarp (2008). In case this result set is still empty, it is returned to the graphical user interface with the appropriate feedback for the user.

In case the initial `SELECT` query or any of the re-processed ones return a result, this is passed on to the *presentation module*. As was mentioned in Section 6.2.3, this step requires input from the representations in the currently selected user profile model (cf. Section 5.4.5 above). In particular, the lexical entities in the result set are filtered according to the specifications in the current user profile model, so that the result that is returned to the graphical user interface consists of only those entities which should be displayed. The results are then displayed to the user as in Figure 6.7 on page 154. Once the user has clicked on one of the items, the corresponding SPARQL `CONSTRUCT` query is generated (cf. (6.16) on page 153) and passed on to the Sesame server, which returns the statements of the constructed graph to the MLR server. These statements are again processed by the presentation module according to the specifications in the user profile model, and then returned to the graphical user interface, where they are displayed to the user in a form like the one suggested on page 158 above.

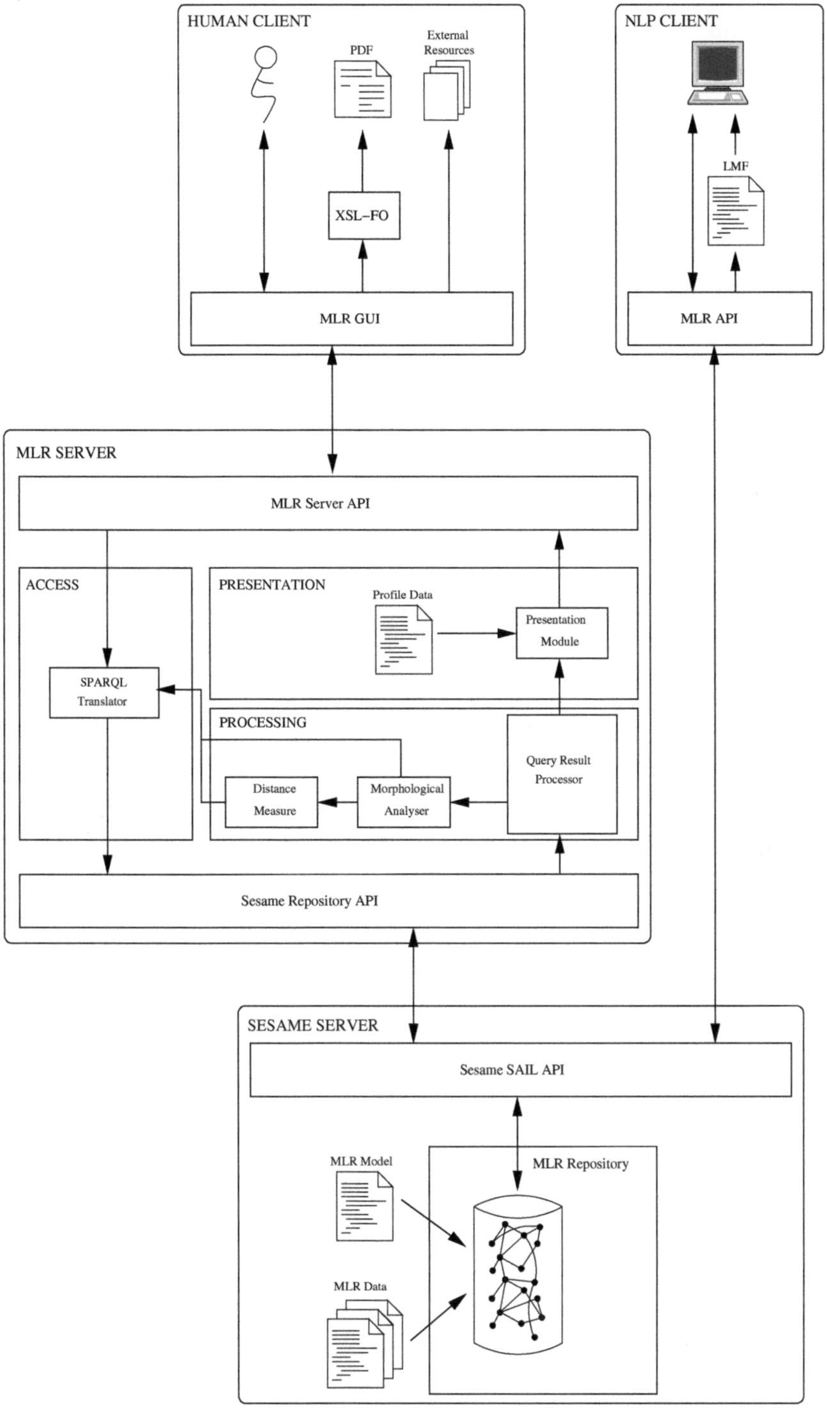

Figure 6.9: High-level architecture of the MLR

7 Conclusion and Future Work

7.1 Conclusion

The central aim of this study has been to design and implement a model for a lexical resource that is *multifunctional* in the sense that it is capable of serving both human users and applications of natural language processing. In order to achieve this goal, this work has integrated research results from two distinct areas. From a theoretical perspective, it has incorporated ideas from general lexicographic theory, in particular *function theory*, into the design of the lexicon model. This aspect has resulted in the design and implementation of a model of user needs on the basis of the function-theoretic account of communicative and cognitive situations in (Tarp, 2008). From a more practical perspective, this study has applied results from research on artifical intelligence to specific problems in the domain of computational lexicography, by using a logic-based formalism for the representation of linguistic phenomena, theorem proving for checking the consistency of the model and data, and graph-based query languages for the formulation of complex queries and integrity constraints.

In order to assess the success of this venture, the conclusions will be formulated with respect to the following points, which have been part of the requirements analysis in Section 3.1.

(1.) The expressivity of the MLR model with respect to being capable of modelling a wide range of linguistic phenomena of varying complexity.

(2.) The accessibility of the representations of these phenomena, in the sense of expressivity of querying, as well as »ease« of extraction.

(3.) The general support given by the MLR model with respect to defining further components in the architecture of a multifunctional dictionary, such as mechanisms for querying and consistency control.

(4.) The scalability of the resulting multifunctional lexical resource.

(5.) The actual multifunctionality of the MLR model, i. e. its actual capability to be used by both human users and NLP applications.

In this book, it has been tried to give answers to all of these points. The main answers with regard to (1.) have been given in chapters 4 and 5. In particular, Section 4.3 has discussed the suitability of OWL for the modelling of lexical data with respect to its formal properties as a typed formalism that has been defined on top of the graph-based RDF. This suitability has then been attested primarily in Sections 5.1 and 5.2, with the discussion of representations for complex linguistic phenomena, such as syntactic and semantic valence descriptions as well as quantitative tendencies with respect to specific morpho-syntactic configurations. Moreover, specific features of OWL which allow for elegant modelling solutions have been discussed, such as multiple inheritance in the hierarchy of lexical and descriptive properties and relations in Section 5.1.3.5. Crucially, all of these representations in the linguistic model remain within the computationally decidable fragment of OWL DL, which enables the use of consistency checking mechanisms based on description logics (see Section 6.1.2 and below).

The accessibility to the representations of these phenomena (cf. (2.)) refers to the »user-friendliness« of the representations, in the sense that their level of complexity should not be too high as to conflict with the nature of the phenomena they are to model. In other words, it should be possible to access and extract specific phenomena in a largely intuitive and comprehensible way. Here, it is believed that the model presented in this study is more "user-friendly" – in the sense just described – than many of the proposed representations in the LMF (ISO/FDIS 24613, 2008). In particular, as was discussed primarily in Sections 3.2.2.1 and 5.2.4.6, LMF's approach to use indirect links e. g. for the representation of valence and multi-word expressions impedes a more intuitive graph-based interpretation. Although it is definitely the case that the representation of valence information as proposed in this book (cf. pages 86 to 99) is highly complex and difficult to comprehend for anyone not directly involved in the development of this model, it is nonetheless assumed that its motivations are transparent enough as to make the representation understandable and reproducible.

Closely related to the previous issue is the desire to hide internal details of the model from the user, and to thereby enable users to query even highly complex representations. This is one of the aspects referred to by point (3.) above, namely the support given by the model in terms of the definition of a query mechanism – primarily with respect to the aforementioned "hiding" of implementation-specific details – and of mechanisms for ensuring the consistency and integrity of model and data. As for the former, Section 6.2.2 has shown how OWL supports the definition of a dynamic query interface. In particular, it has been shown that domain and range information of the properties defined in the model can be used to guide the user through the definition of complex query patterns in at least two respects, namely by offering only the possible values for a property (i. e. the instances in its range) and by constraining the possible continuations after a certain property has been selected (see page 151f for the formal definitions of the relevant sets). This is a major advantage compared to the DiCouèbe query interface, which has the most powerful query mechanism of the dictionaries discussed in Section 3.2.3, but requires the user to have in-depth knowledge of the available data categories.

As for the latter issue, consistency control, Sections 4.3.4 and 6.1.2 have discussed the benefits of being able to formalise the model in terms of description logic axioms (see also Section 5.3). These axioms can be interpreted by a description logic reasoner, which checks whether they are satisfied by both the model and the data. Here, Section 6.1.2 has discussed a current issue of OWL with respect to the open world assumption, which is useful in the context of the semantic web, but in opposition to the closed world typically required in the context of lexical resources. This may lead to counter-intuitive results especially with respect to the definition of data integrity constraints, as missing information does not render the respective item inconsistent. Solutions for overcoming this drawback[1] of OWL have already been proposed (cf. Motik *et al.* (2007a,b); Sirin and Tao (2009)), which – although they have not yet been implemented – seem very promising. For the time being, this issue can be overcome by formulating integrity constraints as SPARQL or SeRQL queries that extract certain configurations and subtract from them the well-formed ones, which has already been

1 Again, it is not a general disadvantage of OWL, since the open world assumption is very useful in the context of the semantic web (cf. page 46 above). It only refers to its use in a lexicographical setting.

successfully used in the development of the SALSA lexicon (Burchardt *et al.* (2008a); see also pages 137ff for details).

In order to assess the scalability of the resource (point (4.) from above), we have created a prototype implementation of a multifunctional lexical resource and filled it with lexical data from two unrelated lexical resources (cf. Section 6.1). In particular, we have extracted and unified lexicographically relevant data from the SALSA corpus release version 1.0 (Burchardt *et al.*, 2006) and the database of collocations from Weller and Heid (2010). The size of the resulting resource comprises almost 14,000 lexemes with roughly 14,500 senses, 3,000 lexical relations, 7,200 valence frame instances and more than 44,000 example sentences (see Table 6.1 on page 135 for a more detailed quantitative overview). In total, these make up over 10,000,000 RDF statements, and can thus be taken to serve as a solid basis for evaluating the scalability of the resource. For storing these statements, it was opted for version 2.3.0 of the Sesame RDF triplestore, in combination with the BigOWLIM 3.2.6 storage and inferencing layer. This combination has already proved to be a very scalable solution, capable of storing billions of RDF statements (see Kiryakov *et al.* (2009)). Compared to the experiments carried out there, the size of the MLR in this study is comparably small, with query evaluation times being typically in the range of milliseconds up to a few seconds.

The final aspect discussed here concerns the actual multifunctionality of the model, in the sense that it allows for the definition of a lexical resource that can be accessed by both human users and NLP applications (cf. (5.)). In order to show this, we have outlined the main aspects of a custom graphical user interface in Section 6.2.2. In addition to allowing for straightforward query access to the data in the sense discussed above[2], this graphical user interface makes use of the model of user needs introduced in Section 5.4 in order to present the lexical data and their descriptions to different types of users in different ways. As a result, the notion of a lexical entry is shifted from a static one that is simply loaded and displayed to the user towards a dynamic one that is generated at runtime. The user model does not only provide formal specifications of primary and secondary needs based on the analysis of Tarp (2008), however, but also multilingual labels for presenting the various indications in the lexicon in different languages. By modelling these specifications on a distinct level, separated from the lexical data, an extensible architecture has been proposed that achieves a complete structural independence of metalanguage, object language and interface language.

As for the computational side, the Sesame repository application programming interface (API) could in principle be used in order to access the data in the MLR. However, as Section 6.3.1 has pointed out, this API would require in-depth knowledge of the model in order to be able to extract information. Therefore, a custom API has been developed which allows for straightforward programmatic access to the data (see Section 6.3 for details). In addition to this, an export routine has been implemented that extracts data from the MLR and outputs them in the LMF standard XML exchange format, which means that they can then be processed by any application that is capable of handling LMF-encoded lexical data. As a result, the data in the MLR can be used by both human users and NLP applications, and thus, the lexicon model proposed in this book is in fact multifunctional.

As the previous paragraphs have shown, the multifunctional graph-based lexicon model as presented in this book is capable of addressing the different points mentioned above in a satisfactory way. Moreover, this study has proposed an architecture that integrates the key

2 The query mask of the graphical user interface as outlined in this book has been developed as part of an undergraduate thesis (cf. Müller, 2010).

aspects of Gouws' notion of a »*mother dictionary*« as well as Tarp's concept of a leximat (cf. Sections 2.2.2 and 2.3). All this has been done by means of a formalism that is – despite its status of a W3C recommendation – not yet widely used in the domain of computational lexicography. By choosing OWL for the definition of the multifunctional lexicon model, as opposed to the common practice of defining yet another custom XML format, this study provides a successful implementation of *actual* reusability of both data and representation formalism in the context of computational lexicographic research.

7.2 Further Lines of Research

In addition to the conclusions presented on the previous pages, there have been issues and questions whose answers have not been given within the scope of this work and which are open for further research. These will be discussed in the following.

Order of Lexicographic Indications in a Lexical Entry

One aspect that has been mentioned several times in this book is that the user model uses Tarp's analysis of primary and secondary user needs in different usage situations. As a result, the corresponding relations in the model specify the status of a property as primary or secondary. While this offers a way for specifying which indications are more (or less) relevant than others in a certain situation, it is not enough to specify e. g. in which order the indication should appear in the entry. Therefore, the model of user needs could be extended such that it allows for the specification of an exact position for each indication. This could be done by defining – similar to the metaproperty *hasStatus* (cf. Section 5.4) – a metaproperty *hasRank* that takes integers as values which represent the absolute position in an entry. However, the problem with this approach would be that it is not extensible, since in case further indications are added at a latter stage, all values of *hasRank* might – in the worst case – need to be changed. A better approach would be to define a strict ordering relation, e. g. an irreflexive transitive metaproperty *precedes*, that specifies the precedence of an indication relative to the other indications. Consider the following configuration, where P_1 to P_3 are properties representing particular indications (e. g. part-of-speech).

(7.1) P_1 *precedes* P_2 *precedes* P_3

If at a later stage a further property P_4 is added and to be displayed between P_2 and P_3, all that is needed to be done is to add the statements P_2 *precedes* P_4 and P_4 *precedes* P_3, and P_4 would receive its correct position between P_2 and P_3[3].

There are several ways to determine which indications should precede which other indications. A very innovative (and promising) one could be to use logged user information from Verlinde (2010) in order to derive statistics as to which indications are most often searched

[3] Note that due to its transitivity, *precedes* does not model direct precedence. Therefore, P_2 *precedes* P_3 and P_2 *precedes* P_4 are consistent.

for. These could then be used to define the relative order – with the most frequent indications appearing at the beginning of the entry – and, in addition to this, give an empirical verification (or falsification) of the user need analysis in Tarp (2008), compensating for the lack of empirical investigation in his account (cf. Piotrowski (2009)).

Adding Further Access Status Values

As was seen in Section 5.4.5.2, the access status has been assumed to be limited to specifying whether an indication should be offered in the drop-down lists of the query form or not (i. e. they have *ignore* as value of the *hasAccessStatus* property). The reason for doing so is that an ordering of the indications in a drop-down list according to principles which – although being justified from a theoretical perspective – is completely opaque to a user may thus lead to confusion rather than support in specifying a query. In particular, users may have to scan the complete list of indications in case they want to specify a value for an indication that is not a primary or secondary need in the profile they have selected. Besides this, it seems hard to predict theoretically which items are typically specified in a query in a specific type of situation. As with the previous issue, quantitative investigation of usage logs may provide insight to some extent and result in a "mild pre-structuring" such that a very small number of frequently specified indications appears before an alphabetically ordered list of all indications which should be offered for querying.

Towards User Individualisation

Closely related to the previous topic is the discussion in Tarp (2011) on the importance of the *specific* needs of *individual* users in *specific* situations, as opposed to the *types* of needs of *types* of users in *types* of situations. Based on this discussion, Spohr (2011) has shown a first approach in the direction of such an individualisation based on the modular architecture presented here. In particular, the Access and Presentation Layer mentioned in Section 5.5.1 can, in addition to the profiles based on user and situation types, further contain files specifying the needs of individual users with respect to access and presentation status of indications, as well as with respect to the labels with which they are displayed. As such, the representation of this information is identical to that of the type-based profile information, as is the mechanism for processing this information in the search and presentation views of the user interface. All that is needed is a straightforward way that would allow users to mark individual indications for their inclusion in the query form or display of lexical entries. As was just mentioned, such individual profiles could on the one hand be stored alongside the type-based profiles. However, since individual users typically find themselves in different consultation situations and may therefore have different needs, this marking of individual indications could be done for each consultation individually – similar to the DiCouèbe interface –, thus allowing users to specify exactly what they want to see in their particular situation.

Publishing Lexical Information as Linked Data

Recent years have seen a rising interest in semantic technologies – in particular the SW –, and subsequently lead to a vast number of resources being available in machine-interpretable form on the internet. The *Linking Open Data (LOD) Project*[4] is all about linking data on the SW and has released principles for publishing data on the SW. Among these are the principles to use uniform resource identifiers (URIs) to identify resources, as well as to make them available in a standard format like RDF/XML. One of the immediate benefits of this is that other resources and services can share and reuse vocabularies defined in other places on the SW. By using OWL for the definition of the MLR model and RDF/XML as possible serialisation, lexical data which are represented according to the definitions in the MLR model can in principle[5] be published on the SW as is and thus be available for other services, e. g. via SW search engines like Sindice[6]. In addition to this, however, the vocabulary defined in the MLR model can be reused by other lexicon developers in order to structure their lexical information according to the definitions in the MLR model. This in turn results in a huge increase in interoperability between lexical information on the SW (cf. Cimiano *et al.*, 2011), allowing for the development of generalised interfaces capable of processing lexical information available in a shared format.

4 http://linkeddata.org/

5 Since there are copyright restrictions underlying the particular data used in this work, they could only be made available "in principle".

6 http://www.sindice.com/

8 Deutsche Zusammenfassung

Dieses Buch befasst sich mit dem Entwurf und der Implementierung eines Modells für eine lexikalische Ressource, die in dem Sinne *multifunktional* ist, als dass sie in der Lage ist, die Bedürfnisse sowohl von verschiedenen Typen von Benutzern als auch von Anwendungen der maschinellen Sprachverarbeitung zu erfüllen. Um dies zu erreichen, verwendet die vorliegende Arbeit Formalismen, die im *Semantic Web* (SW) entwickelt wurden. Hierbei handelt es sich um ein auf dem »World Wide Web« basierendes Projekt des Forschungszweigs der Künstlichen Intelligenz, das zum Ziel hat, Webinhalte mit Bedeutungsannotationen anzureichern. Aufgrund dieses erweiterten Schwerpunktes werden in dieser Arbeit Ziele definiert, die an der Schnittstelle zwischen verschiedenen Forschungsbereichen anzusiedeln sind. Einerseits soll diese Arbeit dazu beitragen, Lösungen zu allgemeinen *lexikographischen* Problemen zu finden, wie z. B. der formalen Erfassung von Benutzerbedürfnissen und der Definition von Mechanismen zur Generierung von Wörterbucheinträgen, die in der Lage sind, diese Bedürfnisse zu erfüllen. Andererseits ist diese Arbeit durch die Verwendung von SW-Formalismen sehr eng mit der *Künstlichen Intelligenz* verbunden. Hier bestehen die wichtigsten Ziele darin, die allgemeine Eignung dieser Formalismen zur Definition eines Lexikonmodells, sowie deren Vorteile im Vergleich zu Formalismen, die sich bisher in der computerlexikographischen Forschung größerer Akzeptanz erfreuen, zu untersuchen. Schließlich zeigt diese Arbeit aufgrund ihrer Zielsetzung, nicht nur die Bedürfnisse »menschlicher« Benutzer, sondern auch die von Anwendungen der maschinellen Sprachverarbeitung zu erfüllen, Anforderungen an die *computerlinguistische* Infrastruktur auf, die notwendig ist, um diese Zielsetzung zu erreichen.

Das erste Kapitel dient der allgemeinen Einführung und Definition der wichtigsten Konzepte, die in diesem Buch verwendet werden. Hierbei handelt es sich insbesondere um das notwendige Hintergrundwissen in allgemeiner Lexikographie und Computerlexikographie, mit besonderem Augenmerk auf die relativ neue *Funktionstheorie* (siehe Bergenholtz und Tarp, 2002; Tarp, 2008). Die Funktionstheorie ist eine allgemeine lexikographische Theorie, die im Unterschied zu eher rekonstruktivistischen Theorien wie der von Wiegand (1988) die Bedürfnisse von *potentiellen* Wörterbuchbenutzern in verschiedenen außerlexikographischen Situationen (d. h. Situationen, die der eigentlichen Wörterbuchbenutzung vorausgehen) als Ausgangspunkt nimmt, und aus deren Analyse Anforderungen an die Präsentation lexikographischer Daten in Wörterbüchern ableitet. Ihre besondere Anziehungskraft zieht die Funktionstheorie im Allgemeinen, und die Arbeit von Tarp (2008) im Speziellen, aus der Tatsache, dass sie die lexikographische Funktion eines Wörterbuchs auf der Basis von Benutzerbedürfnissen definiert (siehe Seite 5), und dass sie diese Definition ergänzt mit einer umfangreichen Analyse dieser Bedürfnisse in verschiedenen kognitiven und kommunikativen Situationen (z. B. Textrezeption oder -produktion in der Muttersprache oder einer Fremdsprache). Obwohl Tarps Analyse an sich nicht unkontrovers diskutiert wird (siehe hierzu z. B. Lew, 2008; Piotrowski, 2009), so bietet sie dennoch eine solide Grundlage für die Definition eines Wörterbuchs, das mehrere dieser Funktionen ausüben soll.

Wie auf Seite 6f dieses Buches diskutiert wird, geht der Begriff *Multifunktionalität*, der Ende der 1980er Jahre im Zusammenhang mit *wiederverwendbaren lexikalischen Ressourcen* geprägt wurde, über die benutzerorientierte Sicht auf lexikographische Funktionen insofern hinaus, als dass er auch Sprachverarbeitungsanwendungen erfasst. Die Definition von Multifunktionalität, die auf Seite 6 gegeben wird, ist im Folgenden wiederholt.

> »Der Begriff ›wiederverwendbare lexikalische Ressource‹ bezeichnet eine linguistische Wissensquelle, die schon von ihrer Konzeption an so spezifiziert und realisiert worden ist, daß die Benutzung in verschiedenen Situationen oder Systemen (sowohl verschiedenen Sprachverarbeitungsanwendungen, als auch verschiedenen (interaktiven) Benutzungssituationen mit ›menschlichen Benutzern‹) in die Design-Kriterien miteinfließt. Solche linguistischen Wissensquellen werden auch als ›multifunktionale‹ Ressourcen bezeichnet.«

Diese Definition von Heid (1997: S. 21), sowie die Überlegungen im Rahmen des von Gouws (2006) erdachten multifunktionalen »Mutterwörterbuchs«, bilden die Grundlage der lexikalischen Ressource, die in dieser Arbeit entwickelt wird.

Kapitel 3 enthält eine Analyse der Anforderungen, die sich im Zusammenhang mit einer multifunktionalen lexikalischen Ressource (MLR) identifzieren lassen, sowie die Auswirkungen, die diese Anforderungen auf den Entwurf der Ressource haben. Die Anforderungsanalyse deckt verschiedene Aspekte einer elektronischen lexikalischen Ressource ab, wie z. B. (i) die Ausführlichkeit und Komplexität der linguistischen Beschreibung, (ii) formale und technische Aspekte, sowie (iii) Anforderungen, die sich direkt aus der beabsichtigten Multifunktionalität der Ressource ergeben. In Bezug auf die linguistische Beschreibung wurde besonderes Augenmerk auf die Wichtigkeit von Mehrwortausdrücken sowie detaillierter Valenzbeschreibungen gelegt, da sich diese als besonders relevant sowohl für Benutzer als auch für Sprachverarbeitungsanwendungen herausgestellt haben (siehe Seite 11f). Im Hinblick auf (ii) befasst sich die in der Literatur am ausführlichsten behandelte Anforderung mit der Zugriffs- und Abfragefunktionalität, die unter anderem benutzerfreundlich und effizient sein und »Ad-hoc-Abfragen« (Heid, 1997) erlauben soll, d. h. Suchanfragen, die nicht notwendigerweise die Spezifikation eines Lemmas beinhalten (siehe auch Atkins, 1992; Spohr und Heid, 2006; de Schryver, 2003). Darüber hinaus wurde jedoch ein weiteres Kriterium identifiziert, das bisher weit weniger Aufmerksamkeit erhalten hat, nämlich das Bedürfnis, Konsistenz und Integrität sowohl des Modells als auch der Daten sicherzustellen. Schließlich begründen die Anforderungen, die sich aus der beabsichtigten Multifunktionalität der Ressource ergeben, das Bedürfnis, ein formales Werkzeug zu definieren, welches die Relevanz bestimmter lexikographischer Angaben in bestimmten Benutzungssituationen angibt. In Bezug auf Anwendungen der maschinellen Sprachverarbeitung ergibt sich aus den multifunktionalen Anforderungen die Wichtigkeit von Austauschformaten sowie die Wichtigkeit der Möglichkeit, z. B. mittels einer Programmierschnittstelle direkten Zugriff auf die Daten in der Ressource zu haben.

Eine der wichtigsten Schlussfolgerungen in Bezug auf den Entwurf einer MLR ist, dass das Modell eine *graphbasierte Sicht* auf das Lexikon erlauben soll, um das relationale Wesen lexikalischer Daten angemessen repräsentieren zu können. Während dies im Einklang mit weiteren aktuellen Ansätzen wie z. B. denen von Polguère (2009) und Trippel (2010) ist, ist eine zusätzliche Bedingung, die sich aus der Anforderungsanalyse ergibt, dass der Formalismus, der zur Definition des Modells verwendet wird, ein stark getypter Formalismus sein muss. Dies ist notwendig, um eine unzweideutige Modellierung linguistischer Informationen sowie die Definition von Mechanismen zu erlauben, die Konsistenz und Integrität sicherstellen. Dies unterscheidet das entwickelte Modell von den eher uneingeschränkten Graphstrukturen der erwähnten Arbeiten.

Weitere Unterschiede zwischen dem hier präsentierten Ansatz und denen, die sich in der Literatur finden lassen, werden auf den Seiten 20 bis 35 diskutiert, hauptsächlich in Bezug auf die oben erwähnten Bedürfnisse. Hier wurde der Schwerpunkt auf den jüngst entwickelten ISO-Standard *Lexical Markup Framework* (LMF; ISO/FDIS 24613, 2008) gelegt, da es sich hierbei um den aktuellsten Ansatz zur Definition eines allgemeinen Frameworks zur Entwicklung von Lexikonmodellen handelt. Zusammengefasst lässt sich sagen, dass sich das Spektrum lexikalischer Ressourcen aufteilt zwischen komputationellen lexikalischen Ressourcen, die nicht auf die Bedürfnisse von verschiedenen Benutzertypen in verschiedenen Situationstypen ausgelegt sind, und elektronischen Wörterbüchern, die nicht im Hinblick auf Sprachverarbeitungsanwendungen entwickelt wurden. Diese beiden Extreme werden ergänzt durch einen Ansatz wie LMF, der – aufgrund seiner abstrakteren Beschaffenheit – in Bezug auf Lösungen, die Probleme auf beiden Seiten des Spektrums betreffen, eher vage bleibt.

Da SW-Formalismen genau diese Eigenschaften besitzen, die für die Definition eines Lexikonmodells als äußerst wichtig erachtet werden – insbesondere die Interpretation als Graph sowie die Typisierung –, werden sie in Kapitel 4 ausführlich behandelt. Im Einzelnen führt das Kapitel diejenigen Technologien ein, die sich auf den unteren Ebenen des sogenannten *Semantic Web Layer Cake* befinden (cf. Seite 41), wie z. B. *Uniform Resource Identifiers* (URIs) und die *eXtensible Markup Language* (XML). Darüber hinaus werden die Vorteile herausgestellt, die sich bei der Verwendung von Formalismen ergeben, die sich auf einer der höheren Ebenen des Diagramms befinden, wie das *Resource Description Framework* (RDF) und die *Web Ontology Language* (OWL). Während diese den Status von *»W3C recommendations«* (d. h. Empfehlungen des World-Wide Web Consortiums[1]) haben, also De-facto-Standards sind und daher insbesondere im Zusammenhang mit ontologischen Ressourcen weit verbreitet sind, ist ihre Verwendung in einem computerlexikographischen Szenario bisher eher wenig dokumentiert – trotz der Vorteile, die ihre Verwendung mit sich bringt. Einer dieser Vorteile ist z. B. die Fähigkeit, Wohlgeformtheitsbedingungen für verschiedene Typen von Lexikonentitäten mit Hilfe von logischen Axiomen zu definieren, die dann von einem Theorembeweiser überprüft werden können[2]. Die Sprache, die zur Definition dieser Axiome verwendet wird, basiert auf einer recht ausdrucksmächtigen *Beschreibungslogik*, d. h. einer Sprache, die auf einem entscheidbaren Fragment der Prädikatenlogik erster Ordnung aufbaut (Baader *et al.*, 2003). Ein weiterer Vorteil beinhaltet die Möglichkeit, den inhärenten Vererbungsmechanismus von RDF Schema und OWL zur Formulierung von unterspezifizierten Suchanfragen zu verwenden, was bereits in Spohr und Heid (2006) erläutert wurde. Dies ist ein wichtiger Vorteil gegenüber der gängigen lexikographischen Praxis, ein anwendungsspezifisches XML-Format für die Modellierung einer lexikalischen Ressource zu definieren, da solche Formate üblicherweise die Implementierung von weiterer Software erfordern, um die gewünschte Interpretation der Vererbungsrelation zu erzielen. Im Gegensatz hierzu ist diese Interpretation bei RDF Schema und OWL praktisch ohne Mehraufwand enthalten, was insbesondere auf deren Status als Web-Standards und die daher verfügbaren Werkzeuge zurückzuführen ist. Weitere Punkte, die in diesem Kontext relevant sind, werden in Abschnitt 4.3 besprochen.

Kapitel 5 stellt den zentralen Teil dieser Arbeit dar, insofern es das graphbasierte MLR-Modell vorstellt. Zusätzlich zu den formalen Einzelheiten zur Implementierung in OWL enthält das Kapitel auch die wichtigsten Designentscheidungen, die Überlegungen, die zu diesen geführt haben, sowie Vergleiche zu Ansätzen wie z. B. LMF.

[1] Siehe http://www.w3.org/.

[2] Vgl. Abschnitt 4.2.7.2 für eine Auflistung solcher Theorembeweiser.

Die grundlegende Unterscheidung, die im MLR-Modell gemacht wird, ist die zwischen *lexikalischen Einheiten* und *beschreibenden Einheiten.* Während lexikalische Einheiten einzelne Lexeme mit ihren verschiedenen Wortformen und Lesarten darstellen, repräsentieren beschreibende Einheiten das, was gängig als *Datenkategorien* bezeichnet wird – m. a. W. Einheiten, die zur Beschreibung lexikalischer Einheiten verwendet werden. Diese umfassen einfache Datenkategorien wie z. B. Wortart oder Genus, die in dieser Arbeit als *linguistische Features* bezeichnet werden (siehe Abschnitt 5.2.2), sowie komplexe Datenkategorien wie Valenzrahmen oder Beispielsätze, die als *»Beschreibungen«* (*»descriptions«*) bezeichnet werden (vgl. Abschnitte 5.2.3 bis 5.2.6). Sowohl der lexikalische als auch der beschreibende Teil des Modells besteht aus Hierarchien, die unter anderem auf dem ISO/FDIS 12620 (2009) und der *General Ontology for Linguistic Description* (GOLD; Farrar und Langendoen, 2010) aufbauen. Während beschreibende Einheiten hauptsächlich nach der Domäne der linguistischen Beschreibung unterschieden werden (z. B. morphologische vs. syntaktische vs. semantische Features; siehe Abbildungen A.2 und A.3 auf den Seiten 199 und 200), werden Lexeme primär auf der Grundlage ihrer morphologischen und syntaktischen Komplexität klassifiziert. Eine dieser Unterscheidungen ist die zwischen *gebundenen* und *freien Einheiten*, die sich wiederum in verschiedene Affixe bzw. syntaktisch einfache oder komplexe freie Einheiten aufteilen (siehe Seite 198 für weitere Einzelheiten). Der Vorteil einer feinkörnigen Klassifizierung von lexikalischen und beschreibenden Einheiten liegt unter anderem in der Fähigkeit, diesen Klassen unterschiedliche Eigenschaften und Relationstypen zuordnen zu können. Wohingegen eine komplexe morphologische Einheit wie ein Kompositum z. B. aus weiteren freien lexikalischen Einheiten besteht, ist dies z. B. bei Präfixen nicht der Fall. Im Gegensatz hierzu kann man jedoch sagen, dass eine Kollokation ebenfalls aus weiteren freien Einheiten besteht. Die Beziehung zwischen einer Kollokation und ihren Bestandteilen ist jedoch nicht notwendigerweise dieselbe wie diejenige, die zwischen einem Kompositum und seinen Bestandteilen besteht. Daher enthält das Modell, ähnlich der reichhaltigen Klassenhierarchie für Entitätstypen, ebenfalls eine Hierarchie lexikalischer Relationen. Diese erlaubt die Definition von spezifischeren und allgemeineren Relationen, die jeweils ihre eigenen Definitions- und Wertebereiche haben. So lassen sich Relationen wie z. B. *isCollocationOf* (*»ist Kollokator von«*) und *isCompoundOf* (*»ist Kompositum aus«*) erstellen, die jeweils für Kollokationen bzw. Komposita definiert sind. Um die Tatsache zu erfassen, dass beide Relationen meronymische Beziehungen beschreiben, werden sie als Subrelationen der oben angedeuteten Relation *»besteht aus«* (*hasComponent*) definiert, was aufgrund des inhärenten Vererbungsmechanismus von OWL zur Folge hat, dass beide Relationen von einer Suchanfrage abgedeckt werden können, welche die allgemeinere, unterspezifizierte *hasComponent*-Relation verwendet.

Zusätzlich zu den lexikalischen Relationen enthält das Modell eine Hierarchie beschreibender Eigenschaften und Relationen. Während sich manche dieser Relationen auf Instanzen der oben erwähnten einfachen Datenkategorien beziehen (z. B. verbindet die *hasGender*-Relation Instanzen der *Lexeme*-Klasse mit Instanzen der *GrammaticalGender*-Klasse), verweisen andere auf komplexere Beschreibungen. Wie bereits erwähnt wurde, handelt es sich bei einer dieser Beschreibungen um die Valenzinformation. Hier schlägt das vorgestellte Modell eine Repräsentation vor, die sich grundlegend von der im LMF-Standard vorgeschlagenen Modellierung unterscheidet, insbesondere in Bezug auf die Darstellung von syntaktischen Funktionen und semantischen Rollen, der Syntax-Semantik-Abbildung, sowie die Relation zwischen den Valenzrahmen eines Mehrwortausdrucks und denen seiner Komponenten. Eine Repräsentation ist auf Seite 100 exemplarisch für die Kollokation *»Kritik üben«* angegeben.

Der letzte Aspekt bezieht sich auf die tatsächliche Multifunktionalität des Modells in Bezug auf dessen Fähigkeit, verschiedene Benutzertypen und Sprachverarbeitungsanwendungen bedienen zu können. Hierfür sieht dieses Buch ein *Metamodell von Benutzerbedürfnissen* vor, welches die Relevanz von bestimmten Angabetypen in einem Wörterbucheintrag in Bezug auf einen bestimmten Benutzertyp in einer bestimmten Benutzungssituation definiert. Kurz zusammengefasst nimmt dieses Metamodell die Analyse von Benutzerbedürfnissen in Tarp (2008) als Grundlage und definiert – mittels zweier Relationen *hasStatus* und *hasLabel* – einerseits den Status einer Angabe als *primary*, *secondary* oder *ignore*, und andererseits die Bezeichnungen, mit denen diese Angabe den Benutzern in verschiedenen Sprachen angezeigt wird. Während eine Angabe wie z. B. *isCollocateOf* für lexikographische Experten relevant ist und diesen in einem englischen Wörterbucheintrag daher z. B. als »*Collocate of:*« bzw. als »*Kollokator von:*« in einer deutschen Version präsentiert werden kann, so stellt sie für Benutzer, die keine besonderen linguistischen oder lexikographischen Vorkenntnisse haben, eine eher unwichtige Angabe dar. Hier kann man nun der *isCollocateOf*-Relation den Status *ignore* zuordnen, und stattdessen einer ihrer übergeordneten Relationen (z. B. *hasCollocation*) primären oder sekundären Status zuweisen, die dem Benutzer dann z. B. als »*Typical word combinations:*« bzw. »*Typische Wortverbindungen:*« präsentiert werden. Darüber hinaus erlaubt die Auszeichnung als primär oder sekundär eine einheitliche Behandlung von Angaben eines bestimmten Angabetyps, z. B. dass primäre Angaben direkt in einem Wörterbucheintrag angezeigt werden, wohingegen sekundäre erst auf Anfrage verfügbar gemacht werden.

Da das Benutzermodell auf einer separaten Ebene getrennt von den lexikalischen Daten definiert ist (in technischer Hinsicht *importiert* es den linguistischen Teil des Modells; vgl. Abschnitt 5.4.5), ist es komplett unabhängig von der im Wörterbuch beschriebenen Sprache. Mit anderen Worten ist es möglich, lexikalische Daten des Deutschen mit Hilfe von z. B. englischen oder französischen Angabebezeichnungen darzustellen, in Abhängigkeit von der Muttersprache oder Präferenz des jeweiligen Benutzers. Aus diesem Grund ist es möglich, *Benutzerprofile* zu definieren, welche sowohl die Bedürfnisse eines bestimmten Benutzertyps in einer bestimmten Situation (z. B. ungeübter Fremdsprachenlerner in einer textrezeptiven Situation in der Fremdsprache), als auch die verschiedenen Sprachen modellieren, in denen die Angaben insbesondere Fremdsprachenlernern der Anfängerstufe präsentiert werden können. Durch den modularen Aufbau des Modells und die dadurch erzielte Unabhängigkeit von Präsentationssprache und Wörterbuchinhalt können weitere Benutzerprofile problemlos zu einem späteren Zeitpunkt hinzugefügt werden.

Nachdem die Einzelheiten des Modells ausführlich behandelt sind, wird in Kapitel 6 über erste Ansätze zur Erstellung einer multifunktionalen lexikalischen Ressource berichtet. Abschnitt 6.1 beschreibt, wie lexikalische Daten aus zwei unterschiedlichen lexikalischen Ressourcen des Deutschen – dem SALSA-Korpus Version 1.0 (Burchardt *et al.*, 2006) und der Kollokationsdatenbank von Weller und Heid (2010) – extrahiert und in das MLR-Modell gespeist wurden. Die entstandene Ressource umfasst etwa 14.000 Lexeme mit 14.500 verschiedenen Lesarten, 44.000 Beispielsätzen und fast 3.000 lexikalischen Relationen. Der Ablaufplan des Lexikonkompilierungsprozesses ist in Abschnitt 6.1.3 dokumentiert, mit besonderem Augenmerk auf der Unifikation der lexikalischen Daten sowie den Mechanismen zur Konsistenzkontrolle. Diese beinhalten einerseits axiombasierte Mechanismen wie die weiter oben erwähnten, bei denen ein Theorembeweiser zur Überprüfung von Inkonsistenzen in Bezug auf die beschreibungslogischen Axiome verwendet wird. Andererseits umfassen sie jedoch auch *abfragebasierte Konsistenzprüfungen* im Sinne von z. B. Burchardt *et al.* (2008a), bei denen mittels Suchanfragen nicht-wohlgeformte Muster aus dem Lexikongraphen extrahiert werden.

Abschnitt 6.2 befasst sich mit dem benutzerorientierten Zugriff auf die Wörterbuchdaten, sowie deren Präsentation. Aufbauend auf den in Abschnitt 5.4 vorgestellten Spezifikationen werden Ansätze entwickelt, wie die in den Benutzerprofilen enthaltenen Informationen dazu verwendet werden können, unterschiedliche Wörterbucheinträge von derselben zugrunde liegenden Datenbasis zu generieren, um die Bedürfnisse der jeweiligen Benutzer zu erfüllen. Zusätzlich zu der Ausarbeitung von Vorschlägen in Bezug auf die Entwicklung einer Suchmaske für eine graphische Benutzeroberfläche werden auch die Einzelheiten der internen Mechanismen diskutiert, die für die profilabhängige Generierung notwendig sind. Wie diese Überlegungen bereits andeuten wird in diesem Zusammenhang die Sicht auf Wörterbucheinträge als *statische* Einheiten durch eine Sichtweise ersetzt, die diese als *dynamische* Einheiten begreift, die zur Laufzeit von den zugrunde liegenden Daten generiert werden, in Abhängigkeit von den Spezifikationen im Modell der Benutzerbedürfnisse.

Im Gegensatz zu diesem benutzerorientierten Ansatz geht es bei der auf die maschinelle Sprachverarbeitung ausgerichteten Sicht hauptsächlich darum, sprachverarbeitenden Anwendungen entweder direkten Zugriff auf die Daten zu erlauben (z. B. mit Hilfe einer Programmierschnittstelle), oder aber indirekten Datenaustausch über Austauschformate zu erlauben. Um die Multifunktionalität der entwickelten Ressource unter Beweis zu stellen, wurden beide Ansätze implementiert. Zum einen behandelt Abschnitt 6.3.1 die Einzelheiten der Java-Programmierschnittstelle, die entwickelt wurde, um direkten Zugriff auf die Daten zu erlauben, ohne vom Anwendungsentwickler detailliertes Wissen über die internen Strukturen des zugrundeliegenden Modells zu verlangen. So wurden z. B. Methoden wie `getLexemes()` oder `Lexeme.getValenceFrames()` implementiert, die es dem Anwendungsentwickler erlauben, auf einfache Weise Informationen aus der MLR zu extrahieren, ohne Graphmuster selbst spezifizieren zu müssen. Zum anderen beschreibt Abschnitt 6.3.2, wie die MLR-Daten in ein standardisiertes Austauschformat überführt werden können. Hierbei wurde exemplarisch auf das nicht-normative LMF-XML-Format zurückgegriffen.

Kapitel 6 schließt mit der Skizze einer möglichen webbasierten Architektur für die lexikalische Ressource, einschließlich einer Beschreibung der grundlegenden Komponenten sowie einem kurzen Überblick über die Verarbeitungsschritte, die an einem Anwendungsszenario beteiligt sind. Zusätzlich zu ersten Überlegungen, wie eine morphologische Analysekomponente in die Benutzeroberfläche des Wörterbuchs integriert werden könnte, werden Vorschläge in Bezug auf die autonomen Verarbeitungsschritte formuliert, die im Falle einer nicht-wohlgeformten Benutzereingabe erforderlich sind, um dennoch sinnvolle Rückmeldung an den Benutzer geben zu können (vgl. hierzu auch das »unsichtbare Wörterbuch« von Bergenholtz, 2005). Zum Zeitpunkt der Fertigstellung dieser Buches ist die Implementierung solcher Rückfallstrategien jedoch noch als Forschungsvorhaben zu betrachten.

Die wichtigsten Schlussfolgerungen dieser Arbeit werden in Kapitel 7 diskutiert, mit einem Ausblick auf mögliche zukünftige Erweiterungen. Auf den Seiten 168 bis 171 wird die Leistung des Modells in Bezug auf die wichtigsten Anforderungen aus Kapitel 3 bewertet. Wie diese Diskussion zeigt sind sowohl die experimentelle multifunktionale lexikalische Ressource als auch das zugrunde liegende Modell in der Lage, die Anforderungen auf zufriedenstellende Weise zu behandeln. Dies wird darüber hinaus durch die Verwendung eines Formalismus erreicht, der – trotz seines Status als W3C-Empfehlung – in der Computerlexikographie bisher noch nicht weit verbreitet ist. Aus diesem Grund liefert die vorliegende Arbeit durch die Definition des multifunktionalen Lexikonmodells unter Verwendung von OWL – im Gegensatz zu der sonst üblichen Entwicklung von eigenen anwendungsspezifischen XML-Formaten –, eine erfolgreiche Implementierung von *tatsächlicher* Wiederverwendbarkeit sowohl der Daten als auch des Repräsentationsformalismus im Rahmen computerlexikographischer Forschung.

9 English Summary

This study deals with the design and implementation of a model for a lexical resource that is *multifunctional*, in the sense that it is capable of serving the needs of different kinds of users as well as applications of natural language processing (NLP). In order to achieve this, this work makes use of formalisms that have been developed in the *Semantic Web* (SW), an artificial intelligence project that builds on the world-wide web and is aimed at the enrichment web content with annotations of meaning. Due to this extended focus, this study defines objectives at the boundary between several research fields. On the one hand, it aims at contributing to solutions to general *lexicographic* problems, such as the modelling of user needs and the definition of mechanisms for generating dictionary entries that are capable of satisfying these needs. On the other hand, by incorporating recent developments from the SW, it is closely linked to the field of *artifical intelligence*. Here, the primary aims are to investigate the general suitability of these formalisms for the definition of a lexicon model, as well as their benefits compared to formalisms which are – up to now – more widely accepted in the *computational lexicographic* community. Finally, due to its aim of serving not only the needs of human users, but also the needs of NLP applications, this study identifies requirements on the *computational linguistic* infrastructure that is necessary in order to achieve this.

The first chapter is devoted to the general introduction and definition of the main concepts used in this book. In particular, it provides the necessary background on computational and general lexicography, with a primary focus on the rather recently developed *function theory* (see Bergenholtz and Tarp, 2002; Tarp, 2008). Function theory claims to be a general lexicographic theory which – in contrast to more reconstructivist theories like the one of Wiegand (1988) – takes as a starting point the needs of *potential* dictionary users in different extra-lexicographic situations (i. e. situations which precede the actual dictionary consultation), and derives from this analysis requirements on the representation of lexicographic data in dictionaries. The major attractiveness of function theory, and in particular of the work presented in Tarp (2008), is that it defines the lexicographic function of a dictionary on the basis of user needs (see page 5), and that it complements this definition with a rich analysis of these needs in different cognitive and communicative situations, e. g. a text-receptive or text-productive situation in the mother tongue or a foreign language. Although the analysis itself is not uncontroversial (see e. g. Lew, 2008; Piotrowski, 2009), it nonetheless provides a solid basis for the definition of a model for a dictionary that is to serve several of these functions.

As discussed on page 6f of this book, the term *multifunctionality*, which has been coined in the context of *reusable lexical resources* in the late 1980's, goes beyond the user-centered view of lexicographic functions in that it covers NLP applications as well. The definition of multifunctionality that has been given on page 6 is repeated below.

> The term "reusable lexical resource" denotes a source of linguistic knowledge whose conception has been specified and realised such that its use in different situations or systems (both different NLP applications and different (interactive) usage situations with "human users") is incorporated in the design criteria. Such sources of linguistic knowledge are also referred to as "multifunctional" resources.

This definition, which has been given by Heid (1997: p. 21), as well as the notion of a multifunctional *»mother dictionary«* conceived of by Gouws (2006), form the basis of the lexical resource that is developed in this study.

Chapter 3 provides an analysis of the main requirements that can be identified in the context of a multifunctional lexical resource (MLR), as well as the implications they have on its design. The requirements analysis covers various aspects of an electronic lexical resource, such as (i) the detail and complexity of the linguistic description, (ii) formal and technical aspects, as well as (iii) requirements which derive from the intended multifunctionality of the resource. As far as linguistic description is concerned, special attention has been paid to the importance of detailed valence information and multi-word expressions. This is due to the fact that both have been identified as particularly relevant for both human users and NLP applications (see page 11f). With regard to (ii), the requirement that has been discussed most prominently in the literature concerns the access and query functionality, which should, among others, be user-friendly as well as efficient, and allow for non-standard access to the data in the dictionary – i. e. access that does not necessarily involve the specification of a lemma (cf. Atkins, 1992; de Schryver, 2003; Spohr and Heid, 2006). In addition to this, however, a further requirement has been identified which has not received as much attention up to now, namely the need to be able to ensure *consistency* and *integrity* of both the lexicon model and the data. Finally, the requirements which originate from the intended multifunctionality of the resource motivate the definition of a formal tool that specifies the relevance of certain lexicographic indications in particular human usage situations. In the context of NLP applications, they indicate the importance of exchange formats and of the possibility to have programmatic access to the resource.

One of the most important implications on the design of an MLR is that in order to be able to represent the highly relational nature of lexical data, the model should allow for a *graph-based view* on the lexicon. While this is in line with other recent proposals such as the ones by Polguère (2009) and Trippel (2010), a further implication derived from the requirements analysis is that the formalism that is used for the definition of the model has to be strongly typed. This is needed in order to allow for unambiguous modelling of linguistic information as well as for the definition of mechanisms for ensuring consistency and integrity, and it distinguishes the proposed model from the rather unconstrained graph structures developed in the works just mentioned.

Further differences between the present approach and related approaches found in the literature are discussed on pages 20 to 35, primarily with respect to the requirements discussed above. Here, particular emphasis has been put on the recently developed ISO standard *Lexical Markup Framework* (LMF; ISO/FDIS 24613, 2008), as it is the most recent approach to defining a common framework for the development of models lexical resources. In sum, the spectrum seems to be divided into computational lexical resources that have not been designed to cater for the needs of different types of users in different types of situations, and electronic dictionaries that have not been developed with a view to NLP applications. These two extremes are complemented by a proposal like LMF, which remains – due to its more abstract nature – rather vague on solutions to particular problems on either side of the spectrum.

Since SW formalisms have exactly those characteristics which have been identified as crucial in a formalism that is used for the definition of a lexicon model – most importantly graph interpretation and typedness –, they are discussed in great detail in Chapter 4. In particular, the chapter introduces technologies located on the lower levels of the so-called *Semantic Web*

Layer Cake (cf. page 41), such as *Uniform Resource Identifiers* (URIs) and the *eXtensible Markup Language* (XML), and highlights the benefits of using formalisms which are located on higher levels, such as the *Resource Description Framework* (RDF) and the *Web Ontology Language* (OWL). While both of these have the status of W3C recommendations (i. e. they are de facto standards) and are thus widely used especially in the context of ontological resources, their reported use in a computational-lexicographic setting is – despite their benefits – rather limited so far. Among these benefits is the possibility to define well-formedness constraints on different types of entities in the lexicon in the form of logic axioms, which can be checked by a theorem prover[1]. The language used for the definition of these axioms is based on a fairly expressive *description logic*, i. e. a language which builds on a decidable fragment of first-order predicate logic (Baader *et al.*, 2003). A further benefit includes the possibility to use the built-in inheritance mechanism of RDF Schema and OWL in order to formulate underspecified queries, which has been presented e. g. in Spohr and Heid (2006). Among others, this is an important advantage over the common lexicographic practice to define a custom XML format for the modelling of a lexical resource, since such formats typically require the implementation of appropriate software in order to achieve the desired interpretation of an inheritance relation. In contrast to this, due to their status as de-facto standards and the wide range of software that is readily available for RDF Schema and OWL, the interpretation of the inheritance relation comes basically for free. Additional points relevant in this context are discussed in Section 4.3.

Chapter 5 represents the core part of this work, as it introduces the graph-based model that has been defined for the MLR. In addition to providing much of the formal detail of the actual implementation in OWL, the chapter also covers the most important design decisions that have been made, the considerations that have motivated them, as well as comparisons to approaches like LMF.

The basic distinction made in the model is that between *lexical entities* and *descriptive entities*. While lexical entities represent individual lexemes, as well as their different forms and senses, descriptive entities represent what is commonly referred to as *data categories* – in other words, those entities which are used for the description of lexical entities. These include simple data categories like part-of-speech or gender (called *linguistic features* in this book; see Section 5.2.2), and complex data categories like valence frames or example sentences (labelled *descriptions*; see Sections 5.2.3 to 5.2.6). Both the lexical and the descriptive part of the model are defined as rich class hierarchies, which are based among others on the ISO standard ISO/FDIS 12620 (2009) as well as the *General Ontology for Linguistic Description* (GOLD; Farrar and Langendoen, 2010). While descriptive entities are structured primarily with respect to their domain of linguistic description (e. g. morphological vs. syntactic vs. semantic features; see Figures A.2 and A.3 on pages 199 and 200 respectively), lexemes are classified primarily on the basis of their morphological and syntactic complexity. One of these distinctions is the one between *bound* and *free units*, which are further subdivided into different kinds of affixes and syntactically simple or complex free units (see page 198 for more details).

The primary benefit of defining such a rich classification of lexical and descriptive entities is to be able to assign different properties and different types of relations to each of these classes. For example, whereas a morphologically complex free unit like a compound can

[1] See Section 4.2.7.2 for a list of such theorem provers.

be said to *consist of* other free lexical units, this is not the case for a prefix. In contrast to this, a collocation can be said to *consist of* other free units as well; however, the relation that holds between a collocation and its components is not necessarily the same as the one holding between a compound and its components. Therefore, similar to the rich hierarchisation of classes of entities, the model also contains a hierarchy of lexical relations. This allows for the definition of more specific relations, each of which has its own domain and range specifications. For example, we can create relations like *isCollocationOf* and *isCompoundOf*, which are defined for collocations and compounds respectively. In order to capture the fact that both of them are meronymic relations, they are defined as subrelations of the *consistsOf* relation just mentioned, which means that – due to the built-in inheritance mechanism of OWL – both of them would be covered by a query which uses the more general, underspecified relation.

Similar to lexical relations, the model contains a hierarchy of descriptive properties and relations. While some of these refer to instances of the simple data categories mentioned above (e. g. the *hasGender* property links instances of the class *Lexeme* to instances of the class *GrammaticalGender*), others link a lexical entity to more complex descriptions. As was mentioned above, one of these deals with the representation of valence information. Here, the presented model proposes a representation that differs considerably from the one proposed in the LMF standard, in particular with respect to the modelling of syntactic functions and semantic roles, the representation of the syntax-semantics mapping, as well as the relation between the valence frames of a multi-word expression and the frames of its components. An example representation has been given on page 100 for the collocation »*Kritik üben*« (»*to criticise*«).

The last aspect of the model concerns its actual multifunctionality with respect to its capability of serving different kinds of users and NLP applications. Here, this study proposes a *metamodel of user needs* that defines the relevance of specific indications in a dictionary entry with respect to a particular type of user in a specific type of situation. In short, the metamodel takes the user need analysis of Tarp (2008) as basis and defines – by means of the properties *hasStatus* and *hasLabel* – the status of an indication as *primary*, *secondary* or *ignore*, as well as the labels with which it is to be presented to the user in different languages. For example, while an indication like *isCollocateOf* is relevant to expert lexicographers and can thus be presented e. g. as »*Collocate of:*« in an English dictionary entry or as »*Kollokator von:*« in its German version, it is not a relevant indication in the context of a linguistically untrained user. Here, the *isCollocateOf* relation can be assigned the status *ignore*, and instead one of its more general superproperties, e. g. *hasCollocation*, receives primary or secondary status and is presented e. g. as »*Typical word combinations:*« or »*Typische Wortverbindungen:*« in the dictionary entry. Moreover, by defining an indication as *primary* or *secondary*, it is possible to assign uniform treatments to the indications of a particular status, e. g. that primary indications should be displayed immediately in the dictionary entry, whereas secondary ones should only be displayed on demand.

Due to the fact that the user model has been defined on a separate layer (technically it *imports* the linguistic part of the model; cf. Section 5.4.5), it is completely independent from the language that is described in the dictionary. In other words, German lexical data can be presented e. g. with English or French labels for indications, depending on the mother tongue or language preference of the respective user. As a result, it is possible to define *user profiles* which model the needs of a specific type of user in a specific type of situation (e. g. untrained language learner in a text-receptive situation in a foreign language), as well as the different presentation languages with which the indications are – especially in the case of language learners at the beginners' level – presented. Due to the modular organisation and thus the independence of presentation languages and dictionary content, further user profile specifications can be added at later stages without any problems.

With the details of the model discussed, Chapter 6 reports on first efforts to compiling an actual MLR on the basis of the model. Here, Section 6.1 describes how lexical data have been extracted from two different German lexical resources, i. e. the SALSA corpus release 1.0 and the collocations database of Weller and Heid (2010), and fed into the MLR. The resulting resource comprises almost 14,000 lexemes with 14,500 different senses, 44,000 example sentences and almost 3,000 lexical relations. The workflow of the lexicon compilation process is documented in Section 6.1.3, focussing on the unification of the lexical data as well as the consistency checking mechanism. On the one hand, this includes axiom-based mechanisms like the ones mentioned above, where a theorem prover checks for inconsistencies with respect to the description logic axioms. On the other hand, however, this further includes *query-based consistency checks* in a manner presented e. g. in Burchardt *et al.* (2008a), where queries extract ill-formed patterns from the lexicon graph.

Section 6.2 deals with the user-oriented lexicon access and the presentation of the dictionary content to the user. Based on the specifications presented in Section 5.4, ideas are developed as to how the information contained in the user profiles can be used to generate different dictionary entries from the same underlying data source in order to satisfy the needs of the respective users. In addition to the formulation of ideas as to the design of the query form of a custom graphical user interface, this section presents details of the internal mechanisms which are needed in order to achieve this. As is suggested by these considerations, the notion of a dictionary entry is shifted from a *static* entity towards a *dynamic* one that is generated from the underlying data at runtime, based on the specifications in the model of user needs.

In contrast to the specification of user needs mentioned above, NLP applications need to have access to the data either directly by means of an application programming interface (API), or indirectly by means of an exchange format. In order to show the multifunctionality of the MLR, both ways have been implemented. On the one hand, Section 6.3.1 provides details on the Java API that has been defined, which allows for programmatic access to the data without demanding too much knowledge of the internal structure of the underlying model. For example, instead of leaving the specification of graph patterns up to the application developer, the API offers methods like `getLexemes()` or `Lexeme.getValenceFrames()`, which allow the developer to extract information from the MLR in a straightforward way. On the other hand, Section 6.3.2 describes how the data can be exported from the MLR into a standard exchange format. Here, the non-normative LMF XML format has been used as an example.

Chapter 6 closes with a sketch of a possible web-based architecture for the lexical resource, including a description of the basic components, as well as an outline of the processing steps that are involved in a human usage scenario. In addition to describing how a morphological analysis of the provided input could be integrated into the dictionary interface, proposals are made as to the different autonomous processing steps that are necessary in order to give meaningful feedback even in case the user input is ill-formed (see also the »invisible dictionary«of Bergenholtz, 2005). At the time of writing, however, the implementation of such backup strategies is still to be considered as future work.

The main conclusions of the work presented in this book are discussed in Chapter 7, with a view to further lines of research. In particular, pages 168 to 171 assess the performance of the model with respect to satisfying the main requirements presented in Chapter 3. As the discussion shows, the MLR model as well as the experimental multifunctional lexical resource that has been defined on its basis are capable of addressing the requirements in a satisfactory way. Moreover, they have done so by means of a formalism that is – despite its status of a W3C recommendation – not yet widely used in the domain of computational lexicography. Therefore, by choosing OWL for the definition of the multifunctional lexicon model, as opposed to the common practice of defining yet another custom XML format, this study provides a successful implementation of *actual* reusability of both data and representation formalism in the context of computational lexicographic research.

10 Bibliography

Abel, Andrea/Weber, Vanessa (2000). ELDIT: A Prototype of an Innovative Dictionary. In U. Heid, S. Evert, E. Lehmann/C. Rohrer (eds.), *Proceedings of the IXth EURALEX International Congress on Lexicography*, pages 807–818. Stuttgart, Germany.

Almind, Richard/Bergenholtz, Henning/Vrang, Vibeke (2006). Theoretical and Computational Solutions for Phraseological Lexicography. In E. Hallsteinsdóttir/K. Farø (eds.), *New Theoretical and Methodological Approaches to Phraseology*, number 27, 2/06 in Linguistik Online, pages 159–181.

Antoni-Lay, Marie-Hélène/Francopoulo, Gil/Zaysser, Laurence (1994). A Generic Model for Reuseable Lexicons: The Genelex Project. *Literary and Linguistic Computing*, 9(1), 47–54, Oxford University Press.

Asmussen, Jørg/Ørsnes, Bjarne (2005). Adapting Valency Frames from The Danish Dictionary to an LFG Lexicon. In *Proceedings of the 8th International Conference on Computational Lexicography (COMPLEX '05)*. Budapest, Hungary.

Atkins, Beryl T. Sue (1992). Putting lexicography on the professional map. In M. Alvar Ezquerra (ed.), *Proceedings of the Vth EURALEX International Congress on Lexicography*, pages 519–526. Barcelona, Spain.

– (1996). Bilingual Dictionaries: Past, Present and Future. In M. Gellerstam, J. Järborg, S.-G. Malmgren, K. Norén, L. Rogström/C. R. Papmehl (eds.), *Proceedings of the VIIth EURALEX International Congress on Lexicography*. Gothemburg, Sweden.

– /Zampolli, Antonio (eds.) (1994). *Computational Approaches to the Lexicon*. Oxford University Press.

– /Rundell, Michael/Sato, Hiroaki (2003). The Contribution of FrameNet to Practical Lexicography. *International Journal of Lexicography*, 16(3), 333–357, Oxford University Press.

Baader, Franz/Nutt, Werner (2003). Basic Description Logics. In F. Baader, D. Calvanese, D. L. McGuinness, D. Nardi/P. F. Patel-Schneider (eds.), *The Description Logic Handbook: Theory, Implementation and Applications*, pages 47–100. CUP.

Baader, Franz/Calvanese, Diego/McGuinness, Deborah L.Nardi, Daniele/Patel-Schneider, Peter F. (eds.) (2003). *The Description Logic Handbook: Theory, Implementation and Applications*. CUP.

Baker, Collin F./Fillmore, Charles J./Lowe, John B. (1998). The Berkeley FrameNet project. In *Proceedings of the joint COLING/ACL 1998*. Montreal, Canada.

Bartels, Hauke/Spieß, Gunter (2002). Das aktive deutsch-niedersorbische Internet-Lernerwörterbuch des verbalen Wortschatzes. Elektronische Medien im Dienste des Erhalts einer bedrohten Minderheitensprache. In A. Braasch and C. Povlsen (eds.), *Proceedings of the Xth EURALEX International Congress on Lexicography*, pages 451–461. Copenhagen, Denmark.

Bechhofer, Sean/van Harmelen, Frank/Hendler, Jim/Horrocks, Ian/McGuinness, Deborah L./Patel-Schneider, Peter F./Stein, Lynn Andrea (2004). OWL Web Ontology Language Reference. W3C Recommendation. http://www.w3.org/TR/owl-ref/.

Beckett, Dave/Broekstra, Jeen (2008). SPARQL Query Results XML Format. W3C Recommendation. http://www.w3.org/TR/rdf-sparql-XMLres/.

– /McBride, Brian (2004). RDF/XML Syntax Specification (Revised). W3C Recommendation. http://www.w3.org/TR/rdf-syntax-grammar/.

Bergenholtz, Henning (2005). Den usynlige elektroniske produktions- og korrekturordbog. In *LexicoNordica, No. 12*, pages 19–40. Nordisk forening for leksikografi in collaboration with Nordisk Språksekretariat, Oslo.

– /Johnsen, Mia (2005). Log Files as a Tool for Improving Internet Dictionaries. *Hermes – Journal of Language and Communication Studies*, 34, 117–141, Aarhus School of Business.

Bergenholtz, Henning/Tarp, Sven (eds.) (1995). *Manual of Specialised Lexicography*. John Benjamins, Amsterdam.

– /Tarp, Sven (2002). Die moderne lexikographische Funktionslehre. Diskussionsbeitrag zu neuen und alten Paradigmen, die Wörterbücher als Gebrauchsgegenstände verstehen. *Lexicographica*, 18, 253–263.

Berners-Lee, Tim (1989). *Information Management: A Proposal*. http://www.w3.org/History/1989/proposal.html.

– /Hendler, James/Lassila, Ora (2001). The Semantic Web: a New Form of Web Content that is Meaningful to Computers Will Unleash a Revolution of New Possibilities. *Scientific American*, 284(5), 34–43, Scientific American, Inc.

– /Fielding, Roy T./Masinter, Larry (2005). *Uniform Resource Identifier (URI): Generic Syntax*. Internet Engineering Task Force. http://www.apps.ietf.org/rfc/rfc3986.html.

Bird, Steven/Day, David/Garofolo, John/Henderson, John/Laprun, Christophe/Liberman, Mark (2000). ATLAS: A Flexible and Extensible Architecture for Linguistic Annotation. In *Proceedings of the 2nd International Conference on Language Resources and Evaluation (LREC 2000)*. ELRA, Athens, Greece.

Bläser, Brigitte/Schwall, Ulrike/Storrer, Angelika (1992). A Reusable Lexical Database Tool for Machine Translation. In A. Zampolli (ed.), *Proceedings of the 14th Conference on Computational Linguistics*. Nantes, France.

Boas, Hans Christian (2002). Bilingual FrameNet Dictionaries for Machine Translation. In M. G. Rodríguez/C. P. S. Araujo (eds.), *Proceedings of the 3rd International Conference on Language Resources and Evaluation (LREC 2002)*, pages 1364–1371. ELRA, Las Palmas de Gran Canaria, Spain.

– (2005). Semantic Frames as Interlingual Representations for Multilingual Lexical Databases. *International Journal of Lexicography*, 18(4), 445–478, Oxford University Press.

Bock, Jürgen/Haase, Peter/Ji, Qiu/Volz, Raphael (2008). Benchmarking OWL Reasoners. In *Proceedings of the Workshop on Advancing Reasoning on the Web: Scalability and Commonsense (ARea08)*.

Bothma, Theo J.D. (2011). Filtering and adapting data and information in the online environment in response to user needs. In P. A. Fuertes-Olivera and H. Bergenholtz (eds.), *e-Lexicography: The Internet, Digital Initiatives and Lexicography*. Continuum, London & New York.

Brants, Sabine/Dipper, Stefanie/Hansen, Silvia/Lezius, Wolfgang/Smith, George (2002). The TIGER treebank. In *Proceedings of the Workshop on Treebanks and Linguistic Theories*. Sozopol.

Bray, Tim/Hollander, Dave/Layman, Andrew/Tobin, Richard (2006). Namespaces in XML 1.0 (Second Edition). W3C Recommendation. http://www.w3.org/TR/xml-names/.

Bray, Tim/Paoli, Jean/Sperberg-McQueen, C. Michael/Maler, Eve/Yergeau, François (2008). Extensible Markup Language (XML) 1.0 (Fifth Edition). W3C Recommendation. http://www.w3.org/TR/xml/.

Bresnan, Joan (1982). Control and Complementation. In J. Bresnan (ed.), *The Mental Representation of Grammatical Relations*, pages 282–390. Cambridge, MA: MIT Press.

Brickley, Dan/Guha, Ramanathan V. (2004). RDF Vocabulary Description Language 1.0: RDF Schema. W3C Recommendation. http://www.w3.org/TR/rdf-schema/.

Broekstra, Jeen/Kampman, Arjohn (2003). SeRQL: A Second Generation RDF Query Language. In *Proceedings of the SWAD-Europe Workshop on Semantic Web Storage and Retrieval*. Amsterdam, The Netherlands.

– /Kampman, Arjohn/van Harmelen, Frank (2002). Sesame: A Generic Architecture for Storing and Querying RDF and RDF Schema. In *Proceedings of the 1st International Semantic Web Conference (ISWC 2002)*. Sardinia, Italy.

Burchardt, Aljoscha/Frank, Anette (2006). Approximating Textual Entailment with LFG and FrameNet Frames. In *Proceedings of the Second PASCAL Recognising Textual Entailment Challenge Workshop*. Venice, Italy.

Burchardt, Aljoscha/Erk, Katrin/Frank, Anette (2005). A WordNet Detour to FrameNet. In B. Fisseni, H.-C. Schmitz, B. Schröder, and P. Wagner (eds.), *Sprachtechnologie, mobile Kommunikation und linguistische Ressourcen*, volume 8 of *Computer Studies in Language and Speech*, pages 408–421. Peter Lang, Frankfurt am Main.

– /Erk, Katrin/Frank, Anette/Kowalski, Andrea/Padó, Sebastian/Pinkal, Manfred (2006). The SALSA Corpus: a German Corpus Resource for Lexical Semantics. In *Proceedings of the 5th International Conference on Language Resources and Evaluation (LREC2006)*. Genoa.

– /Padó, Sebastian/Spohr, Dennis/Frank, Anette/Heid, Ulrich (2008a). Constructing Integrated Corpus and Lexicon Models for Multi-Layer Annotation in OWL DL. *Linguistic Issues in Language Technology – LiLT*, 1(1), 1–33, CSLI publications, Stanford.

– /Padó, Sebastian/Spohr, Dennis/Frank, Anette/Heid, Ulrich (2008b). Formalising Multi-layer Corpora in OWL DL – Lexicon Modelling, Querying and Consistency Control. In *Proceedings of the 3rd International Joint Conference on Natural Language Processing (IJCNLP 2008)*. Hyderabad, India.

Champion, Michael (2004). How much Pain for XML's Gain? In *Proceedings of the XML Conference and Exposition*. Washington, DC.

Chiarcos, Christian (2008). An Ontology of Linguistic Annotations. *LDV Forum on Foundations of Ontologies in Text Technology, Part II: Applications*, 23(1), 1–16, GLDV.

Chiari, Isabella (2006). Performance Evaluation of Italian Electronic Dictionaries: User's Needs and Requirements. In E. Corino, C. Marello, and C. Onesti (eds.), *Proceedings of the XIIth EURALEX International Congress on Lexicography*. Torino, Italy.

Cimiano, Philipp/Buitelaar, Paul/McCrae, John/Sintek, Michael (2011). LexInfo: A declarative model for the lexicon-ontology interface. *Journal of Web Semantics: Science, Services and Agents on the World Wide Web*, 9(1), 29–51.

Cocchi, Gloria (2001). Free Clitics and Bound Affixes: Towards a Unitary Analysis. In B. Gerlach and J. Grijzenhout (eds.), *Clitics in Phonology, Morphology and Syntax*, pages 85–119. Benjamins, Amsterdam.

Copestake, Ann (1992). The ACQUILEX LKB: Representation Issues in Semi-automatic Acquisition of Large Lexicons. In *Proceedings of the 3rd Conference on Applied Natural Language Processing*, pages 88–95. Trento, Italy.

Crowther, Jonathan/Dignen, Sheila/Lea, Diana (eds.) (2003). *Oxford Collocations Dictionary for Students of English*. Oxford University Press.

de Schryver, Gilles-Maurice (2003). Lexicographers' Dreams in the Electronic-Dictionary Age. *International Journal of Lexicography*, 16(2), 143–199, Oxford University Press.

– /Joffe, David/Joffe, Pitta/Hillewaert, Sarah (2006). Do Dictionary Users Really Look Up Frequent Words? – On the Overestimation of the Value of Corpus-based Lexicography. *Lexikos 16 (AFRILEX-reeks/series 16)*, pages 67–83.

Dipper, Stefanie/Hinrichs, Erhard/Schmidt, Thomas/Wagner, Andreas/Witt, Andreas (2006). Sustainability of Linguistic Resources. In E. Hinrichs, N. Ide, M. Palmer, and J. Pustejovsky (eds.), *Proceedings of the LREC 2006 Satellite Workshop on Merging and Layering Linguistic Information*. ELRA, Genoa, Italy.

Dodd, W. Steven (1989). Lexicomputing and the Dictionary of the Future. In G. James (ed.), *Lexicographers and their Works*, volume 14 of *Exeter Linguistic Studies*, pages 83–93. Exeter University Press, Exeter, England.

Duerst, Martin/Suignard, Michel (2005). *Internationalized Resource Identifiers (IRIs)*. Internet Engineering Task Force. http://www.apps.ietf.org/rfc/rfc3987.html.

Edmundson, H. P./Epstein, Martin N. (1969). Computer-Aided Research on Synonymy and Antonymy. In *Proceedings of the International Conference on Computational Linguistics*.

Emele, Martin C. (1994). The Typed Feature Structure Representation Formalism. In *Proceedings of the International Workshop on Sharable Natural Language Resources*. Ikoma, Nara, Japan.

Erjavec, Tomaž/Evans, Roger/Ide, Nancy/Kilgarriff, Adam (2003). From Machine Readable Dictionaries to Lexical Databases: the Concede Experience. In *Proceedings of the 7th International Conference on Computational Lexicography (COMPLEX 2003)*. Budapest, Hungary.

Erlandsen, Jens (2004). iLEX – an ergonomic and powerful tool combining effective and flexible editing with easy and fast search and retrieval. Software demonstration at the *XIth EURALEX International Congress on Lexicography*. Lorient, France.

Evans, Roger/Gazdar, Gerald (1996). DATR: a Language for Lexical Knowledge Representation. *Computational Linguistics*, 22, 167–216.

Evert, Stefan/Heid, Ulrich/Spranger, Kristina (2004). Identifying Morphosyntactic Preferences in Collocations. In M. T. Lino, M. F. Xavier, F. Ferreira, R. Costa, and R. Silva (eds.), *Proceedings of the 4th International Conference on Language Resources and Evaluation (LREC 2004)*, pages 907–910. ELRA, Lisbon, Portugal.

Farrar, Scott/Langendoen, D. Terence (2003). A Linguistic Ontology for the Semantic Web. *GLOT International*, 7(3), 97–100.

– (2010). An OWL-DL Implementation of Gold. An Ontology for the Semantic Web. In A. Witt and D. Metzing (eds.), *Linguistic Modelling of Information and Markup Languages. Contributions to Language Technology*, Text, Speech and Language Technology 40, pages 45–66. Springer Verlag.

Fellbaum, Christiane (ed.) (1998). *WordNet – An Electronic Lexical Database*. MIT Press, Cambridge, MA, USA.

Forgy, Charles L. (1982). RETE: A Fast Algorithm for the Many Pattern/Many Object Pattern Match Problem. *Artificial Intelligence*, 19, 17–37.

Francopoulo, Gil/George, Monte/Calzolari, Nicoletta/Monachini, Monica/Bel, Nuria/Pet, Mandy/Soria, Claudia (2006). Lexical Markup Framework. In *Proceedings of the 5th International Conference on Language Resources and Evaluation (LREC2006)*, pages 233–236. ELRA, Genoa.

Franz Inc. (2006). AllegroGraph RDFStore. http://www.franz.com/agraph/allegrograph/.

Friedman-Hill, Ernest J. (2003). *Jess in Action: Rule-Based Systems in Java*. Manning Publications, Greenwich, CT.

Gelpí, Cristina (2007). Reliability of online bilingual dictionaries. In H. Gottlieb and J. E. Mogensen (eds.), *Dictionary Visions, Research and Practice – Selected papers from the 12th International Symposium on Lexicography, Copenhagen*, pages 3–12. John Benjamins Publishing Company.

Gibbon, Dafydd (2000). Computational Lexicography. In F. van Eynde and D. Gibbon (eds.), *Lexicon Development for Speech and Language Processing*, pages 1–42. Kluwer Academic Publishers, Dordrecht.

Golbreich, Christine/Imai, Atsutoshi (2004). Combining SWRL rules and OWL ontologies with Protégé OWL Plugin, Jess, and Racer. In *Proceedings of the 7th Protégé Conference*. Bethesda, MD.

Görz, Günther (in prep.). Representing Computational Dictionaries in AI-Oriented Knowledge Representation Formalisms. In *Dictionaries. An International Handbook of Lexicography – Supplementary volume: New developments in lexicography, with a special focus on computational lexicography*, HSK – Handbücher zur Sprach- und Kommunikationswissenschaft, pages 10–19. W. de Gruyter, Berlin.

Gouws, Rufus H. (2006). Die zweisprachige Lexikographie Afrikaans-Deutsch – Eine metalexikographische Herausforderung. In A. Dimova, V. Jesenšek, and P. Petkov (eds.), *Zweisprachige Lexikographie und Deutsch als Fremdsprache*, volume 184–185 of *GERMANISTISCHE LINGUISTIK*, pages 49–58. Georg Olms Verlag, Hildesheim, Germany.

– (2007). Sublemmata or main lemmata – A critical look at the presentation of some macrostructural elements. In H. Gottlieb and J. E. Mogensen (eds.), *Dictionary Visions, Research and Practice – Selected papers from the 12th International Symposium on Lexicography, Copenhagen*, pages 55–70. John Benjamins Publishing Company.

Gouws, Rufus H./Prinsloo, Daniel J. (2005). *Principles and Practice of South African Lexicography*. SUN PRESS, AFRICAN SUN MeDIA, Stellenbosch, South Africa.

– /Prinsloo, Daniel J. (2008). What to say about *mañana, totems* and *dragons* in a Bilingual Dictionary? The Case of Surrogate Equivalence. In E. Bernal and J. DeCesaris (eds.), *Proceedings of the XIIIth EURALEX International Congress on Lexicography*, pages 869–878. Barcelona, Spain.

Grishman, Ralph/Macleod, Catherine/Meyers, Adam (1994). COMLEX Syntax: Building a Computational Lexicon. In *Proceedings of the 15th International Conference on Computational Linguistics (COLING 1994)*. Kyoto, Japan.

Haarslev, Volker/Möller, Ralf/Wessel, Michael (2007). RacerPro User's Guide and Reference Manual, Version 1.9.1.

Haß, Ulrike (2005). elexiko – Das Projekt. In U. Haß (ed.), *Grundfragen der elektronischen Lexikographie. elexiko – das Online-Informationssystem zum deutschen Wortschatz*, Schriften des Instituts für Deutsche Sprache, pages 1–17. Institut für Deutsche Sprache.

Hausmann, Franz J. (2004). Was sind eigentlich Kollokationen? In K. Steyer (ed.), *Wortverbindungen – mehr oder weniger fest*, IDS Jahrbuch 2003, 2004, pages 309–334. Institut für Deutsche Sprache.

– /Wiegand, Herbert Ernst (1989). Component Parts and Structures of General Monolingual Dictionaries: A Survey. In F. J. Hausmann, O. Reichmann, H. E. Wiegand, and L. Zgusta (eds.), *Wörterbücher, Dictionaries, Dictionnaires. An International Encyclopedia of Lexicography, First Volume*, HSK – Handbücher zur Sprach- und Kommunikationswissenschaft, Band 5.1, pages 328–361. W. de Gruyter, Berlin/New York.

Hayashi, Yoshihiko/Narawa, Chiharu/Monachini, Monica/Soria, Claudia/Calzolari, Nicoletta (2008). Ontologizing Lexicon Access Functions based on a LMF-based Lexicon Taxonomy. In *Proceedings of the 6th International Conference on Language Resources and Evaluation (LREC 2008)*, pages 916–922. ELRA, Marrakech, Morocco.

Heid, Ulrich (1997). *Zur Strukturierung von einsprachigen und kontrastiven elektronischen Wörterbüchern*, volume 77 of *Lexicographica. Series maior*. Niemeyer, Tübingen.

– (2006). Valenzwörterbücher im Netz. In P. C. Steiner, H. C. Boas, and S. J. Schierholz (eds.), *Contrastive Studies and Valency – Studies in Honor of Hans Ulrich Boas*, pages 69–89. Peter Lang Verlagsgruppe, Frankfurt am Main, Germany.

– (2011). Electronic Dictionaries as Tools: Towards an Assessment of Usability. In P. A. Fuertes-Olivera and H. Bergenholtz (eds.), *e-Lexicography: The Internet, Digital Initiatives and Lexicography*. Continuum, London & New York.

– /Gouws, Rufus H. (2006). A Model for a Multifunctional Electronic Dictionary of Collocations. In E. Corino, C. Marello, and C. Onesti (eds.), *Proceedings of the XIIth EURALEX International Congress on Lexicography*. Torino, Italy.

– /Krüger, Katja (1996). A Multilingual Lexicon based on Frame Semantics. In L. Cahill and R. Evans (eds.), *Proceedings of the AISB Workshop on Multilinguality in the Lexicon*, pages 1–13. Brighton, England.

– /McNaught, John (1991). *Eurotra-7 – Feasibility and Project Definition Study on the Reusability of Lexical and Terminological Resources in Computerized Applications – Final Report*. Commission of the European Communities, Stuttgart/Luxembourg.

– /Spohr, Dennis/Ritz, Julia/Schunk, Christiane (2007). Struktur und Interoperabilität lexikalischer Ressourcen am Beispiel eines elektronischen Kollokationswörterbuchs. In G. Rehm, A. Witt, and L. Lemnitzer (eds.), *Datenstrukturen für linguistische Ressourcen und ihre Anwendungen*. Gunter Narr Verlag, Tübingen, Germany.

Hellwig, Peter (1997). Ein theorie-übergreifender Standard für lexikalische Wissensbasen. In K.-P. Konerding and A. Lehr (eds.), *Linguistische Theorie und lexikographische Praxis. Symposiumsvorträge, Heidelberg 1996*, volume 82 of *Lexicographica. Series Maior*. Niemeyer, Tübingen.

Hendler, James (2001). Agents and the Semantic Web. *IEEE Intelligent Systems*, 16(2), 30–37.

Herbst, Thomas/Heath, David/Roe, Ian/Götz, Dieter (2005). *A Valency Dictionary of English*. Berlin/New York: de Gruyter.

Horridge, Matthew/Knublauch, Holger/Rector, Alan/Stevens, Robert/Woe, Chris (2004). A Practical Guide to Building OWL Ontologies Using the Protégé-OWL Plugin and CO-ODE Tools, Edition 1.0.

Horrocks, Ian (2002). DAML+OIL: A Description Logic for the Semantic Web. *IEEE Data Engineering Bulletin*, 25(1), 4–9.

– /Patel-Schneider, Peter F. (2003). Reducing OWL Entailment to Description Logic Satisfiability. In *Proceedings of the 2nd International Semantic Web Conference (ISWC 2003)*. Sundial Resort, FL.

– /Sattler, Ulrike (2004). Decidability of $\mathcal{SHIQ}$ with complex role inclusion axioms. *Artificial Intelligence*, 160, 79–104.

– /Patel-Schneider, Peter F./Boley, Harold/Tabet, Said/Grosof, Benjamin/Dean, Mike (2004). SWRL: A Semantic Web Rule Language Combining OWL and RuleML. W3C Member Submission. `http://www.w3.org/Submission/SWRL/`.

Hunter, David/Fawcett, Jeff Rafter Joe/van der Vlist, Eric/Ayers, Danny/Duckett, Jon/Watt, Andrew/McKinnon, Linda (2007). *Beginning XML (4th Edition)*. Wiley & Sons.

Hustadt, Ulrich/Motik, Boris/Sattler, Ulrike (2007). Reasoning in Description Logics by a Reduction to Disjunctive Datalog. *Journal of Automated Reasoning*, 39(3), 351–384, Springer Verlag.

Ide, Nancy/Romary, Laurent/de la Clergerie, Éric V. (2003). International Standard for a Linguistic Annotation Framework. In *Proceedings of the HLT-NAACL '03 Workshop on Software Engineering and Architecture of Language Technology*. Edmonton, Canada.

ISO/FDIS 12620 (2009). Terminology and other language and content resources – Specification of data categories and management of a Data Category Registry for language resources. International Organization for Standardization, Geneva, Switzerland.

ISO/FDIS 24613 (2008). Language resource management – Lexical markup framework (LMF). International Organization for Standardization, Geneva, Switzerland.

Joffe, David (2009). TLex: Setting New Standards for a Global, Fully-integrated e-Lexicography Workbench and Electronic Dictionary Publishing System. In *eLexicography in the 21st century: new challenges, new applications (eLEX2009), book of abstracts*. Centre for English Corpus Linguistics, Université catholique de Louvain, Louvain-la-Neuve, Belgium.

Kaplan, Ronald/Bresnan, Joan (1982). Lexical-Functional Grammar: A Formal System for Grammatical Representation. In J. Bresnan (ed.), *The Mental Representation of Grammatical Relations*, pages 173–281. Cambridge, MA: MIT Press.

Karp, Peter D. (1992). The Design Space of Frame Knowledge Representation Systems. SRI AI Center Technical Note #520. SRI International, Menlo Park, CA.

Kepser, Stephan (2004). A Simple Proof of the Turing-completeness of XSLT and XQuery. In *Proceedings of Extreme Markup Languages (EML-2004)*. Montréal, Canada.

Kiryakov, Atanas/Ognyanov, Damyan/Manov, Dimitar (2005). OWLIM – A Pragmatic Semantic Repository for OWL. In M. Dean, Y. Guo, W. Jun, R. Kaschek, S. Krishnaswamy, Z. Pan, and Q. Z. Sheng (eds.), *Web Information Systems Engineering – WISE 2005 Workshops*, volume 3807 of *Lecture Notes in Computer Science*, pages 182–192. Springer Verlag.

– /Peikov, Ivan/Tashev, Zdravko/Ilchev, Atanas (2009). *Knowledge Store: Performance Evaluation*. Deliverable D4.4 (WP 4), EU-IST Project IST-2004-026460 TAO: Transitioning Applications to Ontologies.

Klappenbach, Ruth/Malige-Klappenbach, Helene (1980). Das Wörterbuch der deutschen Gegenwartssprache. Entstehung, Werdegang, Vollendung. In W. Abraham (with the collaboration of Jan F. Brand) (ed.), *Studien zur modernen deutschen Lexikographie. Ruth Klappenbach (1911-1977). Auswahl aus den lexikographischen Arbeiten, erweitert um drei Beiträge von Helene Malige-Klappenbach*, Linguistik aktuell. 1, pages 3–58. John Benjamins, Amsterdam.

Knapp, Judith (2004). *A new approach to CALL Content authoring*. Ph.D. thesis, Institut für Informationssysteme, Universität Hannover, Germany.

Knublauch, Holger/Musen, Mark A./Rector, Alan L. (2004). Editing description logic ontologies with the Protégé OWL plugin. In *Proceedings of DL 2004*. Whistler, BC.

Lenci, Alessandro/Bel, Nuria/Busa, Federica/Calzolari, Nicoletta/Gola, Elisabetta/Monachini, Monica/Ogonowski, Antoine/Peters, Ivonne/Peters, Wim/Ruimy, Nilda/Villegas, Marta/Zampolli, Antonio (2000). SIMPLE: A General Framework for the Development of Multilingual Lexicons. *International Journal of Lexicography*, 13(4), 249–263, Oxford University Press.

Levenshtein, Vladimir I. (1966). Binary Codes capable of Correcting Deletions, Insertions, and Reversals. *Soviet Physics Doklady*, 10(8), 707–710.

Lew, Robert (2008). Lexicographic Functions and Pedagogical Lexicography: Some Critical Notes on Sven Tarp's »Lexicography in the Borderland between Knowledge and Non-Knowledge«. In K. Iwan and I. Korpaczewska (eds.), *Przegląd Humanistyczny. Pedagogika. Politologia. Filologia*, pages 114–123. Szczecin: Szczecińska Szkoła Wyższa Collegium Balticum.

Lüngen, Harald/Storrer, Angelika (2007). Domain ontologies and wordnets in OWL: Modelling options. *LDV Forum on Foundations of Ontologies in Text Technology*, 22(2), 1–19, GLDV.

Manola, Frank/Miller, Eric (2004). RDF Primer. W3C Recommendation. http://www.w3.org/TR/REC-rdf-syntax/.

Mel'čuk, Igor/Žolkovskij, Aleksandr K. (1970). Towards a Functioning Meaning-Text Model of Language. In *Linguistics*, number 57, pages 10–47.

Menon, Bruno/Modiano, Nicole (1993). *EAGLES: Lexicon Architecture*. Technical Report EAG-CLWG-LEXARCH/B.

Motik, Boris (2005). On the Properties of Metamodeling in OWL. In *Proceedings of the 4th International Semantic Web Conference (ISWC-2005)*, pages 548–562. Galway, Ireland.

– /Studer, Rudi (2005). KAON2 – A Scalable Reasoning Tool for the Semantic Web. In *Proceedings of the 2nd European Semantic Web Conference (ESWC'05)*. Heraklion, Greece.

– /Horrocks, Ian/Sattler, Ulrike (2007a). Adding Integrity Constraints to OWL. In C. Golbreich, A. Kalyanpur, and B. Parsia (eds.), *Proceedings of OWL: Experiences and Directions (OWLED 2007)*.

– /Horrocks, Ian/Sattler, Ulrike (2007b). Bridging the Gap between OWL and Relational Databases. In *Proceedings of the 16th International World Wide Web Conference (WWW2007)*, pages 807–816. ACM Press, Banff, Alberta, Canada.

Müller, Pawel (2010). *Entwicklung einer dynamischen Web-Benutzeroberfläche für ein graph-basiertes Lexikonmodell*. Studienarbeit. Institute for Natural Language Processing, University of Stuttgart, Germany.

Müller-Spitzer, Carolin (2005). Die Modellierung lexikografischer Daten und ihre Rolle im lexikografischen Prozess. In U. Haß (ed.), *Grundfragen der elektronischen Lexikographie. elexiko – das Online-Informationssystem zum deutschen Wortschatz*, Schriften des Instituts für Deutsche Sprache, pages 21–54. Institut für Deutsche Sprache.

Nardi, Daniele/Brachman, Ronald J. (2003). An Introduction to Description Logics. In F. Baader, D. Calvanese, D. L. McGuinness, D. Nardi, and P. F. Patel-Schneider (eds.), *The Description Logic Handbook: Theory, Implementation and Applications*, pages 5–44. CUP.

O'Connor, Martin/Nyulas, Csongor/Shankar, Ravi/Das, Amar/Musen, Mark (2008). The SWRLAPI: A Development Environment for Working with SWRL Rules. In *Proceedings of OWL: Experiences and Directions (OWLED 2008)*. Karlsruhe, Germany.

Paprotté, Wolf/Schumacher, Frank (1993). *MULTILEX - Final Report WP 9: MLEXd*. Technical Report MWP 8 - MS.

Piotrowski, Tadeusz (2009). Book review of »Sven Tarp. Lexicography in the Borderland between Knowledge and Non-Knowledge. General Lexicographical Theory with Particular Focus on Learner's Lexicography.«. *International Journal of Lexicography*, 22(4), 480–486, Oxford University Press.

Polguère, Alain (2000). Towards a Theoretically-motivated General Public Dictionary of Semantic Derivations and Collocations for French. In U. Heid, S. Evert, E. Lehmann, and C. Rohrer (eds.), *Proceedings of the IXth EURALEX International Congress on Lexicography*, pages 517–528. Stuttgart, Germany.

– (2006). Structural properties of lexical systems: Monolingual and Multilingual Perspectives. In *Proceedings of the COLING/ACL Workshop on Multilingual Language Resources and Interoperability*. Sydney, Australia.

– (2009). Lexical systems: graph models of natural language lexicons. In G. Sérasset, A. Witt, U. Heid, and F. Sasaki (eds.), *Language Resources and Evaluation*, volume 43, pages 41–55. Springer Netherlands.

Prinsloo, Daniel J. (2005). Electronic Dictionaries viewed from South Africa. *Hermes – Journal of Language and Communication Studies*, 34, 11–35, Aarhus School of Business.

Prud'hommeaux, Eric/Seaborne, Andy (2008). SPARQL Query Language for RDF. W3C Recommendation. http://www.w3.org/TR/rdf-sparql-query/.

Ruimy, Nilda/Corazzari, Ornella/Gola, Elisabetta/Spanu, Antonietta/Calzolari, Nicoletta/Zampolli, Antonio (1998). The Eurpean LE-PAROLE project: The Italian Syntactic Lexicon. In *Proceedings of the 1st International Conference on Language Resources and Evaluation (LREC 1998)*, pages 241–248. ELRA, Granada, Spain.

Ruppenhofer, Josef/Baker, Collin F./Fillmore, Charles J. (2002). The FrameNet Database and Software Tools. In A. Braasch and C. Povlsen (eds.), *Proceedings of the Xth EURALEX International Congress on Lexicography*, pages 371–375. Copenhagen, Denmark.

Schall, Natalia (2007). *Was können elektronische Wörterbücher leisten? Ein Evaluationsverfahren und seine Erprobung an englischen und deutschen einsprachigen Wörterbüchern auf CD-ROM*. Ph.D. thesis, Friedrich-Alexander-Universität Erlangen-Nürnberg, Germany. http://www.opus.ub.uni-erlangen.de/opus/volltexte/2007/701/.

Schöning, Harald (2001). Tamino – A DBMS designed for XML. In *Proceedings of the 17th International Conference on Data Engineering (ICDE'01)*, pages 149–154.

Schunk, Christiane (2006). *Entwicklung eines Kollokationswörterbuchs auf der Basis eines Kollokationsmodells in Beschreibungslogik*. Diploma thesis, Institut für Maschinelle Sprachverarbeitung, Universität Stuttgart, Germany.

Seaborne, Andy (2004). RDQL – A Query Language for RDF. W3C Member Submission. http://www.w3.org/Submission/RDQL/.

Selva, Thierry/Verlinde, Serge/Binon, Jean (2002). Le DAFLES, un nouveau dictionnaire électronique pour apprenants du français. In A. Braasch and C. Povlsen (eds.), *Proceedings of the Xth EURALEX International Congress on Lexicography*, pages 199–208. Copenhagen, Denmark.

Sérasset, Gilles/Mangeot-Lerebours, Mathieu (2001). Papillon lexical database project: Monolingual dictionaries and interlingual links. In *Proceedings of the 6th Natural Language Processing Pacific Rim Symposium*, pages 119–125. Tokyo, Japan.

Siepmann, Dirk (2005). Collocation, Colligation and Encoding Dictionaries. Part I: Lexicological Aspects. *International Journal of Lexicography*, 18(4), 409–443, Oxford University Press.

Sirin, Evren/Tao, Jiao (2009). Towards Integrity Constraints in OWL. In R. Hoekstra and P. F. Patel-Schneider (eds.), *Proceedings of OWL: Experiences and Directions (OWLED 2009)*.

Sirin, Evren/Parsia, Bijan/Grau, Bernardo Cuenca/Kalyanpur, Aditya/Katz, Yarden (2007). Pellet: A practical OWL-DL reasoner. *Journal of Web Semantics*, 5(2).

Soria, Claudia/Monachini, Monica/Vossen, Piek (2009). WordNet-LMF: Fleshing out a Standardized Format for WordNet Interoperability. In *Proceedings of the 2nd International Workshop on Intercultural Collaboration (IWIC-2009)*. Stanford.

Sowa, John F. (2000). *Knowledge Representation: Logical, Philosophical and Computational Foundations*. Brooks/Cole Publishing, Pacific Grove, CA.

Spohr, Dennis (2004). *Using »A Valency Dictionary of English« to enhance the Lexicon of an English LFG Grammar*. Studienarbeit. Institute for Natural Language Processing, University of Stuttgart, Germany.

– (2005). *A Description Logic Approach to Modelling Collocations*. Diploma thesis, Institut für Maschinelle Sprachverarbeitung, Universität Stuttgart, Germany.

– (2008). Requirements for the Design of Electronic Dictionaries and a Proposal for their Formalisation. In E. Bernal and J. DeCesaris (eds.), *Proceedings of the XIIIth EURALEX International Congress on Lexicography*, pages 617–630. Barcelona, Spain.

– (2011). A Multi-layer Architecture for "Pluri-monofunctional" Dictionaries. In P. A. Fuertes-Olivera and H. Bergenholtz (eds.), *e-Lexicography: The Internet, Digital Initiatives and Lexicography*. Continuum, London & New York.

– /Heid, Ulrich (2006). Modeling Monolingual and Bilingual Collocation Dictionaries in Description Logics. In P. Rayson, S. Sharoff, and S. Adolphs (eds.), *Proceedings of the EACL Workshop on Multi-Word-Expressions in a Multilingual Context*, pages 65–72. Trento, Italy.

– /Burchardt, Aljoscha/Padó, Sebastian/Frank, Anette/Heid, Ulrich (2007). Inducing a Computational Lexicon from a Corpus with Syntactic and Semantic Annotation. In J. Geertzen, E. Thijsse, H. Bunt, and A. Schiffrin (eds.), *Proceedings of the Seventh International Workshop on Computational Semantics (IWCS-7)*, pages 210–221. Tilburg, The Netherlands.

Storrer, Angelika (2001). Digitale Wörterbücher als Hypertexte: Zur Nutzung des Hypertextkonzepts in der Lexikographie. In I. Lemberg, B. Schröder, and A. Storrer (eds.), *Chancen und Perspektiven computergestützter Lexikographie. Hypertext, Internet und SGML/XML für die Produktion und Publikation digitaler Wörterbücher*, volume 107 of *Lexicographica. Series Maior*, pages 53–69. Niemeyer, Tübingen.

Stowasser, Joseph Maria/Petschenig, Michael/Skutsch, Franz (1994). *Stowasser: lateinisch-deutsches Schulwörterbuch*. Oldenbourg Schulbuchverlag, München.

Subirats, Carlos (2009). Spanish Framenet: A Frame-semantic Analysis of the Spanish Lexicon. In H. Boas (ed.), *Multilingual FrameNets in Computational Lexicography. Methods and Applications*, pages 135–162. Mouton de Gruyter, Berlin/New York.

Tarp, Sven (2008). Lexicography in the borderland between knowledge and non-knowledge. *Lexicographica. Series Maior*, 134, Niemeyer. [Danish version *Leksikografi i grænselandet mellem viden og ikke-viden* appeared in 2006 as habilitation, Aarhus School of Business, University of Aarhus.].

– (2011). Lexicographical and other e-tools for consultation purposes: Towards the individualization of needs satisfaction. In P. A. Fuertes-Olivera and H. Bergenholtz (eds.), *e-Lexicography: The Internet, Digital Initiatives and Lexicography*. Continuum, London & New York.

ter Horst, Herman J. (2005). Completeness, decidability and complexity of entailment for RDF Schema and a semantic extension involving the OWL vocabulary. *Journal of Web Semantics*, 3(2).

The TEI Consortium (2009). *TEI P5: Guidelines for Electronic Text Encoding and Interchange*. Oxford, Providence, Charlottesville, Nancy.

Trippel, Thorsten (2006). *The Lexicon Graph Model: A generic Model for multimodal lexicon development*. AQ-Verlag, Saarbrücken, Germany.

– (2010). Representation Formats and Models for Lexicons. In A. Witt and D. Metzing (eds.), *Linguistic Modelling of Information and Markup Languages. Contributions to Language Technology*, Text, Speech and Language Technology 40, pages 165–184. Springer Verlag.

Tsarkov, Dmitry/Horrocks, Ian (2006). FaCT++ Description Logic Reasoner: System Description. In *Proceedings of the International Joint Conference on Automated Reasoning (IJCAR 2006)*, volume 4130 of *Lecture Notes in Artificial Intelligence*, pages 292–297. Springer Verlag.

Tutin, Agnès (2008). For an Extended Definition of Lexical Collocations. In *Proceedings of the XIIIth EURALEX International Congress on Lexicography*. Barcelona, Spain.

Unger, Christina/Hieber, Felix/Cimiano, Philipp (2010). Generating LTAG grammars from a lexicon-ontology interface. In S. Bangalore, R. Frank, and M. Romero (eds.), *Proceedings of the 10th International Workshop on Tree Adjoining Grammars and Related Formalisms (TAG+10)*, pages 61–68. Yale University.

Verlinde, Serge (2010). The Base Lexicale du Français: a Multi-purpose Lexicographic Tool. In S. Granger and M. Paquot (eds.), *eLexicography in the 21st century: New challenges, new applications*, Cahiers du CENTAL, pages 335–342. UCL, Presses Universitaires de Louvain.

– (2011). Modelling interactive reading, translation and writing assistants. In P. A. Fuertes-Olivera and H. Bergenholtz (eds.), *e-Lexicography: The Internet, Digital Initiatives and Lexicography*. Continuum, London & New York.

– /Binon, Jean/Ostyn, Stéphane/Bertels, Ann (2007). La Base lexicale du français (BLF): un portail pour l'apprentissage du lexique français. *Cahiers de lexicologie*, 91(2), 251–266.

Vossen, Piek (ed.) (1998). *EuroWordNet: A Multilingual Database with Lexical Semantic Networks*. Kluwer Academic Publishers.

Weller, Marion/Heid, Ulrich (2010). Multi-parametric Extraction of German Multiword Expressions from Parsed Corpora. In *Proceedings of the* Seventh International Conference on Language Resources and Evaluation (LREC 2010). ELRA, Valletta, Malta.

Wiegand, Herbert Ernst (1988). Wörterbuchartikel als Text. In G. Harras (ed.), *Das Wörterbuch: Artikel und Verweisstrukturen*, volume 74 of *Sprache der Gegenwart*, pages 30–120. Schann, Düsseldorf.

– (1989). Der gegenwärtige Stand der Lexikographie und ihr Verhältnis zu anderen Disziplinen. In F. J. Hausmann, O. Reichmann, H. E. Wiegand, and L. Zgusta (eds.), *Wörterbücher, Dictionaries, Dictionnaires. An International Encyclopedia of Lexicography, First Volume*, HSK – Handbücher zur Sprach- und Kommunikationswissenschaft, Band 5.1, pages 246–280. W. de Gruyter, Berlin/New York.

– (1998). *Wörterbuchforschung: Untersuchungen zur Wörterbuchbenutzung, zur Theorie, Geschichte, Kritik und Automatisierung der Lexikographie. 1. Teilband.* de Gruyter, Berlin/New York.

Windhouwer, Menzo A. (2009). ISOcat: Defining widely accepted linguistic concepts. Presentation and tutorial at the *CLARIN metadata project training*.

Appendix

Class and Property Hierarchies

The following pages display the class and property hierarchies in the lexical and descriptive parts of the MLR model. Figure A.1 shows the various subtypes of lexemes (see Section 5.1.2 for more detailed explanations), and Figures A.2 and A.3 display the hierarchies of features and descriptions (cf. Sections 5.2.2 to 5.2.6). The property hierarchies of lexical and descriptive relations are shown in Figures A.4 and A.5 on pages 201 and 202 respectively (see also Sections 5.1.3 and 5.2).

Definition of Valence Description

Figure A.6 on page 203 displays a UML diagram of the valence description. Section 5.2.4 provides the necessary background.

Example Representations

Figures A.7 and A.8 on page 204 contain the representations of the monolingual description of »*Dekor, das/der; -s, -s/-e*« (»*decoration, decor, scenography*«). This item has been chosen because it illustrates different cases of variation in the lexicographic description, namely the plural variants »*Dekors*« and »*Dekore*«, as well as masculine and neuter gender. In addition to this, the neuter variant is only compatible with the reading of »*Dekor*« as »*scenography*« (with domain »*Theater*«), while masculine gender covers the other readings. Finally, the »*scenography*« reading has an absolute number preference for singular. The content of the description itself has been taken from the DWDS[1].

---

1 See http://www.dwds.de/woerterbuch.

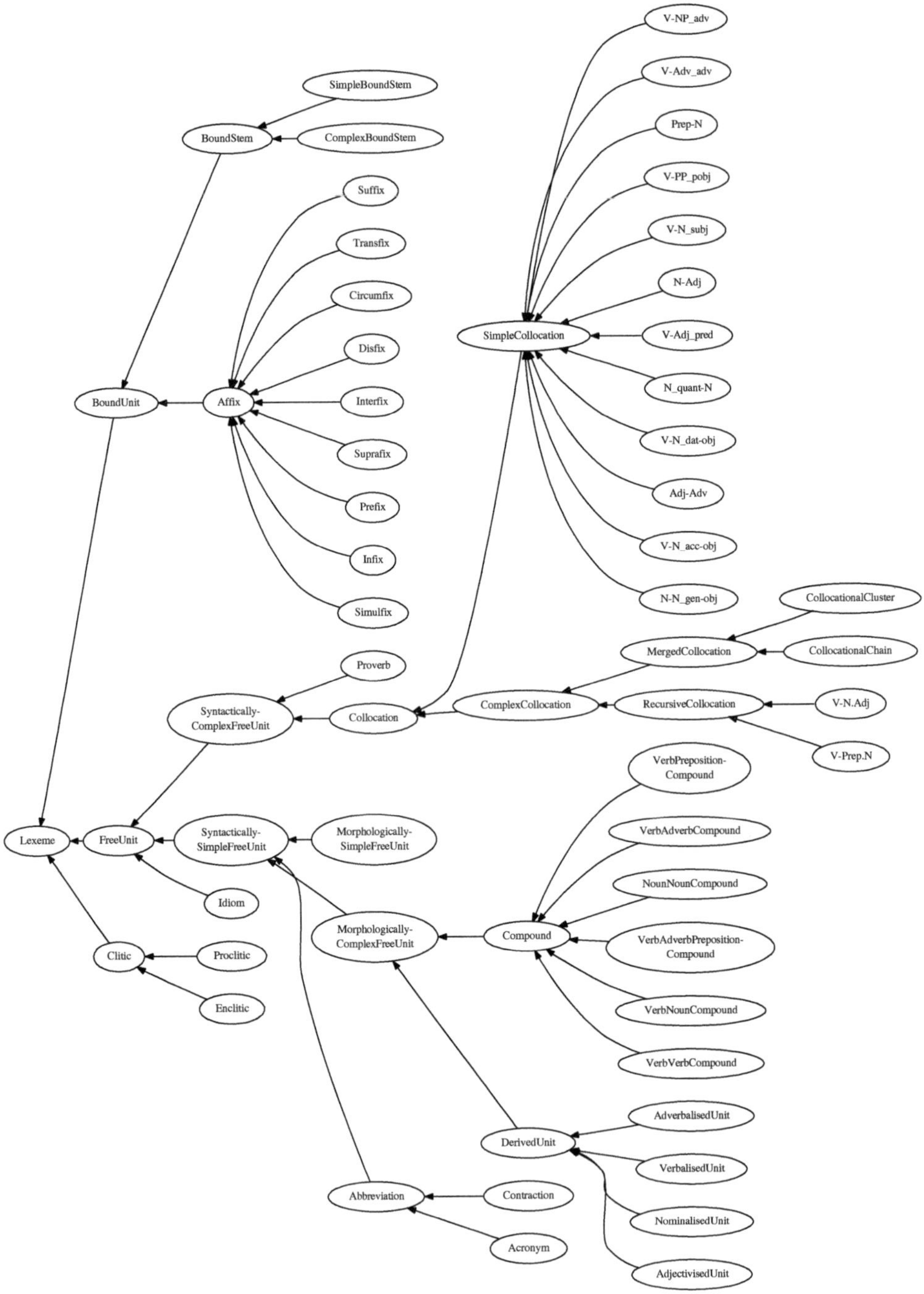

Figure A.1: Subclasses of *Lexeme*

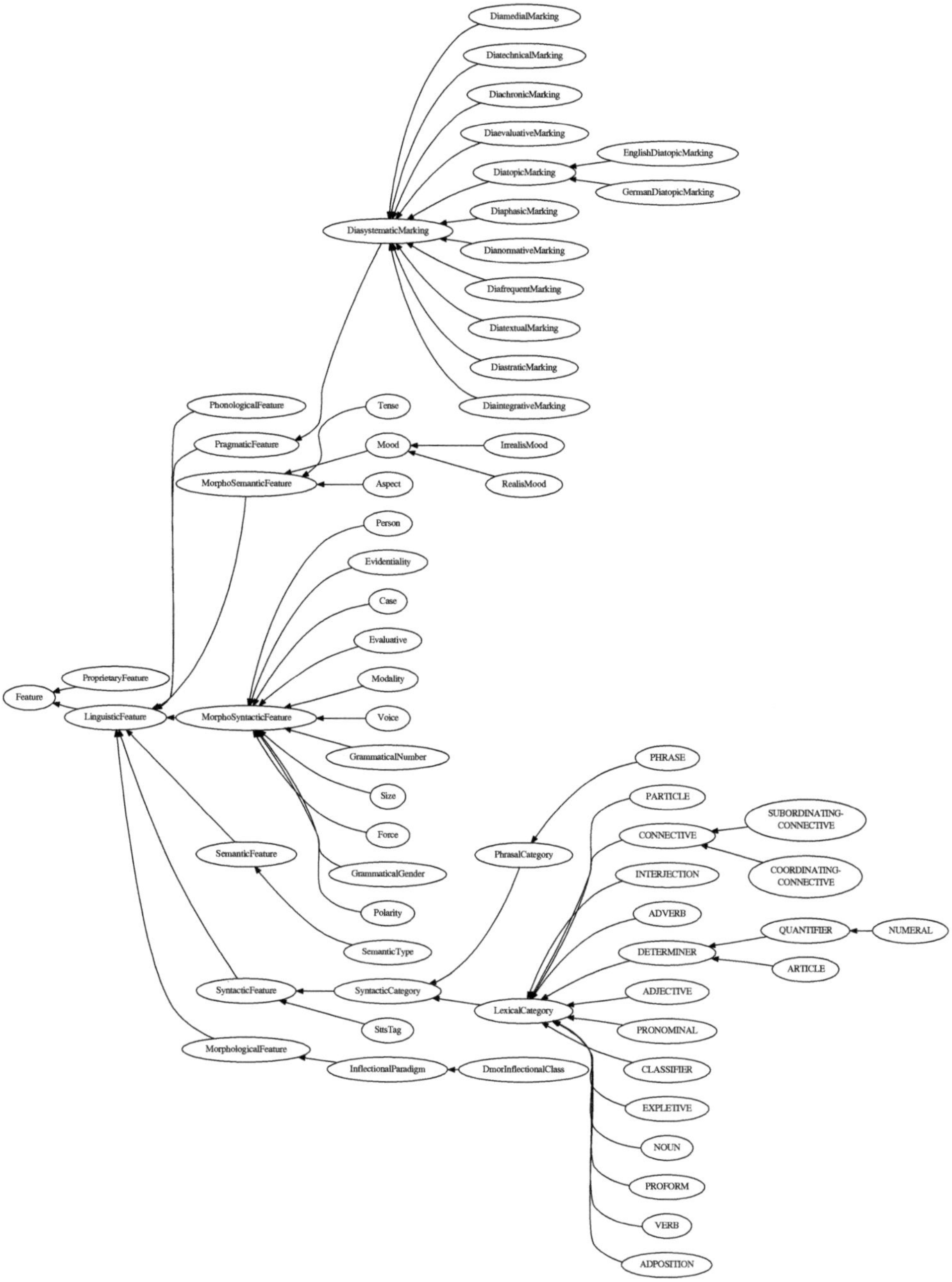

Figure A.2: Subclasses of *Feature*

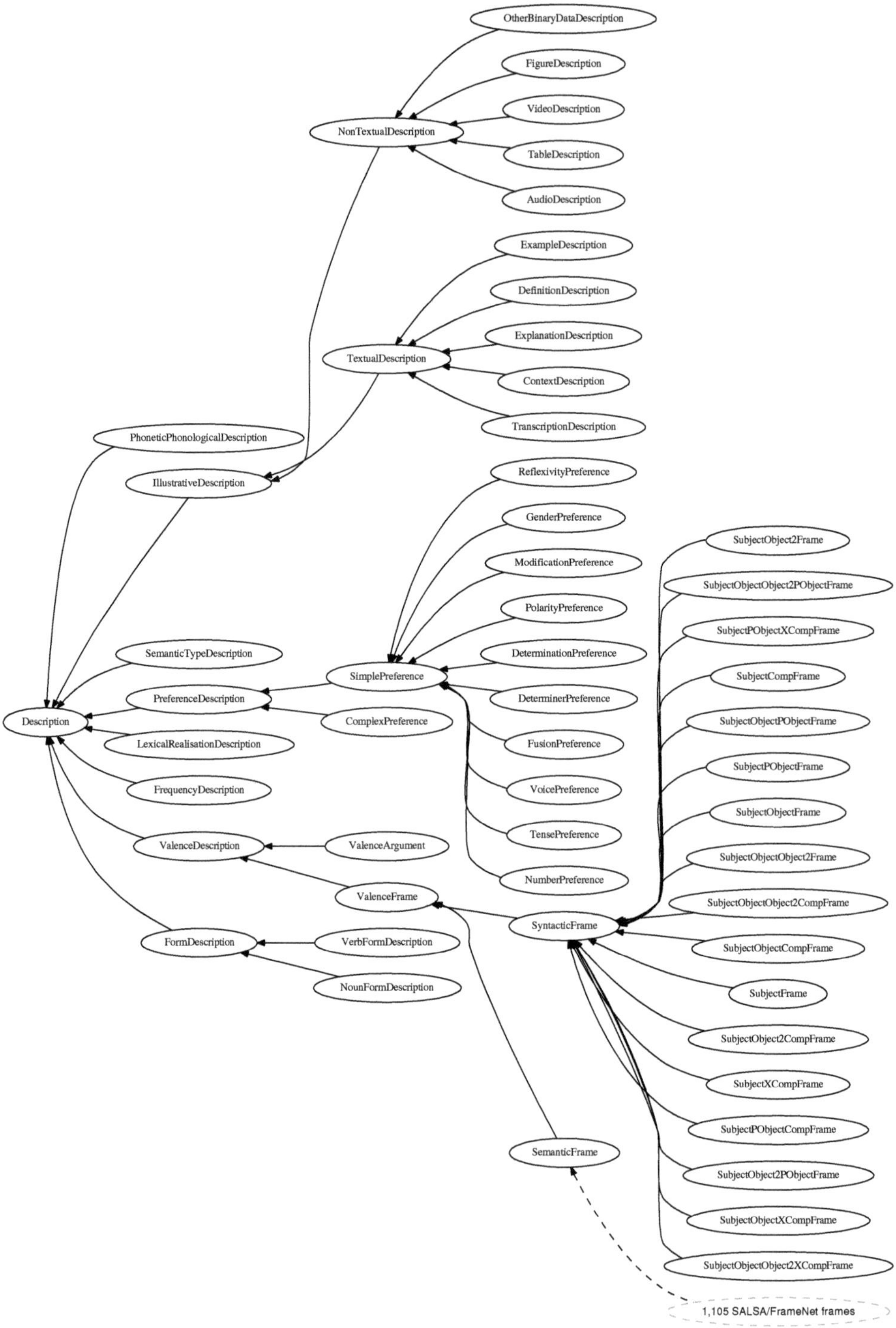

Figure A.3: Subclasses of *Description*

Figure A.4: Subrelations of *hasLexicalRelationTo*

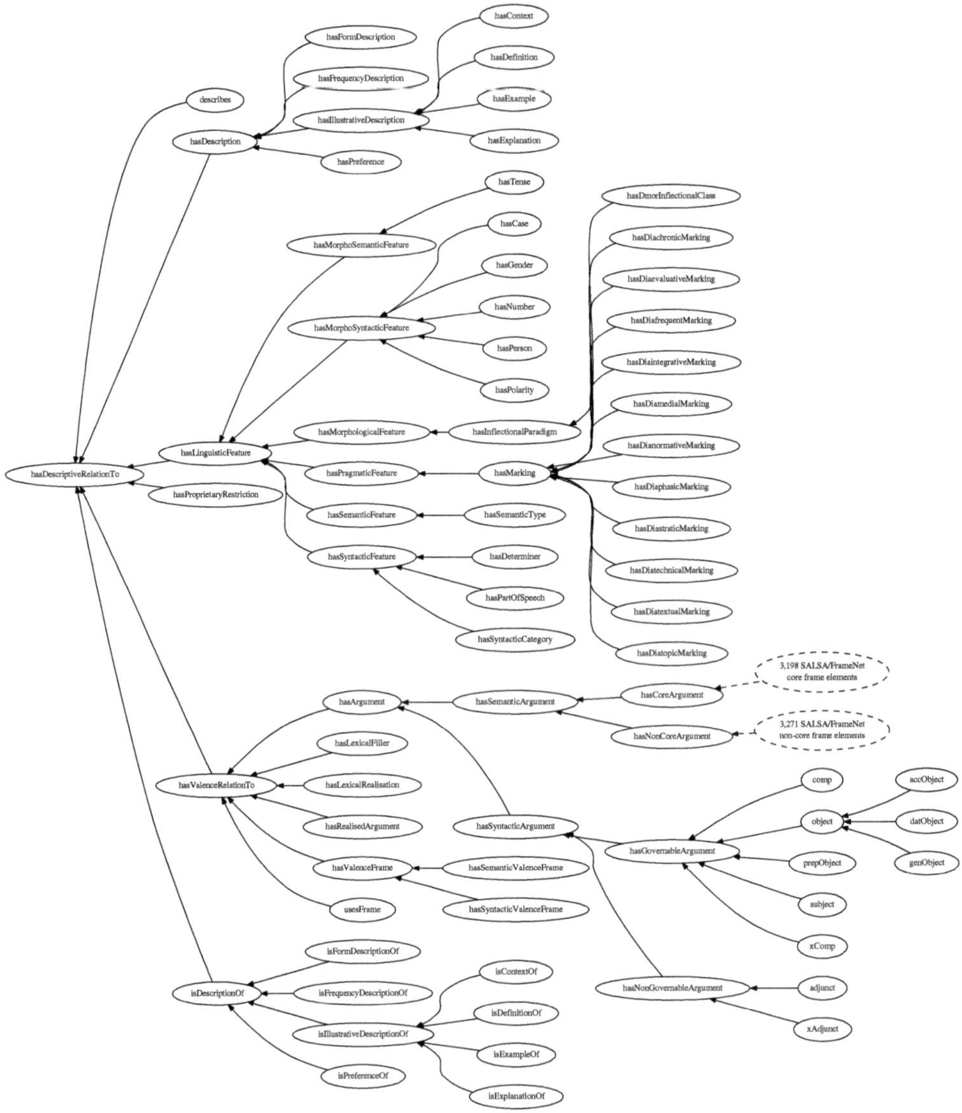

Figure A.5: Subrelations of *hasDescriptiveRelationTo*

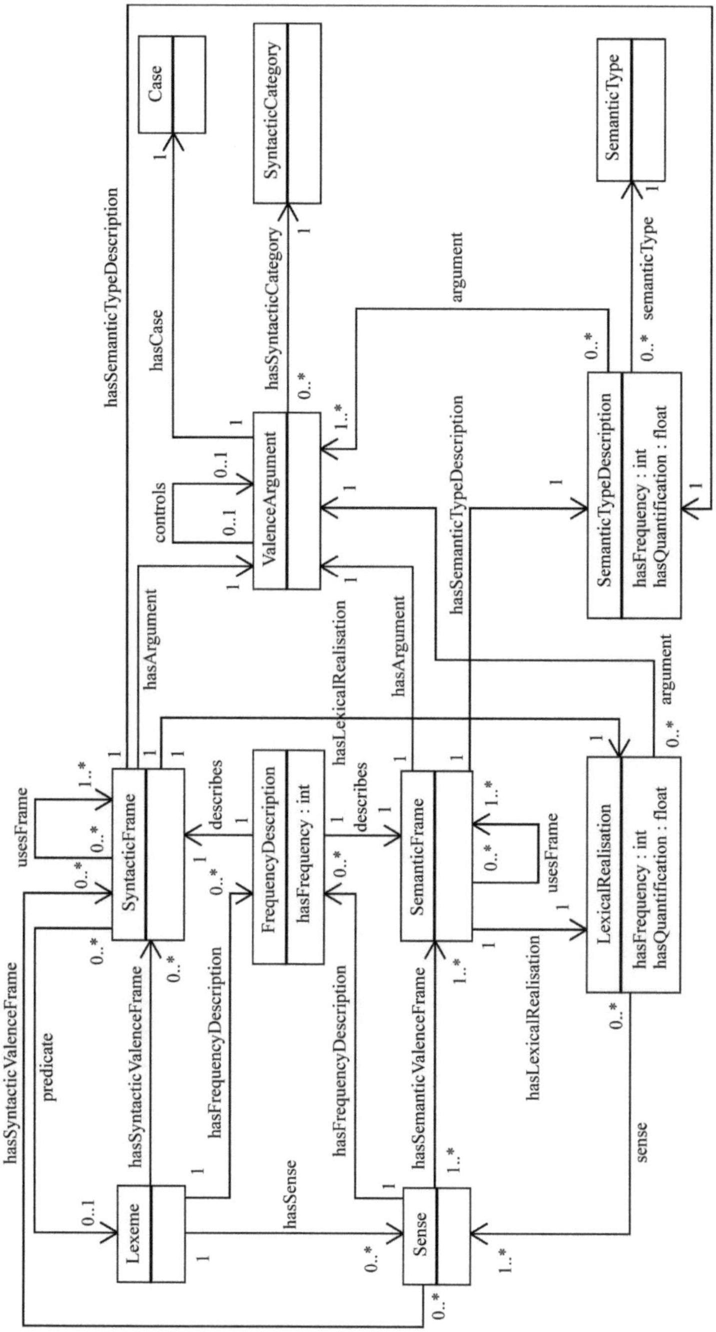

Figure A.6: UML diagram of valence description

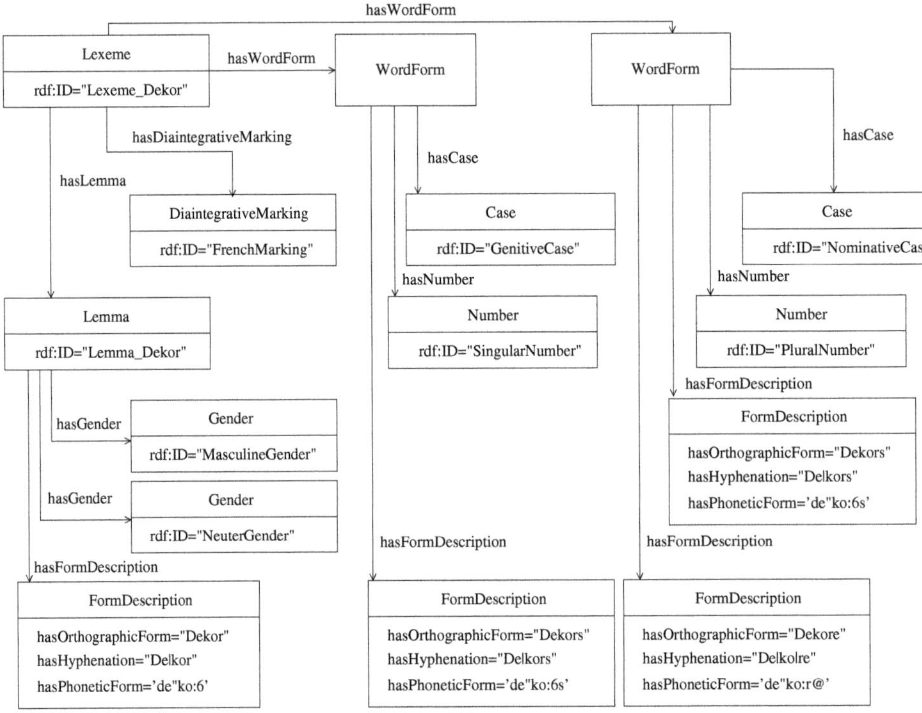

Figure A.7: Form description of *»Dekor, der/das; -s, -s/-e«*

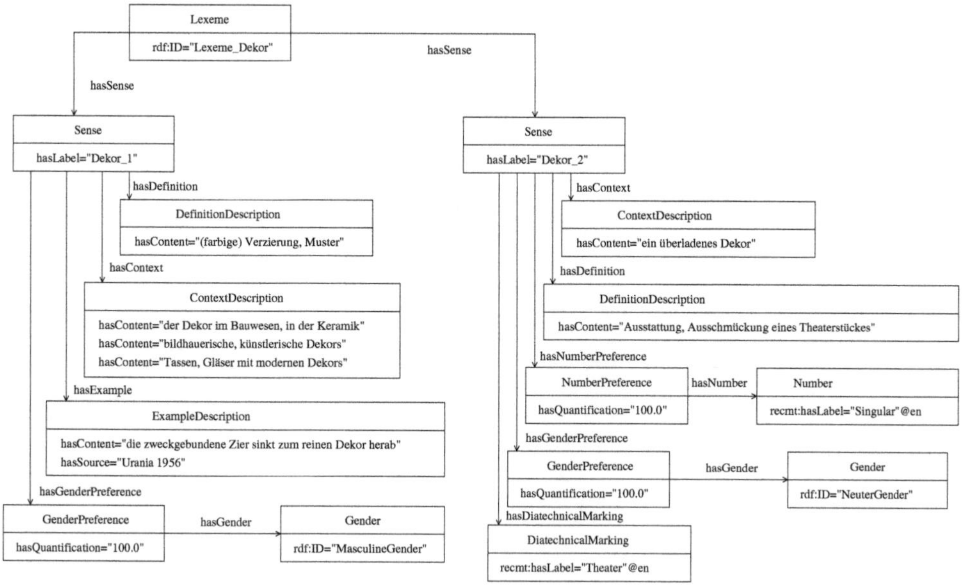

Figure A.8: Sense description of »*Dekor*$_1$« and »*Dekor*$_2$«

Bei Fragen zur Produktsicherheit wenden Sie sich bitte an:
If you have any questions regarding product safety,
please contact:

Walter de Gruyter GmbH
Genthiner Straße 13
10785 Berlin
productsafety@degruyterbrill.com